Mother Nature's Garden

Healthy Vegan Cooking

Florence Bienenfeld, Ph.D.
Mickey Bienenfeld

The Crossing Press • Freedom, CA • 95019

Cover design by Sheryl Karas
Cover and interior illustrations by Mary Azarian
Printed in the U.S.A.

Library of Congress Cataloging-in-Publication Data

Bienenfeld, Florence.
    Mother nature's garden: healthy vegan cooking/Florence Bienenfeld, Mickey Bienenfeld.
       p.cm
    Includes index.
    ISBN 0-89594-702-1 (paper)
    1. Vegetarian cookery. 2. Low-fat diet—Recipes. 3. Salt-free diet—Recipes. 4. Sugar-free diet—Recipes. I. Bienenfeld, Mickey. II. Title.
TX837.B52 1994
641.5'636—dc20

94-16849
CIP

Dedicated to our lovely, sensitive, caring granddaughter, Amanda,
who loves all animals and has been a vegetarian all her life,
to Cousin Ladene, who is allergic to eggs,
to Cousin Mae, who is allergic to all dairy products,
and to all who wish to explore a healthy,
pure way of nourishing the body.

First of all we wish to thank Michael Klaper, M.D., author of *Vegan Nutrition: Pure and Simple*, for honoring us with the foreword for *Mother Nature's Garden*.

A very special thanks to the entire staff at The Crossing Press for producing *Mother Nature's Garden* in such a wonderfully supportive and efficient way.

We also wish to acknowledge all the help and expertise given to us by Renny Klein from Royal House Publishing Company, publishers of our first two cookbooks, *The Vegetarian Gourmet* (1987) and *Healthy Baking* (1992).

To Robin Coleman, we say "thank you" for all your fine secretarial services in connection with *Mother Nature's Garden*.

Last, but not least, we wish to acknowledge and thank our wonderful family and friends who love, encourage and inspire us.

CONTENTS

Foreword... vii

Introduction ix

    Ingredients xi

    Tips xi

Tempting Appetizers, Salads and Dressings 1

Soothing, Satisfying Soups 27

Exciting Entrées, Festive Party and Holiday Dishes
    and Ethnic Specialties...41

Healthful Whole-Grain Breads and Muffins 115

Delicious Cakes, Tortes and Pies 139

Wholesome Cookies, Pastries and Sweets 175

Nourishing Breakfast and Brunch Specialites..............209

FOREWORD

Heart disease and cancer are fast becoming national epidemics. However, there is something we can do to help prevent these scourges:

• By reducing or eliminating our intake of meat, poultry, eggs and dairy products, with their excessive loads of artery-clogging saturated fats and cholesterol, we can minimize our risk of heart attacks, strokes and various kinds of cancers, as well as drastically decrease the amount of pesticides we ingest.

• By reducing our intake of high-sodium foods, many people can help prevent and successfully treat high blood pressure.

• By reducing our intake of refined sugars, we can lessen the damage from tooth decay, calcium loss from bones, and free-radical damage that ages vital tissues, all associated with high-sugar diets.

For those interested in lowering their risk of disease and raising their levels of health and well-being, *Mother Nature's Garden*, by Florence and Mickey Bienenfeld, is an ideal cookbook choice. The recipes contain purely non-animal foods, free of cholesterol and low in sodium and fats. Their baked goods are sweetened mainly with fruit and vegetable sweeteners. They feature a large and exciting variety of vegetarian salads, soups, appetizers, entrées, breads, breakfast and brunch items, and desserts of all kinds. This garden's paths will lead you along a delicious journey toward better health.

Michael Klaper, M.D.
Vegan Nutrition: Pure and Simple

INTRODUCTION

There are many reasons why people choose not to eat meat, eggs, and dairy products. Some do so for religious and moral reasons, others because of allergies and yet others to maintain or recover good health. We have written *Mother Nature's Garden* for all these people.

In the next few pages we wish to expound on the health benefits of a pure vegetarian diet, free of all animal products, which are really quite astounding. According to John Robbins, author of *Diet For a New America* (Stillpoint Publisher, 1987):

- Populations with high meat intakes have correspondingly high rates of colon cancer.
- Women who eat meat daily have a fourfold higher risk of getting breast cancer than do women who eat meat less than once a week.
- Women who eat eggs daily have a threefold higher risk of getting breast cancer than do women who eat eggs less than once a week.
- Women who eat butter and cheese three or more times a week have a threefold higher risk of getting breast cancer than do women who eat these foods less often than once a week.
- Women who eat eggs three or more times a week have a threefold higher risk of getting ovarian cancer than do women who eat eggs less often than once a week.
- Men who consume meat, cheese, eggs, and milk daily are 3.6 times more likely to get prostrate cancer than are men who eat these foods sparingly or not at all.
- Whereas for the average American man the risk of death from heart attack is 50 percent, the risk of death from heart attack for the average American vegetarian man is 15 percent. For the average American pure vegetarian man (who eats no animal products), the risk of death from heart attack is 4 percent. An omnivore who stops eating any meat, dairy products, or eggs reduces his or her risk of heart attack by 90 percent.

- If your blood cholesterol is within the range considered "normal," your risk of dying of a disease caused by clogged arteries is over 50 percent. If you do not consume saturated fat and cholesterol, your risk of dying of a disease caused by clogged arteries is 5 percent.
- Meat supplies 55 percent of the pesticide residues in the average U.S. diet. Dairy products supply 23 percent; vegetables supply 6 percent; fruits supply 4 percent; and grains supply 1 percent. Ninety-nine percent of U.S. mothers (but only 8 percent of U.S. vegetarian mothers) have significant levels of DDT in their breast milk.

Besides being free of all animal products, our recipes are also low in fat and salt, and free of refined sugar. Only whole-grain flours are used in our baked goods.

In *Live Longer Now* (Grosset, 1974), the late Nathan Pritikin, renowned nutritionist and forerunner in the area of preventative health, identified five basic categories of foods as harmful because they can lead to serious degenerative diseases, such as heart disease, atherosclerosis, hypertension and diabetes. These categories are *cholesterol*, *fat*, *salt*, *sugar* and *caffeine*. We therefore suggest the following five rules for healthy eating:

1. The first rule for healthy eating is to reduce your cholesterol intake. Americans consume four times the amount of cholesterol they can handle, and this can lead to illness. Cholesterol is found in all animal products, such as egg yolks, dairy products, meat, and poultry. As blood cholesterol levels rise, the risk of heart disease also goes up. As the arteries become blocked with plaque, blood flow is reduced, less oxygen reaches the body and the brain, and heart attacks become likely. The good news is that plaque in the arteries can regress in time if cholesterol intake is reduced. Every recipe in *Mother Nature's Garden* is cholesterol-free.

2. The second rule for healthy eating is to reduce your intake of *all* kinds of fats as much as possible, and to avoid deep-fried foods entirely. Cook with as little fat as possible. This includes solid as well as saturated liquid or polyunsaturated fat. The average American's diet is 42 percent fat. Most hunting and gathering peoples get about 10 percent of their calories from fat. There is increasing evidence that eating *no* fat is better than eating either saturated or polyunsaturated fat. Recent research shows that hydrogenated fat, found in shortenings and margarines, is especially harmful. When corn or soybean oils are hydrogenated, molecules in the oil are changed into trans-fatty acids. These fatty acids are capable of raising harmful low-density lipoproteins (LDL), the cholesterol-carrying proteins that are associated with the risk of atherosclerosis. Researchers warn anyone at risk of heart disease to avoid a diet high in trans-fatty acids. Most breads, crackers, and pastries found in bakeries and markets are made with hydrogenated fats or partially hydrogenated oils. It pays to check labels before buying. Most health-food stores carry brands of baked goods without hydrogenated fat or oil. Heated and reheated oils, especially those used in frying, are known to contain carcinogens (cancer-producing substances). Our recipes are low in fat, and many are fat-free.

3. The third rule for healthy eating is to eat as little salt as possible. Salt sometimes contributes to hypertension, which can lead to strokes. Northern Japan, where great amounts of salt are used in cooking, has the highest incidence of hypertension in the world.

You *can* enhance the flavors in foods with little or no salt. In our recipes, we call for reduced-salt soy sauce in place of salt. One tablespoon of reduced-salt soy sauce contains less sodium than 1/4 teaspoon of salt. Bragg Liquid Aminos which tastes like soy sauce and contains essential amino acids, is also very low in sodium.

4. The fourth rule for healthy eating is to reduce intake of sugar and alcohol. Consuming sugar (and alcohol) tends to raise levels of blood fat and increase levels of blood cholesterol, and can also lead to diabetes. Sugar, honey, molasses, and syrups are "simple" carbohydrates. Eaten in large amounts, they can overwhelm the body, causing the cholesterol levels in the body to increase very quickly, and they can even cause the person to exhibit diabetic symptoms. "Complex" carbohydrates, found in breads, grains, vegetables, roots, pastas, potatoes and fruits, are broken down by the body into sugar at a slow rate. This sugar trickles into our bloodstreams a little at a time, without overwhelming the body and causing high fat levels or diabetes. Fortunately, both diabetes and hypoglycemia (abnormally low blood sugar) can be prevented and treated by decreasing intake of simple sugars. Our baked goods are sweetened with only fruit, fruit juices, or yams, squash, carrots, and occasionally molasses and maple syrup.

5. The fifth rule for healthy eating is to avoid intake of caffeine, which is found in coffee and tea. Caffeine give a person an energy boost by increasing the free fatty acids in the bloodstream. But continuous high levels of free fatty acids help degenerative diseases to develop. For this reason, caffeine intake is associated with heart disease, atherosclerosis, and diabetes. One study has shown that caffeine intake can lead directly to conditions that bring about the fibrillation type of heart attack. Another study links caffeine to the development of cancer.

Many people are addicted to the caffeine in coffee, tea and colas. If you are planning to give up caffeine, be prepared for a period of withdrawal. Drink decaffeinated teas or coffees, or, preferably, herbal teas or one of the coffee substitutes available in health-food stores.

There are no guarantees in life, but neither is there need to put ourselves at risk. Our fertile planet abounds with a great variety of delicious, wholesome, satisfying, and life-sustaining foods to choose from. And these foods can be prepared in an endless variety of appealing ways.

In *Mother Nature's Garden* you will find exciting recipes that not only taste good and please your palate, but satisfy you and keep you feeling good. Our best wishes to you for good health and good eating!

INGREDIENTS

All of the ingredients called for in our recipes are pure, natural, wholesome and free of eggs, dairy products, honey, and other animal products, and cholesterol, sugar, chemical additives, and preservatives.

In addition, most of the dishes are low in fat and low in salt. Only fruit and vegetable sweeteners are used in most recipes. *A word of caution* to those persons who must avoid salt entirely, and to diabetics who must restrict their use of all sweeteners: Please consult with your physician regarding these ingredients.

Following is a list of the ingredients used. Some of these items are available only in health-food stores.

Sweeteners: Yams and sweet potatoes, banana squash, carrots, dates, black raisins, fresh fruits (choose organically grown fruits whenever possible), frozen concentrated fruit juices, fruit juice sweetened jams, maple syrup, dark molasses, and barley malt.

Flours and Grains: Whole wheat flour, whole wheat pastry flour, brown rice flour, oat flour, rolled oats, oat bran, rye flour, buckwheat, wheat bran, barley, cornmeal, cornstarch, masa harina, soy flour, gluten flour, brown rice, granola, wholegrain cereal flakes, puffed millet, whole-grain pastas and whole wheat matzos.

Proteins: Tofu (soybean curd), beans, lentils, peas, seeds, soy flour (ground dry soy beans), gluten flour (the high-protein part of wheat flour), and soy milk.

Vegetables: Onions, garlic, celery, carrots, mushrooms, bell peppers, asparagus, broccoli, cauliflower, string beans, squash, lettuce, cabbage, tomatoes, green onions, chile peppers, potatoes, corn, eggplant, yams, bean sprouts and Chinese snow peas. Use organic vegetables whenever possible.

Herbs, Seasonings and Spices: Reduced-salt soy sauce contains 85 milligrams sodium per 1/2 teaspoon, whereas regular soy sauce contains 185 milligrams sodium per 1/2 teaspoon. Bragg Liquid Aminos is a low-sodium seasoning that is made of only soybeans and water and it contains 100 milligrams sodium per 1/2 teaspoon, tastes like soy sauce but is not fermented. Sea salt is used only in a few recipes in small quantities. Vegit is another low-sodium seasoning, made from a special yeast grown on blackstrap molasses, sea greens, and a variety of vegetables and herbs. The sodium content is less than 50 milligrams per ounce. Other seasonings are basil, oregano, thyme, cumin, curry powder, chili powder, cayenne, gingerroot, ground ginger, ground coriander, cinnamon, cloves, nutmeg, onion powder and garlic powder.

Fats: Olive oil, safflower or canola oil (cold-pressed oil is preferable), avocado, tahini (ground hulled sesame seeds), nuts, nut butters, and seeds are included only in very small amounts.

Canned or Bottled Goods: Tomato purée, tomato paste, diced green chile peppers, and mustard.

Water: Use bottled spring water whenever possible, because foods taste better without chlorine content found in tapwater.

Miscellaneous: Baking soda, baking powder (a non-aluminum kind is preferable), cream of tartar, carob powder, grain-based coffee substitutes, and, for jelling, agar (seaweed) flakes.

TIPS

Read each recipe through very carefully before beginning, and assemble all the ingredients called for. Preheat the oven before baking. Use level measures. Keep in mind that the amount of time required for cooking or baking and the number of persons each dish will serve is only approximate.

Buying and Storing Foods

Use only black raisins, which contain no preservatives. Cold-pressed oils, available in health-food stores and some supermarkets, retain more of their flavor and vitamins than oils processed with heat and chemicals. In recipes calling for whole grain cereal flakes, use fruit-sweetened, salt-free, and sugar-free products. These are available in health-food stores and some supermarkets.

Yams, called for in many recipes, can be baked until soft ahead of time, then refrigerated or frozen and defrosted as needed. One pound of yams, baked and peeled, yields about 1 cup.

Fresh basil, cilantro, and other herbs, jalapeño peppers, and fresh gingerroot, can be washed, drained and frozen for use as needed. Use them fresh whenever possible, though.

Nuts can be chopped and frozen, then measured out as needed for various recipes.

Buy organically grown produce whenever possible. The price for pesticide-free foods is well worth any additional expense.

Cooking Beans

To cook dry, cover them with water, bring them to a boil, and let them simmer for 10 minutes. Then leave them to soak in the water until they are cool, or overnight. Rinse them well, cover them with fresh water, and cook them until tender. You can store them for a day or two in the refrigerator before using them in a recipe.

Stovetop Cooking Without Oil

To sauté onions or other vegetables without oil, heat a nonstick frying pan over medium heat. Add the onions or other vegetables and 1 to 2 tablespoons water. Sauté uncovered, stir occasionally with a wooden spoon. If the onions or other vegetables begin to stick, add a little more water, stirring to release them from the sides and bottom of the pan. Repeat this process until the onions or other vegetables are softened.

To brown onions or other vegetables without oil, use the same process as for sautéing, but do not add water in the beginning. Stir the onions or other vegetables occasionally with a wooden spoon. After they brown a little and begin to stick, add a little water, and continue sautéing until they are softened.

To fry pancakes without oil, heat a nonstick griddle or a large nonstick frying pan until it is very hot. Fry the pancakes until they are brown on both sides.

To reheat solid foods, such as rice, beans, casseroles, and stir-fried tofu and vegetables: Place the portion you are reheating in a nonstick frying pan or saucepan. Pour 1/4 cup water into the pan, around the edges. Cover the pan, and place it over medium heat for 5 minutes, or over low heat for about 10 to 15 minutes, or until the food is hot. To reheat thick soups or stews: Place the amount you are reheating in a saucepan. Stir in 1/4 cup water. Cover the pan, place it over low heat for about 10 to 15 minutes, or until the soup or stew is hot.

Preparing Tofu

In supermarkets, tofu usually comes in liquid-filled plastic containers. To prepare the tofu for use, place the container in the sink; with a sharp knife slit its plastic top on two adjacent sides and and tilt the container to drain off the liquid. Without removing the tofu, fill the container with fresh water, and drain off the water. Repeat this step twice more. Leaving no water in container, cover it. Place the container in the refrigerator, and leave the tofu to drain in the container for at least 1 hour and for up to several days. Before using the tofu in a recipe, drain off all the liquid that has accumulated in the container. Tofu is now ready to be used in a variety of recipes.

Baking

Use only whole-grain flours. These are available in health-food stores and some supermarkets. To prevent rancidity in whole-grain flours and cereals, store them in the refrigerator.

If possible, use whole wheat pastry flour when it is called for. If you can't get any, substitute regular whole wheat flour, but reduce the quantity of flour by 2 tablespoons per cup, and increase the baking time by 5 to 10 minutes. The product will be moister and slightly heavier.

It is not necessary to sift flour in any of the recipes; however, if your baking soda is lumpy, you may need to put it through a strainer before adding it to the other dry ingredients.

Use a brand of baking powder without aluminum, whenever possible. Such brands are available in health-food stores.

To prepare yeast dough, dissolve the yeast granules into warm water (105°). We advise using a candy thermometer, since hotter temperatures will kill the yeast.

When kneading is called for, knead the dough on a lightly floured board, using as little flour as necessary to keep the dough from sticking. To have time, you may be able to knead dough in your food processor (refer to your food processor instruction booklet).

Yeast dough is normally left to rise, covered, in a warm place until it has doubled in bulk. The bowl need not be oiled. To slow the rising, you can leave the dough in the refrigerator for several hours or overnight. To speed the rising, you can set the oven at 200° (not hotter) for 60 seconds *only*. Turn off the oven, then place in it, on the same shelf, the bowl with dough, covered, and a small pan of boiling water. Dough will rise in one-third to one-half the usual time. This faster-rising method can be used for both the first and second risings. The second rising usually takes less time than the first. Dough has risen sufficiently when a moistened finger poked 1/2 inch into the dough leaves an indentation. Placing dough in the refrigerator or freezer for 30 minutes to 1 hour can make sticky dough easier to handle or knead.

Take care not to overbake the low-fat, low-cholesterol cakes and breads in this book; they can easily become too dry. Remove cakes and breads from the oven as soon as a cake tester shows no sign of wet, raw batter. Don't expect the tester to come out completely clean; a small crumb of dry batter may still cling to it. Cakes and breads become less moist as they cool.

To preserve the freshness and moistness of whole-grain baked goods, especially those low in fat, store them in the refrigerator or freezer until you are ready to use them. Before serving, wrap bread, muffins, scones or pastries in foil, and reheat them in a 350° oven just until they are warm, or toast them in a toaster oven.

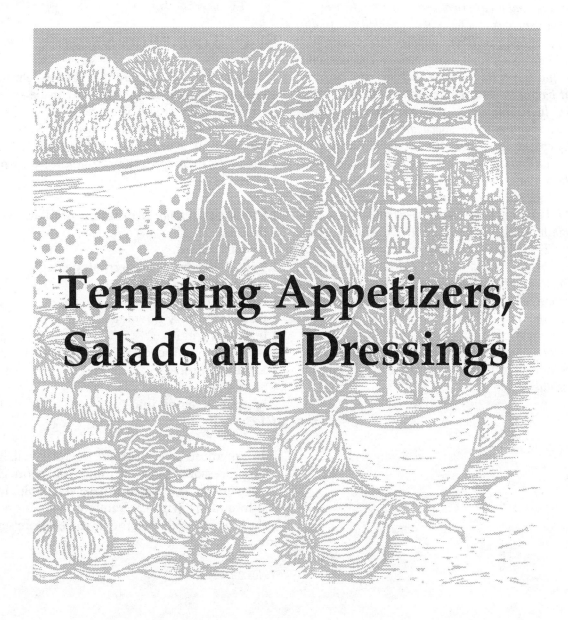

Tempting Appetizers, Salads and Dressings

In this chapter you will find refreshing appetizers, dips, and salads, and a variety of tasty, low-fat dressings.

What may look and taste like egg salad is actually Spicy Tofu "Egg Salad," or sandwich spread. Seasoned with onions, gingerroot, curry powder, cayenne, and lemon juice, it tastes so good that you will want to keep it handy in your refrigerator all the time, yet it takes only 10 minutes to prepare. Other appetizers include an egg-free quiche; Babaganoosh (Middle Eastern Eggplant Appetizer); Sliced Tofu Wieners in Dough; an Indian Garbanzo Bean Dip; and a Fresh Vegetable Platter with Lemon-Tahini-Garlic Dip.

Mother Nature's Garden is resplendent with healthful and refreshing salad vegetables. Whenever possible buy organic produce; it is worth the extra money. The salad recipes here include an easy pasta salad; a broccoli salad with avocado-mustard dressing; Tabouli Bulgar Wheat Salad; Pickled Beet Salad; Moroccan Bell Pepper Salad; and Buckwheat Noodle Salad with Ginger-Orange-Pecan Dressing.

All of these exciting dips, salads and dressings are low in fat and salt, free of cholesterol and sugar, and, except for one, is free of wheat, to which many people may be allergic.

Spicy Tofu "Egg Salad"

This delicious and nourishing spread is delicately spiced with curry and ginger. It can be served on whole-grain bread or crackers, stuffed into celery, or spread on sandwiches with lettuce or sprouts. It takes only about 10 minutes to prepare, and can keep in the refrigerator for up to one week.

1 14-ounce package firm tofu, rinsed and well drained
1/2 small onion
1 1-inch slice fresh gingerroot, peeled
2 celery stalks
1 medium carrot
2 teaspoons curry powder
1 teaspoon Vegit
1 tablespoon reduced-salt soy sauce or Bragg Liquid Aminos
1/8 teaspoon cayenne
2 teaspoons lemon juice
1/4 cup tahini

Into a medium bowl, crumble the tofu well. In a food processor or by hand, mince the onion, ginger, celery, and carrot. Stir these vegetables into the tofu along with the remaining six ingredients. Mix well, and chill the mixture before serving.

Yields 2 1/4 cups

Tofu Onion "Egg Salad"

This mildly flavored high-protein spread is easy to prepare. It makes delicious sandwiches.

1 14-ounce package regular tofu, rinsed and well drained
1 small onion
2 green onions
3 celery stalks
1 large carrot
1/4 teaspoon ground black pepper
1 teaspoon Vegit
1 teaspoon curry powder
1 tablespoon reduced-salt soy sauce or Bragg Liquid Aminos
1/4 cup tahini
1 teaspoon lemon juice

Crumble the tofu into a medium bowl. In a food processor or by hand, coarsely chop the onions, celery, and carrot, and stir the vegetables into the tofu. Stir in the remaining six ingredients, and mix well. Chill the mixture before serving.

Yields 2 1/4 cups

Tofu "Egg Salad" with Dill

Dill and bell pepper give a delightful flavor to this nourishing high-protein spread.

1 14-ounce package regular tofu, rinsed and well drained
1/2 medium onion
2 celery stalks
1 medium carrot
1/4 large bell pepper
1 tablespoon fresh dill (or 2 teaspoons dried dill)
1 teaspoon curry powder
2 tablespoons tahini
2 teaspoons cider vinegar
2 teaspoons maple syrup
1 tablespoon reduced-salt soy sauce or Bragg Liquid Aminos
1 teaspoon lemon juice

Into a medium bowl, crumble the tofu. In a food processor or by hand, mince the onion, celery, carrot, bell pepper, and dill. Stir the minced vegetables into the tofu along with the remaining ingredients. Mix well, and chill the mixture before serving.

Yields 2 1/4 cups

CURRY-GINGER-TOFU-VEGETABLE QUICHE

Note that this quiche is wheat-free.

Crust
2/3 cup brown rice flour
1/2 teaspoon curry powder
1 teaspoon onion powder
2 tablespoons water
1 tablespoon safflower or canola oil
1/2 teaspoon reduced-salt soy sauce or Bragg
   Liquid Aminos

Filling
1 medium onion
3 large garlic cloves
1 large red bell pepper
1 1-1/2 inch slice fresh gingerroot, peeled
2 tablespoons water
2 14-ounce packages regular tofu, rinsed and
   well drained
2 tablespoons tahini
1 1/2 tablespoons reduced-salt soy sauce or
   Bragg Liquid Aminos
1 tablespoon curry powder
2 teaspoons Vegit
1/8 teaspoon cayenne
1 tablespoon lemon juice
3 tablespoons cornstarch

Preheat the oven to 400°.

In a small bowl mix together the rice flour, curry powder, and onion powder. In a cup or a small bowl, mix the water with the oil and soy sauce or Bragg, and stir this mixture into the flour mixture with a fork until the ingredients are blended. Press the dough onto the bottom and 1/2 inch up the sides of a 10-inch ovenproof glass deep-dish pie plate. The dough will be thin. Bake the crust for 12 minutes, remove the crust from oven, then reduce the oven temperature to 325°.

While the crust has been baking, prepare the filling: Mince the onion, garlic, bell pepper, and gingerroot in a food processor or by hand. In a preheated nonstick frying pan, sauté the vegetables over medium heat without oil until the pan becomes dry, stirring occasionally. Stir in 2 tablespoons water, and continue sautéing until the onions are soft. Place vegetables in a large bowl.

Beat the tofu in a food processor or blender until it is smooth. Add the next seven ingredients to the tofu, and beat until the mixture is well blended. Stir the tofu mixture into the sautéed vegetables, and stir to mix well.

Pour the quiche filling into the prebaked crust and bake the quiche for 30 to 35 minutes, or until the filling has set. Allow the quiche to cool for 5 to 10 minutes before serving.

Serves 6

Hummus
(Middle Eastern Dip)

Hummus should be prepared the day before serving.

1 1/2 cups dry garbanzo beans
6 cups water
6 cups water
1 small onion, cut in half
3 large garlic cloves
2/3 cup broth from cooking garbanzo beans
    (in case there is not enough broth, add
    enough water to equal 2/3 cup)
4 large garlic cloves
3/4 cup tahini
1 teaspoon ground cumin
1/3 cup lemon juice
1/4 teaspoon sea salt (optional)
Pinch cayenne
Chopped parsley and paprika for garnish

In a large covered pot, bring the beans and 6 cups water to a boil. Simmer the beans for 10 minutes, then allow them to soak in the hot water until they are cool, or overnight. Drain and rinse the beans well, and return them to the pot. Stir in 6 cups water, the onion, and three cloves of garlic. Bring the beans to a boil, cover them and cook them on low heat for about 3 hours, or until the beans are tender. Toward the end of the cooking time, add 1 cup more water, if necessary, to keep the beans from sticking. Drain the beans, reserving the broth. Add water to the broth, if necessary, to equal 2/3 cup.

In a food processor or blender, purée the beans in batches with the four remaining garlic cloves, the bean broth, and the tahini, dividing the 2/3 cup of broth, garlic and tahini. Put the garbanzo bean-tahini mixture into a large bowl, and stir in the cumin, lemon juice, salt, and cayenne. Chill the hummus well. If the hummus thickens too much as it sets, add 1/4 cup additional water, and stir well. Sprinkle the chopped parsley and paprika on top. Serve with warm pita bread cut into halves or quarters.

Yields 6 cups and serves 12 to 18

Babaganoosh

1 large whole eggplant, with stem intact
2 tablespoons lemon juice
3 tablespoons tahini
4 garlic cloves
1 tablespoon reduced-salt soy sauce or Bragg
    Liquid Aminos

Preheat the oven to 450°.

In a foil-lined 10 x 15-inch baking pan, bake the whole eggplant for about 30 minutes, or until it is very soft. Place the eggplant in a mixing bowl, cut it in half, and let the liquid drain out. Discard the liquid, and peel the eggplant. In a food processor or blender, purée the eggplant with the remaining ingredients until the mixture is smooth. Chill well. Serve with pita bread or crackers.

Serves 6 to 8

WHEAT-FREE LENTIL-NUT-OAT BRAN BALLS

These delicious, high-protein balls make tasty appetizers. Serve them hot with Spicy Barbecue Sauce or Sweet and Sour Sauce (page 81), or in spaghetti sauce over pasta.

3/4 cup dry brown lentils
3 1/2 cups water
1 tablespoon onion powder
1 teaspoon garlic powder
1/2 teaspoon celery seed
1/4 teaspoon ground black pepper
1 tablespoon reduced-salt soy sauce or Bragg
   Liquid Aminos
4 teaspoons Vegit
2 tablespoons cornstarch or potato starch
1/2 teaspoon baking powder
1/2 teaspoon baking soda
1/4 cup water
1/2 teaspoon lemon juice
3 large garlic cloves, minced or crushed
1 tablespoon reduced-salt soy sauce or Bragg
   Liquid Aminos
1/4 teaspoon ground black pepper
1/2 cup minced nuts
1 3/4 cups oat bran
2 teaspoons Vegit

In a 3-quart saucepan, bring the first seven ingredients and 2 teaspoons Vegit to a boil. Lower the heat, cover the pan, and simmer lentils on lowest heat for about 35 minutes, or until they are tender.

Place the lentils and any liquid still remaining in the pan into a medium-size mixing bowl.

Preheat the oven to 400°.

In a small bowl, mix together the cornstarch or potato starch, the baking powder, and the baking soda. Stir in the water and lemon juice. This mixture will foam up, replacing eggs as leavening. Stir the mixture into the lentils, along with the remaining six ingredients and 2 teaspoons Vegit.

Shape the dough into balls the size of walnuts, or larger, if you like. (If the dough is too soft to work with, let it stand for 15 minutes.) Arrange the balls on a nonstick baking sheet. Bake them for 15 minutes, or until they are medium brown.

The balls can be made ahead of time, and kept refrigerated until a half-hour before serving. The balls can also be frozen after they are baked and cooled. Heat the thawed balls at 350° for approximately 8 to 10 minutes, or until they are warmed through.

Yields 36 to 48 balls

INDIAN GARBANZO BEAN DIP WITH CRISPY PITA BREAD

This nutritious dip keeps in the refrigerator for four to five days.

1 1/2 cups Indian-Style Garbanzo Bean Stew
   (page 58)
1/4 cup chopped fresh cilantro
1 tablespoon lemon juice
Crispy Pita Bread (page 8)

Purée the garbanzo bean stew in a food processor until it is smooth. Put the purée in a small mixing bowl, and stir in the cilantro and lemon juice. Chill the dip well. Serve with Crispy Pita Bread.

Serves 6 to 8

OVEN-BARBECUED TOFU APPETIZERS

For a chewier texture, the tofu *must* be frozen and thawed.

2 14-ounce packages firm tofu
Generous sprinkles of onion powder
Generous sprinkles of garlic powder
Generous sprinkles of paprika
Spicy Barbecue Sauce (page 100)

Freeze the tofu in unopened packages for at least one day before preparing this recipe. Allow the tofu to thaw overnight, then rinse and drain it. Cut each tofu block in half lengthwise, then cut each half into twelve squares. Arrange the cubes in a 9- by 13-inch glass baking dish, and sprinkle both sides generously with the onion powder, garlic powder, and paprika. Cover the dish and refrigerate it until 25 minutes before serving time.

Preheat the broiler. Set the oven rack about 6 inches below the broiler. Arrange the seasoned tofu squares on a nonstick cookie sheet, and brush the top sides with barbecue sauce. Broil the tofu 10 minutes. Remove the pan from the oven, turn the tofu squares over, and brush the other sides with sauce. Return the pan to the oven for another 10 minutes.

To serve the tofu squares, fill a small bowl with the remaining barbecue sauce, set the bowl in the center of a small platter, and arrange the tofu squares all around, with toothpicks on the side.

Yields 48 small appetizers

SLICED TOFU WIENERS IN DOUGH

Tofu wieners can be purchased at health-food stores and some supermarkets.

6 tofu wieners
1 cup whole-wheat flour
1/2 teaspoon baking powder
1 tablespoon onion powder
1 teaspoon garlic powder
1/4 cup water
2 tablespoons ~~safflower or canola oil~~ *Soy Spread*
1 teaspoon reduced-salt soy sauce or Bragg Liquid Aminos

Rinse and dry the wieners and set them aside. Preheat the oven to 400°.

In a small mixing bowl, mix together the dry ingredients. In a cup or small bowl, stir together the water, oil, and soy sauce or Bragg with a fork, then stir this into the flour mixture until the dough holds together. Roll out the dough 1/4 inch thick, and cut it into 3 1/2- by 5-inch rectangles. Wrap each dough rectangle around a tofu wiener, and seal the seam with a little water. With a serrated knife, cut each dough-wrapped wiener into six to eight diagonal slices. Arrange the slices on a nonstick baking sheet and bake them for 20 minutes. Serve with mustard and catsup.

Yields 36 to 48

CRISPY PITA BREAD

4 whole wheat pita loaves

Preheat the oven to 325°.

Cut each pita loaf into eight triangles. Arrange them on a 10- by 15-inch baking sheet. Bake for 10 minutes, then turn off the heat. Leave the wedges in the oven until very crisp.

Yields 32 wedges

BULGARIAN EGGPLANT-BELL PEPPER DIP

1 large whole eggplant, stem intact
3 large whole green peppers, stems intact
2 tablespoons tomato paste
1 teaspoon cider vinegar
2 teaspoons reduced-salt soy sauce or Bragg
  Liquid Aminos
About 1/8 teaspoon cayenne, to taste
4 garlic cloves, crushed
1 medium tomato, chopped (about 1/2 cup)

Preheat the oven to 450°.

Bake the eggplant and bell peppers in a foil-lined 10- by 15-inch baking pan until soft. Remove them from the oven and place them in a mixing bowl. Cut the eggplant and peppers in half, and let them drain. Discard all the liquid and peel the eggplant and peppers.

In a food processor or blender, purée the eggplant and bell peppers. Place the mixture in a bowl. Stir in the remaining ingredients. Chill the dip well before serving.

Serves 6

MIDDLE EASTERN APPETIZER PLATTER

2 cups Hummus (page 5)
2 cups Tabouli (page 11)
2 cups Easy Marinated Tomato and
  Cucumber Salad (page 12)
Babaganoosh **(page 5)**
Lettuce leaves or parsley for garnish
Sprinkle of paprika, for the Hummus
8 pita loaves

Preheat the oven to 350°.

Put the Hummus, Tabouli, Tomato and Cucumber Salad and *Babaganoosh* in a partitioned platter or four small serving bowls. If you use separate bowls, place them on a serving tray. Garnish the platter or tray with lettuce leaves or parsley, and sprinkle paprika on top of Hummus.

Heat the pita bread in the oven for 1 minute, or just until it is warm. Cut in halves, quarters, or smaller wedges.

Serves 6 to 8 as an appetizer, or 4 as an entrée

Marinated and Steamed Vegetables

This beautiful platter makes a healthful, delicious appetizer or adjunct to any meal.

6 small (or 2 large) artichokes
1 teaspoon cider vinegar
2 bunches asparagus, bottom ends snapped off
2 large broccoli stalks, large stems cut off
1 red bell pepper or 8 radishes, for garnish
Double recipe Fresh Herb Marinade, chilled

Simmer the artichokes in 3 inches of water with vinegar for 30 to 40 minutes, or just until a leaf can be easily pulled out. Be careful not to overcook them. Cut small artichokes in half. Leave large ones whole.

Steam the asparagus and the broccoli, separately, for 10 minutes or until they are barely tender. Be careful not to overcook them.

Arrange the steamed vegetables in a 9- by 13-inch glass casserole dish. Reserve 1/2 cup of the marinade, and pour the remaining marinade over the vegetables. Cover the dish, and chill the vegetables well.

Arrange the vegetables on a serving platter. Garnish with red bell pepper rings or red radishes. Serve the reserved marinade in a small serving bowl for dipping the artichoke petals.

Serves 8

Fresh Herb Marinade

This fresh-tasting marinade can be used both as a marinade for steamed vegetables and as a dip for raw vegetables.

3 large green onions
1 tablespoon minced fresh dill
1/3 cup parsley leaves
1/4 cup cilantro
1/2 medium green bell pepper
4 large garlic cloves
1 1/2-inch slice gingerroot, peeled
2 teaspoons prepared mustard (preferably stone-ground)
1/3 cup cider vinegar
2 tablespoons lemon juice
1/8 teaspoon ground black pepper
1 tablespoon reduced-salt soy sauce or Bragg Liquid Aminos

In a food processor or blender, blend all the ingredients well. Store in the refrigerator.

Yields 2/3 cup

Fresh Vegetable Platter

Serve this colorful vegetable platter with Lemon-Tahini-Garlic Dip on the side.

6 to 8 romaine lettuce leaves
1 medium tomato, sliced (or 1 cup cherry
   tomatoes)
1 medium cucumber, peeled and diagonally
   sliced
3 medium carrots, peeled and cut into sticks
12 red radishes, trimmed
6 to 8 small white mushrooms
4 celery stalks, cut into sticks
1/2 red bell pepper, sliced, for garnish

On a 12-inch round platter, arrange the romaine leaves in a circular pattern with the stem ends toward the center. Arrange the tomatoes in the center and group the remaining vegetables around the tomatoes. Garnish with the red bell pepper slices.

Serves 8 to 10

Artichokes with Lemon-Tahini Dressing

2 large or 4 small artichokes
2 garlic cloves
1 teaspoon cider vinegar
Lemon-Tahini Dressing (page 16)

Cut the stems from the artichokes, and remove the tough outer leaves. Cut 1/2 inch off the top of each artichoke. In a large pot, set the artichokes stem side down in 2 inches of water. Add the garlic and vinegar, cover the pot, bring the liquid to a boil, and reduce the heat. Simmer the artichokes covered, for 35 to 45 minutes, or until you can easily pull out a leaf. Drain the artichokes, and let them cool. Serve them with Lemon-Tahini Dressing as a dip.

Serves 6 to 8

Lemon-Tahini-Garlic Dip

Serve this delicious dip with fresh vegetables.

1/4 cup lemon juice
1/4 cup tahini
1/4 cup water
2 garlic cloves, crushed
1 teaspoon reduced-salt soy sauce or Bragg
   Liquid Aminos

In a small mixing bowl, stir together all ingredients until they are blended.

Yields 3/4 cup

TABOULI (BULGAR WHEAT SALAD)

1 1/2 cups uncooked bulgar wheat
3 cups water
2 teaspoons reduced-salt soy sauce or Bragg Liquid Aminos
2 cups chopped parsley
1/4 cup lemon juice
2 small tomatoes, chopped
2 large garlic cloves, minced or crushed
1 teaspoon olive oil

In a 3-quart saucepan, soak the bulgar wheat in the water with 2 teaspoons soy sauce or Bragg for 30 to 45 minutes. Bring the mixture to a boil, then reduce the heat and simmer the wheat, covered, for 10 minutes, or until the liquid is absorbed.

Put the cooked bulgar wheat in a bowl. Stir in the remaining ingredients. Toss well and chill before serving.

Serves 8

ROMAINE-TOMATO-AND-CARROT SALAD WITH CREAMY TOFU-CURRY DRESSING

You can turn this salad into an exciting luncheon or dinner entrée by topping each portion with a scoop of Spicy Tofu "Egg Salad."

6 cups bite-size pieces of romaine lettuce, chilled
1 green onion, chopped
1 medium tomato, cut into wedges
1 cup grated carrots
1 cup Creamy Tofu-Curry Dressing, well chilled

Toss all the ingredients in a medium bowl, and serve immediately.

Serves 2 to 4

CREAMY TOFU-CURRY DRESSING (OR DIP)

1 14-ounce package soft tofu, rinsed and well drained
1 tablespoon reduced-salt soy sauce or Bragg Liquid Aminos
2 teaspoons lemon juice
1 tablespoon onion powder
1/2 teaspoon garlic powder
1 teaspoon curry powder

In a food processor or blender, blend all ingredients until the mixture is smooth and creamy.

Yields 1 1/2 cups

EASY MARINATED TOMATO AND CUCUMBER SALAD

This crunchy salad goes especially well with Hummus and pita bread.

2 cups bite-size pieces of cucumber (6 to 8 pickling cucumbers or 3 slicing cucumbers)
3 cups bite-size pieces of tomatoes (from about 8 small tomatoes)
1 medium green pepper, cut in bite-size pieces
2 green onions, chopped
3 tablespoons cider vinegar
2 teaspoons reduced-salt soy sauce or Bragg Liquid Aminos
Pinch ground black pepper

In a medium bowl, mix the ingredients together. Toss them well, cover the bowl, and chill for 2 hours before serving.

Serves 6 to 8

BROCCOLI-VEGETABLE SALAD WITH AVOCADO-MUSTARD DRESSING

6 to 8 romaine lettuce leaves, cut in bite-size pieces and chilled
1 1/2 cups broccoli florets and tender stems, cut into bite-size pieces
1/2 red bell pepper, chopped
1 green onion, chopped
Avocado-Mustard Dressing

Toss the vegetables with the dressing in a medium bowl, and serve immediately.

Serves 2

AVOCADO-MUSTARD DRESSING

This tangy dressing is best made just before serving. It takes only a few minutes to prepare. You can add the ingredients directly to chilled salad, if you prefer, then toss and serve.

1 tablespoon Dijon-type prepared mustard
2 teaspoons lemon juice
1/4 medium avocado, chopped
1/2 teaspoon reduced-salt soy sauce or Bragg Liquid Aminos

Mix the ingredients in a small bowl, or add them directly to the salad. Toss the dressing with the salad, and serve the salad immediately.

Yields enough dressing for a salad for 2

Chopped Salad for Two

This refreshing salad is full of fiber, vitamins, and minerals.

1 large tomato, cut into bite-size pieces
3 romaine lettuce leaves, cut into bite-size
  pieces
1 medium cucumber, cut into bite-size pieces
1 medium carrot, cut into bite-size pieces
2 celery stalks, cut into bite-size pieces
1/4 medium avocado, cut into bite-size pieces
1 teaspoon lemon juice
1 teaspoon cider vinegar
1/2 teaspoon reduced-salt soy sauce or Bragg
  Liquid Aminos
1 teaspoon prepared mustard
1 garlic clove, minced
 1 teaspoon olive oil (optional)

Put the vegetables into a medium bowl, and chill them well.

In a small bowl, mix together the last six ingredients. Toss the salad with the dressing, and serve immediately.

Serves 2

Cucumber Salad with Fresh Dill

The cucumbers and onion can be sliced in a food processor.

3 medium cucumbers, peeled and thinly
  sliced
1/4 large onion, thinly sliced
1 teaspoon reduced-salt soy sauce or Bragg
  Liquid Aminos
2 tablespoons chopped fresh dill
1 tablespoon onion powder
1/4 cup cider vinegar
2 tablespoons frozen or thawed apple juice
  concentrate

Put all the ingredients in a medium bowl, and toss them well. Serve the salad well chilled.

Serves 4 to 6

Easy Colorful Pasta Salad

4 Japanese eggplants, cut into 1/3-inch round slices
1/2 large onion
6 large garlic cloves
1 large red bell pepper
6 fresh basil leaves
8 fresh oregano leaves
3 medium tomatoes, cut into quarters
8 ounces whole-grain rotini spiral pasta, preferably multicolored
2 teaspoons olive oil
2 teaspoons reduced-salt soy sauce or Bragg Liquid Aminos
2 teaspoons cider vinegar

Soak the eggplant slices in cold water for 15 to 20 minutes.

In a food processor or by hand, coarsely chop the next five ingredients. Preheat a large covered nonstick frying pan, and stirring occasionally, sauté the chopped vegetables and drained eggplant slices together without oil, over medium heat uncovered, until the pan becomes dry. Coarsely chop the tomatoes in food processor or by hand, and stir them into the other vegetables. Lower the heat, cover the pan, and simmer the vegetables for 15 minutes, or until the eggplant slices are tender. Put the mixture into a large bowl.

Cook the pasta until it is tender but still firm. Drain and stir it into the vegetables along with the oil, soy sauce or Bragg, and vinegar. Toss the salad well, and chill it before serving.

Serves 6

Lettuce-Broccoli-and-Tomato Salad with Tangy Red Bell Pepper Dressing

This flavorful salad is very low in calories.

1 small head of Boston lettuce, cut into bite-size pieces
1 broccoli stalk, florets only, cut into bite-size pieces
6 cherry tomatoes, cut in half

Into a medium bowl put the lettuce, broccoli, and tomatoes. Chill the salad until you're ready to serve.

Toss the salad with Tangy Red Bell Pepper Dressing, and serve at once.

Serves 2 to 3

Tangy Red Bell Pepper Dressing

1/2 small red bell pepper
1/8 large red onion
1 garlic clove
1 tablespoon lemon juice
2 tablespoons cider vinegar
2 tablespoons water
1 teaspoon reduced-salt soy sauce or Bragg Liquid Aminos
1 teaspoon olive oil

Blend all the ingredients in a food processor or blender, and chill the mixture well.

Yields 1/2 cup

CUCUMBER-CHERRY TOMATO-AND-ROMAINE SALAD WITH VINAIGRETTE DRESSING

This salad takes only minutes to prepare.

12 romaine lettuce leaves, chilled
1 medium-size cucumber, peeled, sliced, and chilled
24 cherry tomatoes, chilled

Arrange three lettuce leaves on each of four salad plates. Over the lettuce, on one half of the plate, arrange one-fourth of the cucumber slices; on the other half place six cherry tomatoes. Spoon Vinaigrette Dressing over each serving.

Serves 4

VINAIGRETTE DRESSING

Enjoy this light vinaigrette over crisp, fresh vegetables or salads. Use the dressing sparingly, because its flavor is quite strong.

1/2 cup cider vinegar
4 garlic cloves, crushed or finely minced
4 teaspoons Dijon-type mustard
2 teaspoons reduced-salt soy sauce or Bragg Liquid Aminos
1 to 2 teaspoons olive, safflower or canola oil
Pinch ground black pepper

In a small bowl, beat all the ingredients with a fork until they are well blended.

Yields 2/3 cup

EASY HEARTS OF ROMAINE SALAD

1 large romaine lettuce, rinsed and drained

Cut the lettuce head lengthwise into four equal wedges, leaving the stem intact. Chill the lettuce wedges well in the refrigerator, or to save time, in ice water. Serve one wedge on each of four salad plates. Spoon Vinaigrette Dressing sparingly over each serving.

Serves 4

ROMAINE SALAD WITH LEMON-DIJON DRESSING

The dressing can be made ahead of time and stored in the refrigerator.

1 large head romaine lettuce, rinsed, cut into bite-size pieces
2 tablespoons lemon juice
2 tablespoons cider vinegar
1 tablespoon olive oil
1 tablespoon onion powder
1 teaspoon garlic powder
1/8 teaspoon pepper
2 teaspoons Dijon-type mustard
1 tablespoon water
1 teaspoon reduced-salt soy sauce or Bragg Liquid Aminos

Chill the lettuce well. In a small bowl, mix together all the remaining ingredients. Toss the salad in a large bowl, and serve immediately.

Serves 4

CHOPPED VEGETABLE SALAD FOR TWO WITH LEMON-TAHINI DRESSING

Enjoy this crunchy, satisfying salad for lunch or dinner.

8 lettuce leaves, cut into bite-size pieces
3/4 cup thinly sliced carrots
1 cup chopped broccoli
2 red radishes, chopped
1 green onion, chopped
1 celery stalk, chopped
2 to 3 tablespoons Lemon-Tahini Dressing

Toss all the ingredients together in a medium bowl. Serve immediately.

Serves 2

CHOPPED VEGETABLE-PASTA SALAD WITH LEMON-TAHINI DRESSING

Chopped Vegetable Salad for Two
4 cups cooked whole wheat or brown-rice pasta, rinsed in cold water
4 to 6 tablespoons Lemon-Tahini Dressing

Toss together all the ingredients in a large bowl. Chill the salad before serving.

Serves 6 to 8

LEMON-TAHINI DRESSING

This sesame-flavored dressing keeps in the refrigerator up to two weeks. Use it sparingly on your favorite vegetable salad or on cold pasta.

2 large garlic cloves, minced or crushed
1/4 cup tahini
4 teaspoons reduced-salt soy sauce or Bragg Liquid Aminos
1/4 cup lemon juice
2 tablespoons water

Mix together all the ingredients. Store the dressing in the refrigerator in a small covered jar.

Yields 2/3 cup

ROMAINE AND TOMATO SALAD WITH AVOCADO-LEMON-HERB DRESSING

The mildly flavored herb dressing should be mixed in the salad bowl shortly before serving. The salad takes only a few minutes to prepare.

1/2 large head (10 to 12 leaves) romaine
   lettuce, rinsed, drained, cut into bite-size
   pieces and chilled well
2 small tomatoes, cut into wedges
1/4 medium avocado, chopped
1 garlic clove, minced
1 tablespoon lemon juice
1 tablespoon cider vinegar
1/2 teaspoon reduced-salt soy sauce or Bragg
   Liquid Aminos
Pinch oregano
Pinch thyme
Pinch basil

In a medium bowl mix together the lettuce, tomato wedges, and the remaining ingredients. Toss the salad well and serve immediately.

Serves 2

EXOTIC EGGPLANT SALAD

This salad can be made a day or two before serving. Serve it as a salad or as an appetizer.

1 large eggplant, peeled and cut into 1/2-inch
   cubes
1/2 medium onion
2 large garlic cloves
1/2 large red or green bell pepper
3 celery stalks
1 medium tomato, chopped
1/2 cup tomato purée
1/8 teaspoon cayenne
1 teaspoon cumin
2 tablespoons frozen or thawed apple juice
   concentrate
1/4 cup cider vinegar
1 teaspoon reduced-salt soy sauce or Bragg
   Liquid Aminos

Soak the eggplant cubes in enough water to cover them for 20 minutes. Drain and cook it in a large, covered, nonstick frying pan with 2 tablespoons of water over medium heat for about 15 minutes, or until the eggplant is tender.

Remove the eggplant to a bowl, and set the bowl aside. In a food processor or by hand, coarsely chop the onion, garlic, pepper, and celery. In the pan in which you cooked the eggplant, stir-fry these vegetables without oil for about 10 minutes, or until they are tender.

Return the eggplant to the pan, and stir in the remaining ingredients. Cook eggplant and vegetables uncovered for 20 minutes.

Let the mixture cool, and chill it until you're ready to serve.

Serves 8 to 10

Tasty Red Coleslaw

This salad is easy to prepare and stores well in the refrigerator for several days.

1 medium red cabbage, shredded
2 tablespoons frozen or thawed apple juice
   concentrate
2 tablespoons cider vinegar
1 tablespoon lemon juice
1 teaspoon reduced-salt soy sauce or Bragg
   Liquid Aminos
1/4 teaspoon ground black pepper
1/4 teaspoon dried oregano
1/4 teaspoon garlic powder
1/4 teaspoon celery seed
1 teaspoon onion powder

Toss all ingredients together in a large bowl. Let the cabbage marinate for several hours before serving.

Serves 6 to 8

Tangy Eggplant Zucchini Salad

This cooked vegetable salad can be served as an appetizer. It keeps well in the refrigerator for up to one week.

1 medium (1 1/4 pounds) eggplant, sliced 1/2
   inch thick
1 medium zucchini
1/2 large onion, chopped
3 garlic cloves, minced
1/4 green bell pepper, chopped
1/4 red bell pepper, chopped
2 tablespoons water
1 small tomato, chopped
3 tablespoons tomato paste
1/4 cup water
1 teaspoon reduced-salt soy sauce or Bragg
   Liquid Aminos
1 teaspoon olive oil
1/4 teaspoon dried oregano
1/4 teaspoon ground coriander
1 tablespoon lemon juice
1 tablespoon frozen or thawed apple juice
   concentrate
2 tablespoons chopped parsley

Soak the eggplant slices in cold water for 15 to 20 minutes.

Cut the zucchini lengthwise into four slices. Preheat a nonstick griddle or frying pan. Fry the eggplant and zucchini slices on both sides, without oil, until they are brown. Cut the eggplant and zucchini into bite-size pieces, and set them aside. Preheat a nonstick frying pan, cook the onion, garlic, and bell pepper uncovered until the vegetables begin to stick, for about 5 minutes. Stir in 2 tablespoons water, and sauté until the onion is soft, then stir in the next seven ingredients, along with the eggplant and zucchini. Cover the pan, and simmer until the eggplant and zucchini are tender.

Put the vegetables into a medium bowl, and stir in lemon juice, apple juice, and chopped parsley.

Serves 4

COLESLAW WITH CARROTS, GINGER, AND SUNFLOWER SEEDS

This coleslaw keeps in the refrigerator for several days. It makes a good between-meals snack.

1/2 large green cabbage, shredded (about 8 cups)
2 large carrots, grated (about 1/2 cup)
1 1-inch slice gingerroot, grated
2 tablespoons sunflower seeds
1 tablespoon prepared mustard
1 teaspoon onion powder
1 tablespoon lemon juice
2 tablespoons frozen or thawed apple juice concentrate
3 tablespoons cider vinegar

In a large bowl, toss all the ingredients. Chill the salad well before serving.

Serves 6 to 8

EASY COLESLAW WITH CARROTS

This healthy salad can be made in minutes using a food processor.

4 cups coarsely chopped cabbage
4 cups grated carrots
1/4 cup minced onion
1/4 cup frozen or thawed apple juice concentrate
1/4 cup cider vinegar

In a medium bowl, toss all the ingredients. Chill the salad for at least 2 hours before serving.

Serves 6

EASY GRATED CARROT-CELERY-RAISIN SALAD

This is a refreshing, crunchy salad.

3 cups grated carrots
1 1/2 cups finely sliced celery
1/4 cup black raisins
2 tablespoons frozen or thawed pineapple juice concentrate
2 tablespoons cider vinegar

Toss all the ingredients together in a large bowl. Chill the salad well before serving.

Yields 4 3/4 cups

Easy Chopped Vegetable Salad

All the vegetables for this healthful salad can be quickly chopped in a food processor.

1/4 medium onion, coarsely chopped
2 red radishes, coarsely chopped
1/2 small red bell pepper, coarsely chopped
2 carrots, coarsely chopped
4 celery stalks, coarsely chopped
1/2 small cabbage, coarsely chopped
1/3 cup cider vinegar
3 tablespoons frozen or thawed apple juice
  concentrate
1/4 teaspoon ground black pepper
2 teaspoons onion powder

In a large bowl, toss the chopped vegetables with the vinegar, apple juice, black pepper, and onion powder. Chill the salad well before serving.

Serves 4 to 6

Easy Grated Raw Vegetable Salad

Raw beets make this salad colorful and naturally sweet. You can grate the vegetables in a food processor.

1 medium raw beet, peeled and grated
1 medium zucchini, unpeeled, grated
2 medium carrots, peeled and grated
2 teaspoons cider vinegar
1 teaspoon reduced-salt soy sauce or Bragg
  Liquid Aminos
6 chilled lettuce leaves

Put the grated vegetables into a small bowl, and stir in the vinegar and soy sauce or Bragg. Chill the mixture.

To serve, arrange the lettuce leaves on two salad plates, and mound the grated vegetables in the center.

Serves 2

Grated Fresh Vegetable Salad

You can use a food processor for both grating and chopping in this recipe.

4 to 6 medium carrots, grated
4 small zucchini, grated
1/2 green bell pepper, coarsely chopped
2 green onions, coarsely chopped
4 celery stalks, coarsely chopped
1 1/2-inch slice gingerroot, coarsely chopped
2 tablespoons lemon juice
1 tablespoon cider vinegar
1/8 teaspoon ground black pepper
1 teaspoon reduced-salt soy sauce or Bragg
  Liquid Aminos

In a medium bowl, toss all the ingredients well. Chill the salad before serving.

Serves 4

CRUNCHY MARINATED CUCUMBER SALAD

This unusual salad features tiny slices of pickling cucumbers. The cucumbers can be sliced in a food processor.

10 small pickling cucumbers, unpeeled and thinly sliced
1/4 medium onion, chopped
1/4 medium red pepper, chopped
1/4 cup frozen and thawed apple juice concentrate
1/4 cup cider vinegar
2 teaspoons onion powder

Toss all the ingredients in a large bowl. Chill the salad for at least six hours before serving.

Serves 6

MOROCCAN BELL PEPPER SALAD

This variation on a traditional pepper salad makes a good addition to any buffet table.

3 large tomatoes, peeled and chopped
3 large garlic cloves, minced
2/3 cup minced parsley
2 large red bell peppers, cut into bite-size pieces
2 large green bell peppers cut into bite-size pieces
1 teaspoon reduced-salt soy sauce or Bragg Liquid Aminos

In a large frying pan over medium heat, sauté the chopped tomatoes without oil until the pan becomes dry. Stir in the remaining ingredients, and sauté the vegetables over low heat, uncovered, for about 25 minutes, or until the peppers are softened and most of the moisture is absorbed. Refrigerate the salad until serving time.

Yields 3 1/2 cups

MARINATED GREEN BEAN SALAD

This tasty salad of crunchy green beans is lovely to serve at a summer buffet or picnic.

1 cup water
1 teaspoon onion powder
1/2 teaspoon garlic powder
1/4 teaspoon dried oregano
1/4 teaspoon celery seed
1 teaspoon reduced-salt soy sauce or Bragg
  Liquid Aminos
2 pounds fresh green beans, tips removed
1/4 cup cider vinegar
1/4 cup chopped onion

In a 4 to 5-quart covered saucepan, bring the first six ingredients to a boil over medium heat. Stir in the green beans, and return the mixture to a boil. Lower the heat, and simmer the beans, covered, for 8 to 15 minutes, or until they are barely tender. Be careful not to overcook them.

Remove the beans from the heat, and place them with the broth in a large bowl. Stir in the vinegar and chopped onion. Toss the mixture well, and let it marinate in the refrigerator for 2 to 8 hours. Toss the beans several times while they are marinating, and toss them again well before serving.

Serves 6 to 8

BUCKWHEAT-NOODLE SALAD WITH GINGER-ORANGE-PECAN DRESSING

Serve this unusual noodle salad at a party or potluck brunch or supper.

1 1-inch slice gingerroot, peeled
1/2 cup pecans or macadamia nuts
1/3 cup frozen and thawed orange juice
  concentrate
1/3 cup water
2 teaspoons reduced-salt soy sauce or Bragg
  Liquid Aminos
1 tablespoon safflower or canola oil
1 8-ounce package Japanese buckwheat
  noodles, cooked according to package
  directions and rinsed in cold water

Blend all the ingredients but the noodles in a food processor until the nuts and ginger are finely chopped; or mince the ginger and nuts by hand, and combine them with the other ingredients.

In a medium bowl, stir the dressing into the noodles. Chill the salad well before serving.

Serves 6 to 8

GREEK POTATO SALAD WITH FRESH MINT

Chopped fresh mint leaves make this potato salad very refreshing.

6 medium boiling potatoes (2 1/2 to 3
 pounds), scrubbed and unpeeled
3 cups water
1 medium onion, chopped
2 large garlic cloves, minced
2 tablespoons water
1/2 large green or red bell pepper
8 large fresh mint leaves, minced
2 teaspoons reduced-salt soy sauce or Bragg
 Liquid Aminos
1 1/2 teaspoons olive oil

In a 4- to 5-quart saucepan, simmer the whole potatoes in the water, covered, for about 30 to 40 minutes, or until they are just tender.

Drain the potatoes, and set them aside to cool.

In a medium nonstick frying pan, sauté the onion and garlic without oil over medium heat until the onion begins to stick. Stir in the water and bell pepper, and cook for 3 minutes longer, stirring occasionally. Remove the pan from the heat, and set aside.

Peel the potatoes, and cut them into large bite-size pieces. In a large bowl, mix together the cut potatoes, the onion and pepper, and the mint, soy sauce or Bragg, and oil. Toss the salad well, and chill well before serving.

Serves 6 to 8

TASTY POTATO SALAD

6 medium red potatoes (about 2 pounds),
 scrubbed and peeled
3 cups water
1 14-ounce package soft tofu, rinsed, drained
 well, and crumbled
2 teaspoons prepared mustard (preferably
 stone-ground)
1 tablespoon reduced-salt soy sauce or Bragg
 Liquid Aminos
1 tablespoon cider vinegar
2 teaspoons curry powder
1/8 teaspoon ground black pepper
4 celery stalks, coarsely chopped
1 small onion, coarsely chopped
2 medium carrots, peeled and coarsely
 chopped
1 1-inch slice gingerroot, peeled and coarsely
 chopped
Generous sprinkle paprika, for garnish

In a 4- to 5-quart covered saucepan, simmer the potatoes in the water for about 40 minutes, or until they are just tender.

Drain the potatoes, and rinse them in cold water. Peel them, cut them into bite-size pieces, and put them in a medium bowl. Stir in the next six ingredients, then stir in the chopped vegetables. Sprinkle with paprika, and chill the salad well before serving.

Serves 8

Chinese-Style Salad with Marinated Tofu

This salad is especially good when you use a variety of lettuce.

6 cups bite-size pieces of lettuce, chilled
1/4 pound mung bean sprouts
1/4 pound snow peas
4 green onions, chopped
1 8-ounce can sliced water chestnuts, drained
1 14-ounce package firm tofu, rinsed, drained well, and cut into 1/2-inch cubes
1 teaspoon lemon juice
1 teaspoon curry powder
1 teaspoon dark molasses
1 teaspoon onion powder
2 teaspoons reduced-salt soy sauce or Bragg Liquid Aminos
1 1-inch slice gingerroot, peeled and grated
Sesame-Ginger Dressing
Sprinkle of paprika, for garnish

In a large bowl, mix together the first five ingredients. Chill them well. (If you're in a hurry, cover the bowl and place it in the freezer for 15 minutes.)

In a small bowl, marinate the cubed tofu in the lemon juice, curry powder, molasses, onion powder, soy sauce or Bragg, and grated gingerroot for at least 15 minutes.

Toss the salad vegetables with the Sesame-Ginger Dressing. Arrange the salad on two large, chilled dinner plates, and place a mound of marinated tofu in the center of each. Sprinkle paprika over the tofu, and serve.

Serves 2

Sesame-Ginger Dressing

This exotically flavored dressing can keep in the refrigerator for up to one week.

1/4 cup tahini
1 1-inch slice gingerroot, peeled and grated
1 teaspoon dark molasses
1 tablespoon reduced-salt soy sauce or Bragg Liquid Aminos
2 garlic cloves, crushed or minced

In a food processor or blender, blend all the dressing ingredients. Chill the dressing well before serving.

Yields 2/3 cup

Flavorful Celery-Root Salad

Celery root, or celeriac, can be eaten raw or cooked. Its intense celery flavor is complemented by the lemon and tahini in this recipe.

1 large celery root, peeled and grated (about 8 cups)
1/4 cup lemon juice
1/4 cup cider vinegar
1/2 cup water
1/4 cup tahini
2 teaspoons reduced-salt soy sauce or Bragg Liquid Aminos
1 teaspoon Dijon-type prepared mustard
1 garlic clove, crushed
1/2 cup chopped parsley

In a medium bowl, mix all the ingredients together. Chill the salad well before serving.

Serves 12

FRUIT AND VEGETABLE SALAD

This salad requires no dressing. You can mince the ingredients in a food processor.

1/2 apple, unpeeled, and minced
1 wedge fresh pineapple (one-twelfth of a pineapple), cut away from peel and minced
3 carrots, minced
1 wedge red cabbage, minced
10 red seedless grapes, minced

In a medium bowl, combine all the ingredients. Chill the salad well before serving.

Serves 3 to 4

SWEET CUCUMBER SALAD

Prepare this salad one day before serving. It takes only minutes to prepare.

8 medium pickling cucumbers, unpeeled and thinly sliced
2 tablespoons minced fresh dill, or 2 teaspoons dried dill
1 cup water
1/2 cup frozen or thawed apple juice concentrate
1 garlic clove, cut into pieces
1/2 medium onion, cut into 4 wedges, then sliced thin crosswise
1/4 teaspoon ground black or white pepper
1/4 teaspoon ground ginger
1 teaspoon reduced-salt soy sauce or Bragg Liquid Aminos

Put all the ingredients into a 1/2-gallon jar or large bowl. Allow the cucumbers to marinate overnight in the refrigerator. Drain them before serving, saving the brine.

Return any leftover salad to the brine and let them marinate for 3 to 7 days, or until the pickles have the desired taste and texture.

Serves 10 to 12

PICKLED BEET SALAD

2 bunches beets, trimmed
1/2 medium onion, thinly sliced
1/3 cup thawed apple juice concentrate
3 tablespoons cider vinegar
1 teaspoon reduced-salt soy sauce or Bragg Liquid Aminos

Place the beets in a 3-quart saucepan, and cover them with water. Cover the pan, bring the water to a boil, and reduce the heat. Simmer the beets for about 30 minutes, or just until they are tender. Be careful not to overcook them.

Drain the beets, peel them, and cut them into thin slices. Put the sliced beets in a medium bowl along with the remaining four ingredients. Toss well, and chill the salad well before serving.

Serves 6

COLORFUL GRATED VEGETABLE SALAD

This salad is packed full of vitamins, minerals, and fiber. You can grate the vegetables in a food processor.

4 cups mixed greens, cut into bite-size pieces
1 cup coarsely shredded red cabbage
1 medium raw or cooked beet, grated
1 large carrot, grated
1 medium zucchini, grated
1/4 large green bell pepper, grated
1/4 large red bell pepper, grated
2 tablespoons lemon juice
2 tablespoons cider vinegar
2 garlic cloves, minced or crushed
1/4 teaspoon dried oregano, crushed
1/4 teaspoon dried thyme, crushed
1/4 teaspoon dried rosemary, crushed
8 whole lettuce leaves

Place the greens and red cabbage in a large salad bowl. Add the beet, carrot, zucchini, and bell peppers. Toss the grated vegetables into the mixed greens and red cabbage. In a small bowl, blend the lemon juice, vinegar, garlic, and herbs. Add the dressing to the salad and toss well. Place two lettuce leaves on each plate, and mound a portion of the salad in the center.

Serves 4

SWEET AND SOUR HIGH-ENERGY SALAD

This delicious, tangy salad tastes best after marinating for several days. You can use a food processor to slice the carrots.

1 large onion, chopped
4 large garlic cloves, minced
2 tablespoons water
4 to 5 medium carrots, diagonally sliced into thin ovals
6 1/2-inch High-Energy Protein Loaf or Spicy High-Energy Protein Loaf (pages 82 and 83), thawed and cut into strips
1 tablespoon reduced-salt soy sauce or Bragg Liquid Aminos
2 teaspoons apple cider vinegar
2 teaspoons ground black pepper
3 tablespoons cider vinegar
2 tablespoons maple syrup
3 tablespoons water
1 teaspoon cornstarch

Preheat a nonstick frying pan over medium heat. Sauté the onion and garlic without oil until the pan becomes dry. Stir in the 2 tablespoons water, and cook until the onion is soft. Stir in the carrots and the strips of High-Energy Protein Loaf, along with the soy sauce or Bragg, the vinegar and the pepper. Cover the pan, and cook over medium heat for 15 to 20 minutes, or until the carrots are tender.

Mix together the last four ingredients and stir this into the carrot mixture in the pan. Place the mixture in a medium bowl, and marinate it in the refrigerator for at least one day, but preferably longer.

Serves 6 to 8

Soothing, Satisfying Soups

What could be more satisfying than a big, steaming bowl of nutritious, delicious soup? In this chapter you will find a wide variety of healthful soup recipes. All our soups are low in fat, low in salt, and free of wheat and dairy products. The soups are very easy to prepare, especially if you have a food processor. For working people, we suggest cooking soups in the evening for the next day's meal, or on weekends for weekday dinners. Most soups keep well in the refrigerator for up to one week, and can be frozen and left out to thaw during the day.

Hearty soups, especially those with beans, lentils, or peas, are an important part of most vegetarian diets. Beans, lentils, and peas supply protein as well as complex carbohydrates and minerals. A thick lentil or bean soup, with a raw vegetable salad and good whole-grain bread, makes a complete, healthful, balanced meal.

Spicy Dal (Indian Lentil Soup)

For a treat, enjoy this Indian soup with Paratha.

1 cup dry orange lentils (*masoor dal*)
1/2 cup dry yellow split peas (*toor dal*)
4 cups water
1/2 medium onion, chopped
1/2 teaspoon turmeric
1 cup chopped fresh tomatoes (or 1/4 cup tomato paste and 3/4 cup water)
4 garlic cloves, minced
1 1/2 tablespoons grated or chopped gingerroot
1/4 cup chopped cilantro leaves
1/2 teaspoon ground coriander
1/4 teaspoon chili powder
1 1/2 teaspoons ground cumin
2 1/2 cups water
2 teaspoons reduced-salt soy sauce or Bragg Liquid Aminos
2 tablespoons lemon juice
1/2 cup chopped cilantro leaves
1 tablespoon safflower or canola oil

In a 4- to 5-quart covered saucepan, bring the lentils and split peas, 4 cups of water, the onion and the turmeric to a boil. Lower the heat and simmer, stirring occasionally, for 35 minutes, or until the lentils are tender.

Purée the lentils in a food processor or blender, and return them to the saucepan. Stir in the next nine ingredients. Bring the mixture to a boil, then reduce the heat and simmer, covered, for 15 minutes.

Just before serving the soup, stir in the lemon juice, the remaining cilantro leaves, and the oil, and simmer for 5 minutes.

Serves 6 to 8

Easy Brown-Lentil Dal (Indian-Style Lentil Soup)

Serve this mildly seasoned *dal* with paratha either as the first course of an Indian meal or as a meal in itself.

2 cups dry brown lentils
10 cups water
1 large onion, chopped
3 garlic cloves, minced
1 1/2 cups carrots, thinly sliced
1 1/2 cups tomato purée
2 teaspoons reduced-salt soy sauce or Bragg Liquid Aminos
6 pitted dates, chopped
3 garlic cloves, minced
1 1-inch slice gingerroot, peeled and grated or chopped
1/4 jalapeño pepper, seeded and chopped
1/2 teaspoon ground coriander
1 teaspoon ground cumin
1 tablespoon safflower or canola oil
1/2 cup chopped cilantro leaves

In a large, covered pot, bring the first seven ingredients to a boil. Reduce the heat to low, and simmer the lentils covered, for 1 hour.

Stir into the lentils the chopped dates, garlic, ginger, jalapeño, coriander and cumin. Cover the pot, and simmer the mixture 20 minutes longer.

Purée half of the soup in a food processor or blender, and return it to the pot. Reheat the soup briefly, stir in the oil and chopped cilantro, and serve.

Serves 8 to 10

Easy Lentil Soup

This soup is easy to prepare, satisfying, and good for you.

2 cups dry brown lentils
10 cups water
1 large onion, cut in half
3 large whole garlic cloves
1 6-ounce can tomato paste
3 bay leaves
1 tablespoon reduced-salt soy sauce or Bragg Liquid Aminos
6 small carrots, thinly sliced
4 celery stalks, thinly sliced
2 small yellow crookneck or summer squashes, thinly sliced

Bring the first seven ingredients to a boil in a large, covered soup pot. Reduce the heat, simmer the lentils for about 1 1/2 hours, or until they are tender.

With a slotted spoon, remove the onion, garlic, and about half of the lentils. Purée them in a food processor or blender, and return them to the soup. Stir in the vegetables, return the soup to a boil, and reduce the heat. Simmer the soup, covered, for about 30 minutes, or until the vegetables are tender.

Serves 10

Easy Lentil-Vegetable Soup

This delicious hearty soup takes very little time to prepare. It keeps in the refrigerator for up to one week, and also freezes well.

1 pound dry brown lentils (2 1/2 cups)
10 cups water
1 teaspoon cider vinegar
1 tablespoon reduced-salt soy sauce or Bragg Liquid Aminos
1 tablespoon chili powder
3 large whole garlic cloves
1 large onion, cut into quarters
1 large tomato, cut in half
4 large whole carrots
4 whole celery stalks
1/2 large red or green bell pepper
1 teaspoon dried dill
1 teaspoon dried basil

Bring all the ingredients to a boil in a large, covered pot. Lower the heat, and simmer the mixture, covered, for 1 1/2 to 2 hours, or until the lentils are soft.

With a slotted spoon, remove the vegetables and some of the lentils. Purée these in a food processor or blender in batches, and return the purée to the pot. Reheat the soup briefly, and serve.

Yields 3 quarts

Easy Italian-style Lentil Soup

This soup is economical and easy to prepare. You can chop the vegetables in a food processor. Enjoy it with a salad and pasta.

2 cups uncooked brown lentils
8 cups water
1 tablespoon reduced-salt soy sauce or Bragg Liquid Aminos
3 bay leaves
1 medium onion, coarsely chopped
3 large garlic cloves, coarsely chopped
1/2 large green bell pepper, coarsely chopped
4 medium tomatoes, chopped (about 2 cups)
4 large fresh basil leaves, chopped (or 2 teaspoons dried basil)
1/4 cup chopped Italian parsley
1 tablespoon olive oil

Bring the lentils, water, soy sauce or Bragg, and bay leaves to a boil in a large, covered pot. Lower the heat, and cook the lentils, covered, for 1 hour.

Stir the chopped vegetables into the soup, return the soup to a boil, and reduce the heat. Simmer the soup, covered, for another hour, or until the lentils and vegetables are tender.

Stir in the olive oil, and serve.

Serves 8 to 10

LENTIL-SPINACH SOUP

This Italian-style lentil soup is both wholesome and delicious.

2 cups dry brown lentils
1 medium onion, chopped
3 large garlic cloves, minced
8 cups water
2 cups chopped fresh tomatoes (2 large
   tomatoes)
1/2 large green bell pepper, chopped
2 cups chopped fresh spinach (or 1 10-ounce
   frozen chopped spinach package)
4 chopped fresh basil leaves (or 1 teaspoon
   dried basil)
6 chopped fresh oregano leaves (or 1
   teaspoon dried oregano)
Leaves from 2 sprigs thyme (or 1 teaspoon
   dried thyme)
1 tablespoon olive oil
1 tablespoon reduced-salt soy sauce or Bragg
   Liquid Aminos

Bring the lentils, onion, garlic, and water to boil in a large, covered pot. Reduce the heat, and simmer the lentils, covered, for 1 1/2 hours.

Stir in the remaining ingredients. Return the soup to boil, then lower the heat and simmer the soup, covered, for about 1/2 hour longer. Purée half the soup in a food processor or blender and combine it with the rest, or serve the soup as it is.

Yields 3 quarts

HEARTY BEAN AND PASTA SOUP

This Italian-style soup is a meal in itself.

1 cup dry garbanzo beans
1 cup dry kidney beans
6 cups water
7 cups water
2 bay leaves
1 large onion, chopped
4 large garlic cloves, minced
4 carrots, thinly sliced crosswise
2 celery stalks, thinly sliced crosswise
1 1/2 cups tomato purée
1 teaspoon cider vinegar
1 tablespoon olive oil
1 tablespoon reduced-salt soy sauce or Bragg
   Liquid Aminos
8 fresh basil leaves, chopped (or 2 teaspoons
   dried basil)
6 fresh oregano leaves, chopped (or 1
   teaspoon dried oregano)
4 ounces (1 1/2 cups) dry whole wheat or rice
   spaghetti, broken into bite-size pieces

Bring the beans and 6 cups water to a boil in a large, covered pot. Reduce the heat, and simmer the beans for 10 minutes.

Remove the pot from the heat, and allow the beans to soak in the water until they are cool, or overnight. Drain the beans, rinse them well, and return them to the pot. Cover the beans with 7 cups water, and add the bay leaves, onion, and garlic. Bring the mixture to a boil. Reduce the heat, and simmer the beans, covered, for 2 hours.

Stir in all the remaining ingredients, return the soup to a boil, and lower the heat. Simmer the soup, covered, for another 30 minutes or until the carrots and celery are tender.

Serves 6 to 8

White-Bean Soup with Leeks and Vegetables

This is a delicious and hearty Greek-style soup.

1 pound (2 1/4 cups) dry Great Northern
  white beans
6 cups water
10 cups water
1 large onion, thinly sliced
1 bunch leeks, white part only, thinly sliced
3 large garlic cloves, minced
2 tablespoons water
6 young medium carrots, thinly sliced
  crosswise
6 celery stalks with leaves, thinly sliced
  crosswise
2 small tomatoes, cut into bite-size pieces (1
  cup)
1/4 large red bell pepper, coarsely chopped
1 bay leaf
1/4 cup (packed) chopped fresh basil leaves
1/8 teaspoon cayenne
2 tablespoons reduced-salt soy sauce or Bragg
  Liquid Aminos
1 tablespoon olive oil
1 teaspoon cider vinegar

Bring the beans and 6 cups water to a boil in a large covered pot. Reduce the heat, and simmer the beans for 10 minutes. Remove the pot from the heat, and allow the beans to soak in the hot water until they are cool, or overnight.

Drain the beans, rinse them well, and return them to the pot. Add the remaining 10 cups water. Bring the mixture to a boil, and reduce the heat. Simmer the beans, covered, for about 1 1/2 hours, or until they are tender.

While the beans are cooking, sauté the onion, leeks, and garlic in a large nonstick frying pan without oil, until the vegetables begin to stick. Stir in 2 tablespoons water, and cook until the vegetables are soft and slightly browned. Stir in the next seven ingredients, sauté for 5 minutes, and remove the pan from the heat.

When the beans are tender, stir into them the sautéed vegetables, along with the soy sauce or Bragg, the olive oil, and the cider vinegar. Bring the soup to a boil, reduce the heat to low, and simmer the soup for about 15 minutes, or until the vegetables are tender.

Serves 8

THREE-BEAN VEGETABLE SOUP

This satisfying soup freezes well, and keeps in the refrigerator for up to one week.

3/4 cup dry kidney beans
3/4 cup dry red beans
3/4 cup dry garbanzo beans
8 cups water
8 cups water
1 large onion, cut into quarters
4 large whole garlic cloves
1/3 cup tomato paste
1 tablespoon reduced-salt soy sauce or Bragg Liquid Aminos
5 large fresh basil leaves, chopped (or 1 1/2 teaspoons dried basil)
1/4 cup chopped parsley
4 celery stalks, thinly sliced crosswise
4 carrots, thinly sliced crosswise
~~1 tablespoon olive oil~~

In a large, covered pot, bring the beans and 8 cups water to a boil. Reduce the heat, and simmer the beans for 10 minutes. Remove the pot from the heat, and allow the beans to soak in the hot water until they are cool or overnight.

Drain the beans, rinse them well, and return them to the pot. Add 8 cups water along with the onion, garlic, tomato paste, and soy sauce or Bragg. Bring the mixture to a boil. Lower the heat, and cook the beans, covered, for 1 1/2 hours.

Remove the onion, garlic and half the beans with a slotted spoon. Purée these in a food processor or blender, and return the mixture to the pot. Stir in the remaining ingredients, and cook for about 45 minutes over low heat, or until the

vegetables and beans are tender. Stir occasionally toward the end of the cooking time to keep the soup from sticking. If the soup is too thick, add a little water.

Serves 10 to 12

HEARTY SPLIT-PEA SOUP

This soup can be stored for up to one week in the refrigerator. It freezes well.

2 cups dry green split peas
8 cups water
1 large onion, chopped
1/4 cup chopped fresh parsley
2 tablespoons chopped fresh dill (or 2 teaspoons dried)
2 celery stalks, sliced
6 carrots, sliced
1 tablespoon reduced-salt soy sauce or Bragg Liquid Aminos
1 teaspoon cider vinegar
1/4 teaspoon ground black pepper
~~1 tablespoon safflower or canola oil (optional)~~

Bring to a boil all the ingredients except the oil in a large, covered pot. Lower the heat, and simmer the soup, covered, for about 1 1/4 hours, or until the split peas are very tender.

Purée half the soup in a food processor or blender, and return the mixture to the pot. Stir in the oil, heat the soup briefly, and serve.

Serves 8

GREEN SPLIT-PEA SOUP

This soup takes only minutes to prepare. Since it is puréed after cooking, the vegetables need not be sliced or chopped.

1 1/2 cups dry green split peas
6 cups water
1 medium onion, cut in half
1/2 cup chopped fresh parsley leaves
1 heaping tablespoon chopped fresh dill
   (or 1 1/2 teaspoons dried)
2 celery stalks, cut in half
2 large carrots, cut in half
2 teaspoons reduced-salt soy sauce or Bragg
   Liquid Aminos

Bring all the ingredients to a boil in a 4- to 5-quart covered saucepan. Lower the heat, and simmer the soup, covered, for about 1 1/4 hours, or until the split peas are very tender.

Purée the soup in a food processor or blender. Reheat the soup briefly, and serve.

Serves 4

SPLIT PEA SOUP WITH FRESH PEAS

1 pound dry green split peas
1 large onion, cut into quarters
1/2 cup chopped parsley
6 whole carrots
4 whole celery stalks
1 tablespoon dried dill
1/2 teaspoon ground black pepper
1 tablespoon reduced-salt soy sauce or Bragg
   Liquid Aminos
10 cups water
1 cup fresh or frozen green peas
1 tablespoon safflower or canola oil

Bring the first nine ingredients to a boil in a large, covered pot. Lower the heat, and cook the soup, covered, for about 1 1/4 hours, or until the split peas are tender.

Remove the carrots from the soup, and set them aside. Purée the soup in batches, and return the soup to the pot. Slice the carrots into rounds and stir them into the soup along with the fresh or frozen peas and oil. Heat the soup briefly and serve.

Yields 3 quarts; serves 12

MUSHROOM-BARLEY SOUP

This hearty soup can be made in 2 hours.

6 carrots, sliced
6 celery stalks, sliced
1/2 pound mushrooms, chopped
1 large onion, chopped
1/2 teaspoon ground black pepper
2 large garlic cloves, minced
8 cups water
3/4 cup barley
1 tablespoon reduced-salt soy sauce or Bragg
   Liquid Aminos
2 cups fresh or frozen lima beans
2 cups fresh or frozen green peas
2 heaping tablespoons chopped fresh dill (or
   2 teaspoons dried)
1 tablespoon safflower or canola oil

In a large covered pot, bring the first nine ingredients to a boil. Lower the heat, and simmer the soup, covered, for 45 minutes. Stir in the lima beans, peas, dill, and oil. Return the soup to a boil, reduce the heat, and simmer the soup, covered, for 30 minutes longer.

Purée half the beans and vegetables in a food processor or blender. Return the mixture to the pot. Reheat the soup briefly, and serve.

Serves 8 to 10

Note: This soup can be cooked in an electric crockpot set on high for 24 hours. Use boiling water, and add all the ingredients at once. Before serving, purée half the soup, and return it to the crockpot.

MUSHROOM-BARLEY-LENTIL SOUP

This delicious soup is great for cold weather.

6 cups water
1 pound mushrooms, sliced
1 large onion, chopped
1 cup dry lentils
4 carrots, thinly sliced crosswise
4 celery stalks, thinly sliced crosswise
1/2 cup barley
1 tablespoon reduced-salt soy sauce or Bragg
   Liquid Aminos
2 teaspoons Vegit
1 tablespoon safflower or canola oil
2 tablespoons brown-rice flour or cornstarch
1/4 cup water

In a 4- to 5-quart covered saucepan, bring 6 cups water, the mushrooms, the onion, and the lentils to a boil. Reduce the heat, and simmer the ingredients, covered, for 1 hour.

Purée half the mixture in a food processor or blender, and return the purée to the pot. Stir in the carrots, celery, barley, soy sauce or Bragg, and Vegit. Return the mixture to a boil, then lower the heat, and simmer, covered, for about 30 minutes, or until the vegetables are tender.

Stir in the oil. Mix the rice flour or cornstarch with 1/4 cup water, and stir this mixture into the soup. When the soup has thickened, remove it from the heat and serve.

Yields 8 cups; serves 6 to 8

FLAVORFUL VEGETABLE BROTH OR SOUP STOCK

The vegetables in this recipe give the broth a golden color and a good, strong flavor.

4 quarts water
1 pound celery root, peeled and cut in half
3 large parsley roots, peeled
1 pound whole carrots, peeled
4 whole celery stalks
2 whole large onions, peeled

In a large, covered pot, bring all the ingredients to a boil. Reduce the heat and simmer the mixture, covered, for 2 hours or longer.

Strain the broth and discard the vegetables. Store the broth in airtight containers in the refrigerator or freezer.

Yields 3 quarts

FLAVORFUL VEGETABLE BROTH WITH NOODLES

1 quart Flavorful Vegetable Broth
2 teaspoons reduced-salt soy sauce or Bragg Liquid Aminos
1 teaspoon Vegit
1 1/2 cups cooked noodles

In a 2-quart covered saucepan, heat the broth, soy sauce or Bragg, Vegit, and noodles, covered, until the soup is hot.

Serves 2 to 3

THICK ITALIAN-STYLE LENTIL SOUP

This soup makes a hearty meal when served with a raw vegetable salad and whole-grain bread.

1 pound uncooked brown lentils
8 cups boiling water
2 cups tomato purée
1 medium onion, chopped
1/2 large green bell pepper
2 celery stalks. sliced
3 large garlic cloves, minced
1/4 cup chopped parsley
1/4 teaspoon ground black pepper
2 fresh basil leaves (or 1/2 teaspoon dried basil)
4 fresh oregano leaves (or 1/2 teaspoon dried oregano)
1/2 teaspoon fresh thyme leaves (or 1/2 teaspoon dried thyme)
1 teaspoon cider vinegar
1 tablespoon reduced-salt soy sauce or Bragg Liquid Aminos
1 1/2 teaspoons olive oil
2 cups chopped fresh spinach (or 1 10-ounce package frozen chopped spinach)

Bring all the ingredients except the olive oil and spinach to a boil in a large, covered soup pot. Lower heat, and simmer the soup, covered, for about 1 1/2 hours, or until the lentils are tender. Purée half the soup in a food processor or blender, and return the mixture to the pot. If the soup is too thick, add water to taste. Stir the oil and spinach into the soup. Heat the soup and serve it.

Serves 6 to 8

MUSHROOM-POTATO-VEGETABLE SOUP

This hearty soup provides protein from soy milk and carbohydrates from both potatoes and barley.

1 large onion, chopped
4 garlic cloves, chopped
4 celery stalks, chopped
1/2 large green bell pepper, chopped
8 cups water
1 pound mushrooms, coarsely chopped
    (about 3 cups)
6 medium carrots, coarsely chopped
    (about 1 1/2 cups)
2 1/2 pounds potatoes, coarsely chopped
    (about 3 cups)
1/3 cup barley
1/8 teaspoon ground black pepper
2 teaspoons reduced-salt soy sauce or Bragg
    Liquid Aminos
2 teaspoons cider vinegar
1 teaspoon curry powder
1/8 teaspoon dried thyme
2 cups soy milk

Over medium heat, sauté the onion, garlic, celery, and bell pepper in a 4- to 5-quart covered saucepan, uncovered, without oil, stirring occasionally, until the pan becomes dry and the vegetables begin to brown. Add the remaining ingredients, bring the mixture to a boil, then simmer the soup, covered, for 30 minutes.

Remove half the vegetables with a slotted spoon, purée them in a food processor or blender, and return them to the pot. Stir in the soy milk. If the soup is too thick, add a little

water. Simmer the soup, covered, for another 10 minutes, and serve.

Serves 10

HEARTY CABBAGE-POTATO SOUP

This soup takes less than 30 minutes to prepare. All vegetables can be chopped in a food processor.

1 medium onion, minced
2 tablespoons water
6 cups water
1/2 to 3/4 large cabbage (5 cups minced)
4 celery stalks diced (about 1 1/2 cups)
1 small red bell pepper, diced
5 medium potatoes, diced (about 4 cups)
Pinch cayenne
3 tablespoons reduced-salt soy sauce or Bragg
    Liquid Aminos
~~1 tablespoon safflower or canola oil~~

In a preheated, covered 4- to 5-quart nonstick pot, sauté the chopped onion uncovered over medium heat without oil until the onion begins to stick. Stir in 2 tablespoons water, and cook until the onion is soft. Stir in 6 cups water along with the next six ingredients. Bring the mixture to a boil, then lower the heat, and simmer the soup, covered, for 30 minutes.

With a slotted spoon, remove 2 cups of vegetables, purée the vegetables in a food processor or blender, and return them to the pot. Stir the oil into the soup. Bring the soup to a boil, and simmer it, covered, over low heat for 15 minutes. Serve the soup hot.

Serves 8 to 10

POTATO-LEEK SOUP

This soup is soothing either as it is or puréed.

1 bunch leeks, white part only, chopped
2 celery stalks, thinly sliced
2 large garlic cloves, minced
1 large onion, chopped
2 tablespoons water
6 cups water
4 medium boiling potatoes (about 2 pounds),
    peeled, and coarsely chopped
2 tablespoons reduced-salt soy sauce or Bragg
    Liquid Aminos
1/4 teaspoon dried thyme
1/8 teaspoon cayenne
1/8 teaspoon ground nutmeg
1/2 tablespoon safflower or canola oil

In a 4- to 5-quart nonstick saucepan, sauté the first four ingredients, uncovered over medium heat without oil. When the vegetables begin to stick, add 2 tablespoons water, and cook until the vegetables are soft, stirring occasionally. Stir in 6 cups water, potatoes, soy sauce or Bragg, thyme, cayenne, nutmeg, and oil. Bring the soup to a boil, lower the heat, and simmer, covered, for about 30 minutes, or until the vegetables and potatoes are very soft. If the soup is too thick, stir in 1/2 to 1 cup more water. Purée the soup and reheat it, or serve it as it is.

Yields 2 1/2 quarts

LEEK-POTATO-ONION SOUP

This creamy soup is enriched with soy milk.

2 medium onions, sliced
1/2 green or red bell pepper, sliced
3 medium leeks, white part only, sliced
3 garlic cloves, minced
10 cups water
6 medium potatoes, sliced thin or chopped
4 celery stalks, sliced
Pinch cayenne
1/4 teaspoon dried thyme
2 teaspoons Vegit
2 tablespoons reduced-salt soy sauce or Bragg
    Liquid Aminos
1 1/2 cups soy milk
Chopped parsley or dill, for garnish

In a preheated, covered 4- to 5-quart saucepan, sauté the onions, bell pepper, leeks, and garlic without oil, stirring occasionally, until the vegetables begin to stick. Stir in the next seven ingredients. Bring the mixture to a boil, reduce the heat, and simmer the soup, covered, for about 45 minutes, or until the potatoes are tender.

Remove the vegetables with a slotted spoon, and purée them in a food processor or blender. Return the puréed vegetables to the pot, and stir in the soy milk. Heat the soup, and serve it with chopped parsley or dill.

Serves 12

THICK RED BEAN-BARLEY-VEGETABLE SOUP

This soup makes a delicious one-dish meal.

2 cups dry small red beans
6 cups water
8 cups water
1 large onion, coarsely chopped
3 large garlic cloves, minced
5 small ripe tomatoes, coarsely chopped
  (about 1 1/2 cups)
1/2 small red bell pepper, chopped
1/2 small green bell pepper, chopped
1/2 cup barley
6 medium carrots, thinly sliced
4 celery stalks, thinly sliced
2 tablespoons reduced-salt soy sauce or Bragg
  Liquid Aminos
1 teaspoon Vegit
1 teaspoon dried dill

Bring the beans and 6 cups water to a boil in a large pot. Boil the beans over medium heat, covered, for 10 minutes, then remove the pot from the heat, and allow the beans to soak in the hot water until they are cool, or overnight. Drain the beans, rinse them well, and return them to the pot.

Bring the soaked beans, 8 cups water, and the next five ingredients to a boil. Lower the heat, and simmer the beans, covered, for 1 hour.

Stir in the barley, and continue cooking the beans, covered, for about 30 minutes longer, or until the beans are tender.

Stir in the last five ingredients, return the soup to a boil, then lower the heat. Simmer the soup, covered, for about 30 minutes longer, or until the carrots and celery are tender. Serve the soup hot.

Serves 6 to 8

LIGHT SWEET AND SOUR CABBAGE BORSCHT

This soup is satisfying despite its low calorie-count.

1/3 cup tomato paste
1 medium cabbage, finely shredded or grated
2 medium onions, chopped
6 cups water
2 teaspoons reduced-salt soy sauce or Bragg
  Liquid Aminos
2 1/2 tablespoons lemon juice or cider vinegar
1/2 cup frozen apple juice concentrate
Pinch ground black pepper

Bring all the ingredients to a boil in a large, covered pot. Lower the heat, simmer, covered, for 2 to 3 hours.

Yields 8 cups

QUICK AND EASY BROTH

This flavorful broth can be ready to drink in 15 minutes or less.

2 cups boiling water
1 tablespoon onion powder
1/2 teaspoon garlic powder
1/4 teaspoon celery seed
1 tablespoon reduced-salt soy sauce or Bragg Liquid Aminos
1 teaspoon Vegit
Pinch black or white pepper
1/2 teaspoon cider vinegar

In a covered medium saucepan, bring all the ingredients to a boil and simmer the broth, covered, for 10 minutes.

Yields 2 cups

QUICK AND EASY BROTH WITH BUCKWHEAT NOODLES

This delicious noodle soup can be ready to serve in the time it takes to cook the noodles. Buckwheat has more protein than any other grain, and it has a particularly interesting flavor.

4 cups boiling water
1 teaspoon cider vinegar
1/2 package Japanese buckwheat noodles with lotus root (available in health-food stores and Asian markets)
Double recipe Quick and Easy Broth, heated
1/4 cup chopped parsley

Break the noodles into shorter lengths (thirds or fourths). In 4 cups boiling water to which the vinegar has been added, cook the noodles for 7 to 10 minutes, or until the noodles are tender.

Drain the noodles, and add them to the broth. Sprinkle chopped parsley in each bowl.

Serves 4

Exciting Entrées, Festive Party and Holiday Dishes and Ethnic Specialties

If you are wondering what to fix for dinner tonight and feel in the mood for Italian food, you might consider tofu lasagna, eggplant-tofu casserole, or potato gnocchi.

For Indian dishes, you'll find curried vegetables, rice dishes, and garbanzo bean and lentil stews.

For Mexican food, you might consider our recipes for vegetarian burritos, tamales, tostadas, chilies, salsas, Mexican-style beans and casseroles, and flavorful Spanish rice.

Asian food? Consider Chinese Vegetables with Tofu; Steamed Vegetables with Easy Peanut Sauce; Fried Rice; or Steamed Rice with Buckwheat or Barley.

Especially in cool weather, what could be better than a piping-hot nourishing stew? Here you will find various combinations of lentils, beans, split peas, barley, and vegetables.

For a holiday or other celebration you might consider a Brown Rice-Vegetable Casserole; Kasha (buckwheat kernels) with Noodles Served with Squash-Stuffed Orange Halves or with Tzimmes, a stew of carrots, sweet potatoes, and prunes; Baked Squash Stuffed with Curried Rice; Prakus (Stuffed Cabbage Rolls); or Polenta with Vegetables and Pine Nuts.

Middle Eastern appetizers and salads also make delicious and nutritious lunch or dinner entrées. You can find Middle Eastern recipes in the first chapter.

All of these exciting dishes are free of animal products, cholesterol, and sugar; all are low in fat and salt, and many are wheat-free. The choice is yours. We wish you and your loved ones bon appétit!

PASTA PRIMAVERA WITH PINE NUTS

**1 cup plus 2 tablespoons water
4 medium carrots, thinly sliced
1 large or 2 medium zucchini, thinly sliced
1 small onion, chopped
4 large garlic cloves
2 cups bite-size pieces of tomato
2 tablespoons chopped fresh basil
2 teaspoons reduced-salt soy sauce or Bragg Liquid Aminos
1 teaspoon olive oil
2 to 4 tablespoons pine nuts
6 ounces dry whole wheat pasta, preferably fettucine or spaghetti
1 1/2 teaspoons cider vinegar**

In a 4- to 5-quart saucepan bring 1 cup water and carrots to a boil. Reduce the heat and simmer the carrots, covered, for 5 minutes. Add the zucchini and simmer for 5 more minutes. Drain the vegetables. Set aside.

In a preheated large nonstick frying pan, sauté the onion and garlic uncovered until the onion begins to stick. Stir in 2 tablespoons of water, and sauté until onion is soft. Stir in the chopped tomatoes and basil, sauté for 5 minutes, then stir in the soy sauce or Bragg, the oil, the pine nuts, and the steamed carrots and zucchini. Remove the pan from the heat.

While the vegetables are cooking, cook the pasta in boiling water according to the directions, but with the vinegar added to the cooking water. Drain and rinse the pasta, and stir it into the heated sauce. Serve the pasta hot.

Serves 3 to 4

Pasta with Eggplant and Tomato Bell Pepper Sauce

The eggplant sauce can be prepared a day ahead of time, then heated in the same time as it takes to cook the pasta.

2 medium (1 to 1 1/4 pounds each) eggplants

Sauce

1 medium onion, coarsely chopped
3 large garlic cloves, minced
2 tablespoons water
3/4 cup tomato purée
1 cup chopped fresh tomatoes (about 2 1/2 medium tomatoes)
3 fresh basil leaves, chopped
1/2 large red or green bell pepper, chopped
1 cup water
1/2 teaspoon cider vinegar
1/2 teaspoon frozen or thawed apple juice concentrate
1 teaspoon reduced-salt soy sauce or Bragg Liquid Aminos
~~1 1/2 teaspoons olive oil~~
8 ounces dry whole wheat or brown-rice pasta, (preferably *rotini*)
1 teaspoon cider vinegar

Peel the eggplants, and cut them into slices 1/2 inch thick. Soak them in water for 15 to 30 minutes, and drain them well.

Fry the eggplant slices on a preheated non-stick griddle, without oil, until they are brown on both sides and tender. Remove them from the heat and let them cool. Cut the eggplant slices into thin strips, and set them aside.

In a 4- to 5-quart saucepan, sauté the onion and garlic without oil over medium heat, stirring occasionally, until the onion begins to stick.

Stir in 2 tablespoons water, and continue cooking until the onions are soft. Stir in the remaining nine ingredients. Bring the sauce to a boil, and simmer it uncovered over medium heat for 5 minutes, stirring occasionally. Remove the pan from the heat.

While the sauce is cooking, or about 20 minutes before serving, cook the pasta according to the package instructions, adding the vinegar to the water in the pot. Drain the pasta, and gently stir it into the heated sauce. Serve the pasta hot.

Serves 4

Spaghetti with Lentil Balls

For a special treat serve Wheat-Free Lentil-Nut-Oat Bran Balls with Tomato Basil Sauce over steamy hot spaghetti.

Tomato Basil Sauce (page 46)
18 to 24 Wheat-Free Lentil-Nut-Oat Bran Balls (1/2 recipe; page 6), with 1 teaspoon Italian Seasoning added to the dough
12 ounces dry spaghetti

Heat the sauce, and, at the same time, heat the water for cooking the spaghetti. Just after you put the spaghetti into the boiling water to cook, put the oven-baked lentil balls into the sauce. Simmer the sauce on low heat until the balls are heated through. Do not allow the sauce to boil. If it becomes too thick, add a little more water.

When the spaghetti is done, drain it. Serve the sauce and lentil balls on top of each plate of hot spaghetti.

Serves 6

Pasta Pomodora

The fresh tomatoes, bell peppers and herbs give this pasta a marvelous flavor.

4 large garlic cloves, crushed or minced
1 large onion, coarsely chopped
1/2 large green or red bell pepper, coarsely chopped
2 tablespoons water
6 plum tomatoes, coarsely chopped
1/2 teaspoon dried basil
2 teaspoons reduced-salt soy sauce or Bragg Liquid Aminos
8 ounces dry whole wheat pasta or brown rice pasta
1 1/2 teaspoons olive oil

In a large nonstick frying pan, sauté the garlic, onion, and bell pepper over medium heat, without oil, stirring occasionally, until the pan becomes dry. Stir in 2 tablespoons water, and continue cooking over medium heat, stirring occasionally until the onion softens. Stir in the next three ingredients and sauté over medium heat for 5 minutes. Remove the pan from the heat, and set it aside.

While the vegetables cook, cook the pasta as directed on the package. Drain pasta well, and return it to the pot. Stir in the olive oil, and then stir in the tomato-bell pepper sauce. Toss well before serving.

Serves 4

Pasta with Tomatoes, Garlic, and Basil

This sauce is easy to prepare and delicious.

1 medium onion, chopped
3 large garlic cloves, minced
1/4 cup chopped red bell pepper
5 fresh basil leaves
2 cups chopped fresh tomatoes
3/4 cup tomato purée
1 tablespoon olive oil
1/2 cup water
1 teaspoon reduced-salt soy sauce or Bragg Liquid Aminos
12 ounces whole wheat, or brown rice pasta

In a preheated 4- to 5-quart saucepan sauté the first four ingredients over medium heat until the onion begins to stick. Stir in the chopped tomatoes, and cook until the pan becomes dry. Stir in the tomato purée, olive oil, water, and soy sauce or Bragg. Reduce the heat to low, and simmer the sauce for 15 to 20 minutes, uncovered.

Cook the pasta according to the directions on the package. Drain the pasta, return it to the pot, and toss the hot sauce into the hot pasta. Serve immediately.

Serves 4

Pasta Marinara with Zucchini and Asparagus

The marinara sauce in this dish can be made ahead of time. Steam the zucchini and asparagus while the pasta is cooking.

4 large garlic cloves, crushed or minced
1 large onion, coarsely chopped
2 tablespoons water
2 cups (1 pound) fresh coarsely chopped tomatoes
1/4 bell pepper, minced
1/4 cup chopped fresh basil leaves
2 teaspoons reduced-salt soy sauce or Bragg Liquid Aminos
1 teaspoon ground dried oregano
1/2 cup tomato purée
1/2 cup water
1 cup water
2 medium zucchini, sliced
8 asparagus stalks, cut into eighths
8 ounces whole wheat pasta or brown rice pasta
1 teaspoon cider vinegar
1 1/2 teaspoons olive oil

In a large nonstick frying pan over medium heat, sauté the garlic and onion without oil, stirring occasionally until the pan becomes dry. Stir in 2 tablespoons water, and continue cooking over medium heat, stirring occasionally until the onion is soft. Stir in the next seven ingredients. Bring the sauce to a boil, reduce the heat, and simmer the sauce, uncovered, for 15 minutes. At this point you can leave the sauce to cool, if you wish, then chill it for later use. Warm the sauce while you cook the vegetables and the pasta.

In a medium saucepan over low heat, bring 1 cup water to a boil. Add the zucchini and asparagus, and cook them for about 10 minutes, or until they are barely tender. Drain them and set aside.

While the vegetables are steaming, cook the pasta in rapidly boiling water in a large pot as directed on the package, but with the vinegar added to the pot. Drain the pasta well, return it to the pot, and toss it with olive oil.

Stir the steamed zucchini and asparagus into the sauce. Serve the sauce and the vegetables over the hot pasta.

Serves 4

Pasta with Tomatoes, Basil, and Pine Nuts

6 large garlic cloves, crushed or minced
1 medium onion, minced
2 tablespoons water
3 cups (1 1/2 pounds) coarsely chopped fresh
    tomatoes
1/4 cup chopped fresh basil leaves
1/4 teaspoon ground black or white pepper
1 tablespoon reduced-salt soy sauce or Bragg
    Liquid Aminos
1/3 cup (1 1/2 ounces) pine nuts
12 ounces whole wheat pasta or brown rice
    pasta
1 teaspoon cider vinegar
1 tablespoon olive oil

In a large nonstick frying pan, sauté the garlic
and onion over medium heat without oil, stirring occasionally until the pan becomes dry. Stir
in 2 tablespoons water, and continue cooking
over medium heat, stirring occasionally until the
onion is soft. Stir in the next five ingredients,
and sauté over medium heat for 5 minutes. Keep
the sauce warm while you cook the pasta.

Cook the pasta as directed on the package,
but add the vinegar with the pasta to the rapidly boiling water. Drain the pasta well. Return
it to the pot, stir in the olive oil, and then stir in
the tomato-pine nut sauce. Toss the pasta and
sauce well before serving.

Serves 6

Tomato Basil Sauce

1 medium onion, coarsely chopped
3 large garlic cloves, minced
2 tablespoons water
1 2/3 cups (16-ounce can) tomato purée
1 1/2 cups water
1 teaspoon reduced-salt soy sauce or Bragg
    Liquid Aminos
5 fresh basil leaves
1 teaspoon frozen or thawed apple juice
    concentrate or maple syrup
1 teaspoon cider vinegar
1 1/2 teaspoons olive oil

In a 4- to 5-quart saucepan, over medium heat,
sauté onion and garlic without oil, stirring occasionally, until the onion begins to stick. Stir in 2
tablespoons water, and continue cooking until
the onions are soft. Stir in the remaining ingredients. Bring the sauce to a boil over medium
heat, then reduce the heat to low, and simmer
the sauce, uncovered, for 25 to 30 minutes, stirring occasionally.

Yields 3 cups

Classic Tofu Lasagna

This large lasagna dish is great for parties. You can prepare it the day before and store it in the refrigerator. Let it stand at room temperature for 1 hour before baking. The lasagna also freezes well before or after baking. Spoon heated Tomato Basil Sauce over each portion.

2 14-ounce packages soft or regular tofu, rinsed and well drained
1/2 medium onion
6 large garlic cloves
1 tablespoon dried basil
1 tablespoon dried oregano
2 tablespoons reduced-salt soy sauce or Bragg Liquid Aminos
2 tablespoons cornstarch
2 teaspoons curry powder
1 tablespoon Vegit
3 teaspoons cider vinegar
1 pound dry whole wheat lasagna noodles
Double recipe (6 cups) Tomato-Basil Sauce (page 46)

In a food processor or blender, blend the tofu with the next eight ingredients, and 2 teaspoons cider vinegar, and set the mixture aside.

Into a large pot of rapidly boiling water, drop the lasagna noodles, one at a time, and stir in the remaining 1 teaspoon vinegar. Cook the noodles according to the instructions on the package, or until they are just tender. Rinse the noodles, and leave them in cold water until you're ready to use them. Drain the noodles well before assembling the lasagna.

Preheat the oven to 350°.

Layer the lasagna in a lightly oiled 9- by 13-inch ovenproof glass baking pan in the following fashion: First, spread 1 cup sauce on the bottom of the pan. Lay one-third of the noodles on top of the sauce, then spread 3/4 cup sauce over the noodle layer. Spread half the tofu filling evenly over the sauce, and one-third of the noodles over the filling. Layer sauce, filling, and noodles again, then top with 1 cup sauce. Bake the lasagna for about 1 hour, or until it is hot and bubbly and light brown on top. Heat the remaining sauce to spoon over each portion.

Serves 10 to 12

Tofu-Broccoli Lasagna

With whole wheat noodles, tofu, broccoli, and tomatoes, this lasagna is a meal in itself. You can prepare it the day before serving, and store it in the refrigerator. Let it remain out at room temperature for 1 hour before baking.

1 14-ounce package soft or regular tofu,
** rinsed and well drained**
3 large garlic cloves
1/4 medium onion
5 fresh basil leaves
1 1/2 tablespoons reduced-salt soy sauce or
** Bragg Liquid Aminos**
2 tablespoons cornstarch
1 teaspoon curry powder
1 teaspoon Vegit
1 teaspoon cider vinegar
1 1/2 cups coarsely chopped broccoli florets
1/2 pound dry whole wheat lasagna noodles
1 teaspoon cider vinegar
3 cups Tomato-Basil Sauce (page 46)

In a food processor or blender, blend the tofu with the next seven ingredients and 1 teaspoon cider vinegar.

In a medium bowl, stir the broccoli into the tofu mixture, and set the mixture aside.

In a large pot of rapidly boiling water, drop the lasagna noodles, one at a time, and stir in the remaining 1 teaspoon vinegar. Cook the noodles according to the instructions on the package, or until they are just tender. Rinse the noodles, and leave them in cold water until you're ready to use them. Drain the noodles well before assembling the lasagna.

Preheat the oven to 350°.

Layer the lasagna in a lightly oiled 9- by 9-inch ovenproof glass baking pan in the following fashion: First, spread 1 cup sauce on the bottom of the pan. Lay one-third of the noodles on top of the sauce, then spread 1/2 cup sauce over the noodle layer. Spread half the tofu-broccoli filling evenly over the sauce, and one-third of the noodles over the filling. Layer sauce, filling, and noodles again, then top with the remaining sauce.

Bake the lasagna for about 45 minutes, or until it is hot and bubbly and light brown on top.

Serves 6

LASAGNA FLORENTINE

This lasagna is made with a light mixture of vegetables and tofu.

1 small onion, chopped
4 garlic cloves, minced
2 tablespoons water
1 14-ounce package soft tofu, rinsed and
    drained well
2 teaspoons curry powder
1 1/2 tablespoons reduced-salt soy sauce or
    Bragg Liquid Aminos
2 tablespoons tahini or olive oil
1 teaspoon Vegit
1 teaspoon cider vinegar
2 medium-large carrots
1/2 large green or red bell pepper
2 cups chopped fresh spinach (or 1 10-ounce
    package frozen chopped spinach,
    thawed and drained)
6 ounces dry whole wheat lasagna noodles
1 teaspoon cider vinegar

In a medium nonstick frying pan, sauté the onion and garlic over medium heat until the pan becomes dry. Stir in 2 tablespoons water and sauté until the onion is soft. Put the onion into a medium bowl.

In a food processor or blender, blend the tofu with the next five ingredients. Stir the tofu mixture into the onion in the bowl. In a food processor or by hand, grate the carrots and bell pepper, and add them to the tofu along with the spinach.

In a large pot of rapidly boiling water to which the vinegar has been added, drop the lasagna noodles, one at a time. Cook the noodles according to the instructions on the package, or until they are just tender. Rinse the noodles, and leave them in cold water until you are ready to use them. Drain the noodles well before assembling the lasagna.

Preheat the oven to 350°.

In a lightly oiled 9- by 9-inch ovenproof glass baking dish, lay one-third of the noodles on the bottom, and spread one-third of the tofu-vegetable mixture over them. Repeat this layering twice more, ending with filling on top. Cover the dish with foil, pierce the foil in several places, and bake the lasagna for 35 to 40 minutes, or until it is well heated through.

Serves 4 to 6

Italian-style Eggplant-Tofu Casserole

Serve this vegetarian version of eggplant parmesan with pasta and a big salad.

1 14-ounce package regular tofu, rinsed and well drained
2 teaspoons onion powder
1 teaspoon garlic powder
2 teaspoons reduced-salt soy sauce or Bragg Liquid Aminos
1 teaspoon dried oregano
1 teaspoon cider vinegar
2 medium eggplants (about 2 pounds)
2 cups Tomato-Basil Sauce (page 46)
1 large red or green bell pepper, chopped
4 large mushrooms, sliced

Crumble the tofu in a medium bowl. Stir in the next five ingredients and mix well. Set the bowl aside. Cut the eggplants into 1/2-inch round slices, discarding the ends, and soak the slices in water for 20 minutes. Drain the slices well, and fry them without oil on a preheated non-stick griddle or in a large frying pan until they are brown on each side and tender.

Preheat the oven to 400°.

In a lightly oiled 9- by 9-inch ovenproof glass baking dish, spread 3/4 cup of sauce. Layer half the eggplant slices over the sauce. Sprinkle half the tofu, and half the chopped bell pepper, evenly over the eggplant slices. Spread 1/2 cup sauce over this layer. Lay the remainder of the eggplant slices over the sauce, and sprinkle the remaining tofu and bell pepper over the eggplant. Cover the dish with 3/4 cup sauce, and decorate the top with the sliced mushrooms.

Cover the dish with foil, pierce several holes in the foil, and bake the casserole for about 35 minutes, or until it is bubbly.

Serves 4

Salaan Vegetables (Curried Cauliflower & Peas)

Enjoy this vegetable curry over Indian-Style Brown Rice and Barley.

2 medium cauliflowers, including white stems, cut into bite-size pieces
2 teaspoons reduced-salt soy sauce or Bragg Liquid Aminos
2 tablespoons water
1 cup coarsely chopped tomatoes
2 large garlic cloves, minced
1 teaspoon grated fresh gingerroot
2 tablespoons chopped cilantro
1 teaspoon ground cumin
1/2 teaspoon ground coriander
1/4 teaspoon paprika
2 cups fresh green peas (or 1 12-ounce package frozen peas)
1 tablespoon safflower or canola oil

In a covered 4- to 5-quart saucepan, heat the cauliflower, soy sauce or Bragg, and water over medium heat, stirring occasionally, for 5 minutes. Stir in the next seven ingredients, and cook the mixture over medium heat, uncovered, for 15 minutes. Stir in the peas and oil, cover the pan, and lower heat. Simmer the vegetables for 15 minutes longer, or until they are tender.

Serves 8

Wheat-Free Potato-Oat Bran Gnocchi with Spinach Pesto

This marvelous Italian specialty is worth the time it takes to prepare. Gnocchi can keep in the refrigerator for several days and can be heated in a sauce before serving.

3 medium boiling potatoes, scrubbed and
   unpeeled
2 tablespoons onion powder
2 tablespoons reduced-salt soy sauce or Bragg
   Liquid Aminos
1/2 teaspoon ground black pepper
2 teaspoons Vegit
2 1/2 cups oat bran
1/2 cup oat bran for board
1 quart water
1 tablespoon onion powder
2 teaspoons reduced-salt soy sauce or Bragg
   Liquid Aminos
1 teaspoon cider vinegar
Spinach Pesto Sauce (page 52)
1/4 cup pine nuts, for garnish

Boil the potatoes until they are tender. Rinse them in cold water, and peel them. In a food processor, purée the potatoes until they are smooth, or put them through a ricer. Measure out 1 1/2 cups potatoes. Put them in a large bowl, and, with a fork, blend in 2 tablespoons onion powder, 2 tablespoons soy sauce or Bragg, the black pepper, and the Vegit. Stir in 1 1/4 cups oat bran, then knead in 1 1/4 cups more.

Cut the dough into eight parts, and roll each piece of dough into a long, thin roll about 1/2 inch in diameter, using a little of the remaining oat bran on the board as needed. With a sharp knife, cut each roll into 1/2-inch lengths.

In a 4- to 5-quart saucepan, bring 1 quart water to a boil. Season the water with 1 tablespoon onion powder, 2 teaspoons soy sauce or Bragg, and 1 teaspoon cider vinegar. Cook half the gnocchi at a time, uncovered, over medium heat for 10 minutes. Remove the gnocchi with a slotted spoon. Stir them into hot Spinach Pesto, and heat the mixture, uncovered, just until the gnocchi are heated through, or store the gnocchi in the refrigerator, to be reheated in the sauce before serving.

Serve the gnocchi topped with the pine nuts.

Serves 4 to 6

Spinach Pesto Sauce

This rich-tasting pesto can be served with gnocchi or pasta.

4 cups fresh spinach leaves, coarsely chopped
2 cups fresh basil leaves, coarsely chopped
6 large garlic cloves, coarsely chopped
2 cups water
2 teaspoons cornstarch
2 teaspoons reduced-salt soy sauce or Bragg Liquid Aminos
1/4 teaspoon ground black pepper
2 tablespoons tahini
1/4 cup pine nuts for garnish

Sauté the spinach, basil, and garlic in a preheated large nonstick frying pan, over medium heat, for 5 minutes, stirring occasionally.

Stir in the next five ingredients, and stir constantly as the sauce comes to a boil. Lower the heat, and simmer 5 minutes longer, stirring occasionally. Remove the pan from the heat. The sauce can be made ahead to this point; before serving, heat it over medium heat, stirring occasionally, and stir in 1/4 cup water if the sauce becomes too thick. Serve the sauce steaming hot. Sprinkle pine nuts on top before serving.

Serves 4 to 6

Classic Pesto

This variation on the traditional uncooked sauce of basil, garlic, and olive oil takes only minutes to prepare.

2 cups loosely packed fresh basil leaves
6 large garlic cloves
2 tablespoons olive oil
1 teaspoon reduced-salt soy sauce or Bragg Liquid Aminos
1/4 teaspoon ground black pepper
1/2 cup pine nuts
1/4 cup water

Blend all the ingredients but the water in a food processor for 2 minutes. Add the water, and blend again for 1 minute. Refrigerate the sauce until just before serving.

Stir the sauce into hot cooked pasta, and serve at once.

Serves 4 to 6

Sweet Mango Chutney

Serve this with curries and whole wheat Indian bread (*paratha*, page 127).

1 large mango, coarsely chopped (1 1/2 cups)
1/3 cup frozen and thawed apple juice
   concentrate
Pinch cayenne
1/4 teaspoon ground cumin
1/4 teaspoon ground coriander

Cook all the ingredients uncovered in a small saucepan over medium heat for 5 minutes. Reduce the heat, cover, and simmer the mixture for about 25 minutes, or until the mango is softened. Chill and store in the refrigerator.

Yields 1 1/2 cups

Coconut Chutney

This flavorful chutney adds zest to any curry.

1/2 large coconut, separated from shell, skin
   pared off, and meat cut into small pieces
1 jalapeño pepper, seeds removed
2 garlic cloves
1 1/2 tablespoons cumin seed, or 1 tablespoon
   ground cumin
1/4 teaspoon ground black pepper
1 teaspoon reduced-salt soy sauce or Bragg
   Liquid Aminos
1 1/2 cups chopped cilantro
2 tablespoons water
2 tablespoons lemon juice

Put all ingredients into a food processor, and process until the coconut is finely chopped. Store the chutney in a covered glass jar in the refrigerator for up to one month.

Yields about 3 cups

Indian-Style Brown Rice and Barley

Serve this with Indian curries.

1 1/2 cups long grain brown rice
1/2 cup barley
4 cups water
1 tablespoon reduced-salt soy sauce or Bragg
   Liquid Aminos
1 teaspoon ground cardamon or coriander
1/4 teaspoon ground black pepper, or 6 black
   peppercorns
1/2 tablespoon safflower or canola oil

In a covered 3-quart saucepan, bring all the ingredients to a boil. Lower the heat, and simmer the rice, covered, for about 35 minutes, or until the rice and barley are tender and all the liquid is absorbed.

Serves 6 to 8

Mushroom-Potato Curry

This delicately spiced curry tastes delicious over Indian-Style Brown Rice and Barley.

1 medium onion (1 cup)
1 1/2 cups chopped tomatoes
4 garlic cloves, minced
1 teaspoon grated gingerroot
2 tablespoons chopped cilantro
1 1/2 teaspoons ground cumin
1 teaspoon ground coriander
1/4 cup chopped pitted dates
4 small boiling potatoes, peeled and diced (2 cups)
1/2 teaspoon paprika
1/8 teaspoon turmeric
2 teaspoons reduced-salt soy sauce or Bragg Liquid Aminos
1 pound fresh mushrooms, chopped into bite-size pieces
1 tablespoon safflower or canola oil

In a 4- to 5-quart saucepan, cook all the ingredients except the mushrooms and oil over medium heat, uncovered, for 10 minutes. Then cover the pan, and simmer the mixture for 20 minutes over low heat, stirring occasionally. Stir in the mushrooms and oil, and continue cooking over low heat, covered, for 20 to 30 minutes longer, or until the potatoes are tender. Serve the curry hot.

Serves 4

Curried Cauliflower, Potatoes and Peas

1 large onion, chopped
4 large garlic cloves, minced
1 1-inch slice fresh gingerroot, grated
2 tablespoons water
2/3 cup tomato purée
1/2 cup chopped pitted dates
1 teaspoon ground coriander
1 1/2 teaspoons ground cumin
1/4 cup chopped cilantro leaves
1 tablespoon reduced-salt soy sauce or Bragg Liquid Aminos
1/3 cup water
2 pounds red or white rose potatoes, peeled and cut into large bite-size pieces
Florets and stems of 1 medium to large cauliflower, cut into large bite-size pieces
2 cups fresh or frozen (unthawed) peas

In a 4- to 5-quart covered saucepan sauté the chopped onion, garlic and ginger over medium heat without oil until the onion begins to stick and turn brown. Stir in 2 tablespoons water, and continue sautéing uncovered until onion softens. Stir in the next eight ingredients, and cook, uncovered, for 15 minutes.

Add the cauliflower, cover the saucepan, and simmer the vegetables for about 30 to 40 minutes, or until the potatoes are tender.

Five minutes before serving stir in the peas, and simmer until the peas are hot. Serve the curry immediately, or let it cool to serve later as a salad.

Serves 8

EGGPLANT CURRY

You can chop the dates, cilantro, garlic, and gingerroot in a food processor.

2 medium eggplants, peeled, cut in large bite-size pieces, soaked in water for 10 minutes, and drained
4 medium boiling potatoes, peeled and cut into small bite-size pieces (4 cups)
1/2 cup water
2 teaspoons reduced-salt soy sauce or Bragg Liquid Aminos
1 1/2 cups coarsely chopped tomatoes
1/8 teaspoon ground black pepper
1 tablespoon lemon juice
8 pitted dates, chopped, or 3 tablespoons grated coconut
1/4 cup chopped fresh cilantro
3 garlic cloves, minced
1 1-inch slice fresh gingerroot, grated or chopped
1 1/2 teaspoons curry powder
1 1/2 teaspoons ground cumin
1 teaspoon ground coriander
1/2 teaspoon paprika
1/8 teaspoon turmeric

In a 4- to 5-quart saucepan, cook the eggplant, potatoes, water, and soy sauce or Bragg over low heat, covered, for about 30 minutes, or until the eggplant and potatoes are tender.

Stir in the remaining ingredients, and simmer the mixture over low heat, covered, for 25 to 30 minutes, stirring occasionally. Serve the curry hot.

Serves 6

CURRIED RICE AND EGGPLANT CASSEROLE

2 1/2 cups uncooked brown rice
4 3/4 cups water
2 teaspoons cider vinegar
1/2 teaspoon ground coriander
1/4 teaspoon ground black pepper
2 large eggplants, peeled and cut into 1/2-inch cubes
1 1/2 large onions
1/2 cup sliced almonds or chopped walnuts
2/3 cup frozen and thawed apple juice concentrate
1 teaspoon ground cumin
2 tablespoons curry powder
3/4 cup black raisins
1 teaspoon cider vinegar

In a 3-quart covered saucepan, bring the rice, water, vinegar, coriander, and black pepper to a boil. Lower the heat, and simmer the rice for 30 minutes, covered, or until all liquid is absorbed.

While the rice cooks, soak the eggplant cubes in cold water for 20 minutes. Drain them well.

Preheat the oven to 350°. In a 4- to 5-quart preheated saucepan, sauté the onions over medium heat, uncovered, until they begin to stick. Add the eggplant cubes, and sauté, stirring occasionally, until the eggplant is soft.

Stir in the remaining ingredients, and simmer for 5 minutes longer. Stir in the steamed rice, and mix well. Remove the pan from the heat. Spread the curried rice mixture evenly in a 9- by 13-inch ovenproof glass baking dish. Bake the casserole for about 30 minutes, or until the rice is piping hot. Serve the casserole hot.

Serves 8 to 10

MASALA DOSA
(INDIAN-STYLE POTATO CRÊPES)

These mildly spiced, low-fat potato-filled crêpes make a good entrée or appetizer. You can prepare both crêpes and filling the day before serving, if you like.

Filling

4 large boiling potatoes (about 2 pounds)
2 large onions, thinly sliced
2 tablespoons water
1 jalapeño pepper, seeded and coarsely chopped
1 1-inch slice fresh gingerroot, coarsely chopped
1/2 cup firmly packed cilantro leaves, chopped
1/2 teaspoon ground cumin
1/4 teaspoon turmeric
2 teaspoons safflower or canola oil
1/4 teaspoon sea salt

Crêpes

1/2 cup uncooked orange lentils (*masoor dal*)
1 1/2 cups water
1/2 jalapeño pepper, seeded and minced
1/2 cup firmly packed cilantro leaves
1/2 medium onion, minced
1 1/2 cups water
2 cups brown rice flour
3 tablespoons cornstarch
2 teaspoons safflower or canola oil
1 tablespoon reduced-salt soy sauce or Bragg Liquid Aminos
1/4 teaspoon baking soda
1 teaspoon oil, for the pan

To make the filling, boil the potatoes. Reserve the cooking water. When the potatoes have cooled, peel them. Cut each potato into eight pieces and coarsely chop half the pieces in a food processor or by hand with 1/4 cup liquid from the potatoes. Repeat this process with the rest of the potatoes. (Or chop the potatoes by hand, and combine them with 1/2 cup cooking liquid.) Place the chopped potatoes in a large bowl.

In a large, preheated nonstick frying pan, sauté the onions without oil until they begin to stick and brown. Stir in 2 tablespoons water, and continue to cook the onions over low heat until they are soft. Stir in the jalapeño, gingerroot, cilantro, cumin and turmeric, and simmer for 5 minutes longer.

Mix the onion-cilantro mixture into the potatoes, then mix in the oil and salt.

To make the crêpes, soak the lentils in 1 1/2 cups water for 1 hour or longer. In a food processor or blender, purée the lentils with the water they have soaked in. Put the lentil purée into a medium bowl. Stir in the jalapeño, cilantro, and onion. Blend the remaining crêpe ingredients in a food processor or blender, and mix them well into the lentil mixture.

Preheat a 9-inch nonstick frying pan or a 7-inch crêpe pan over medium heat until the pan is hot. With a piece of paper towel or kraft paper, lightly oil the pan with 1 teaspoon oil. Stir the batter well, and measure out 1/4 cup. Pour the batter into the center of the pan, and quickly tilt the pan to allow the batter to spread. The crêpes need not be perfectly round. When a crêpe is golden brown on the bottom, gently turn it over, and cook it on the other side for about 1 minute. It should not brown very much on the second side. Stir the batter well between crêpes. The batter will make about twenty.

You can stack the cooked crêpes and store them in the refrigerator for a day or two, if you like, before assembling the dish.

To assemble the *Masala Dosa*, lay each crêpe pale side up. Spread 1 heaping tablespoon of filling in a strip down the center third of the crêpe. Gently fold one side of the crêpe over the filling, and carefully roll up the crêpe so the seam side is down. Handle the crêpes carefully, but don't worry about small tears.

You can heat the filled crêpes on the stove or in the oven. To heat them on the stove, use a nonstick frying pan or a griddle without oil. Turning once, heat the crêpes until the filling is well heated through. To heat the crêpes in the oven, preheat the oven to 400°, place the crêpes on a 10- by 15-inch nonstick baking sheet, and heat them for 15 to 20 minutes, or until they are well heated through.

Yields 20 filled crêpes

INDIAN-STYLE GARBANZO BEAN STEW

This spicy stew, served over brown rice, makes a nourishing entrée. Add more cayenne if you would like the stew spicier.

2 cups dry garbanzo beans
8 cups water
7 cups water
1 large onion, chopped
3 large garlic cloves, minced
1 1-inch slice fresh gingerroot
2 tablespoons water
3 tablespoons tomato paste
6 pitted dates, chopped
2 teaspoons curry powder
1 teaspoon ground coriander
2 teaspoons ground cumin
1/4 teaspoon cayenne
1 tablespoon reduced-salt soy sauce or Bragg
    Liquid Aminos
1/4 cup chopped cilantro leaves
2 teaspoons lemon juice

In a large, covered pot bring the beans and 8 cups water to a boil. Boil for 10 minutes, then remove the pot from the heat and let the beans soak in the water until they are cool, or overnight.

Drain and rinse the beans well, and return them to the pot. Add 7 cups water. Bring the beans and water to a boil, reduce the heat, and simmer the beans, covered, for 2 to 3 hours, or until they are tender. Drain the beans, reserving 1 cup broth (if there isn't this much broth, add water to equal 1 cup). Refrigerate the beans until the next day, if you like.

In a preheated nonstick frying pan, sauté the onion, garlic, and ginger over medium heat until the onion begins to stick. Stir in 2 tablespoons water and cook until the onion softens. Stir in the next seven ingredients and the 1 cup reserved bean broth. Simmer for 5 minutes.

Put the drained garbanzo beans into a 4- to 5-quart saucepan. Stir in the tomato-date mixture, bring the stew to a boil, then reduce the heat and slowly simmer the stew, covered, for 25 minutes, stirring occasionally. Stir in the cilantro and lemon juice, simmer the stew 5 minutes more, and serve.

Serves 8

SPICY LENTIL STEW

Enjoy this hearty stew over brown rice.

1 pound dry lentils
4 1/2 cups water
2 bay leaves
1/2 green bell pepper, cut into large bite-size
pieces
1 large onion, coarsely chopped
6 garlic cloves, minced
4 carrots, cut crosswise into 1/2-inch slices
4 celery stalks, cut crosswise into 1/2-inch
slices
6 pitted dates, chopped
2 teaspoons chili powder
1 tablespoon reduced-salt soy sauce or Bragg
Liquid Aminos
1 teaspoon cider vinegar
1 tablespoon curry powder
1/4 cup chopped fresh cilantro leaves

In a large, covered pot, bring the lentils, water, and bay leaves to a boil over medium heat. Lower the heat, and simmer the lentils, covered, for about 1 hour, or until they are tender. If necessary, add a little more water during the cooking.

Stir in the remaining ingredients, cover the pot, and simmer the stew for about 45 minutes, or until the vegetables are tender and the stew has thickened.

Serves 8

QUICK AND EASY CURRIED LENTILS

This dish can be served hot with brown rice or cold with salad or raw vegetables.

1 1/2 cups dry brown lentils
3 cups water
4 teaspoons reduced-salt soy sauce or Bragg
Liquid Aminos
4 teaspoons onion powder
1 teaspoon garlic powder
1/2 teaspoon ground black pepper
1/2 teaspoon celery seed
1 teaspoon dried oregano
2 teaspoons Vegit
2 teaspoons curry powder
1 teaspoon ground coriander

In a 4- to 5-quart covered saucepan, bring all the ingredients to a boil. Lower the heat, and simmer the lentils, covered, for about 25 minutes, or until all the liquid is absorbed. Serve the lentils hot or cold.

Serves 4

HEARTY CROCKPOT BEAN-BARLEY STEW

This nourishing, economical stew is very easy to prepare as a main course or side dish. You can use leftovers to make Bean-Barley-Oat Bran Burgers (page 109).

2 cups dry pinto beans
2 cups dry small red beans
10 cups water
1 cup dry barley
3 cups chopped onions
6 to 8 large garlic cloves, minced
2 1/2 tablespoons reduced-salt soy sauce or Bragg Liquid Aminos
2 teaspoons Vegit
1/2 teaspoon ground black pepper
2 teaspoons cider vinegar
6 cups boiling water

Bring the beans and water to a boil in a large pot, and boil the beans for 10 minutes. Remove the pot from the heat, and let the beans soak in the hot water until they are cool, or overnight. Drain the beans, rinse them well, and put them into a large crockpot. Stir in the remaining ingredients, and set the temperature on high. Cook the beans, covered, for 8 to 10 hours.

If the stew is too thick, add 1/2 to 1 cup boiling water. Serve the stew hot.

Serves 12

EASY LENTIL CABBAGE STEW

Serve this tasty, nourishing entrée over brown rice or noodles.

1 large onion, cut in half and sliced
1/2 large cabbage, coarsely sliced
1 cup dry brown lentils
3 1/2 cups water
1/3 cup tomato paste
2 tablespoons lemon juice
1/4 cup frozen or thawed apple juice concentrate
1 tablespoon reduced-salt soy sauce or Bragg Liquid Aminos
2 teaspoons cider vinegar
1 teaspoon Vegit
1/2 teaspoon ground ginger

In a 4- to 5-quart preheated nonstick saucepan, sauté the onion over medium heat, uncovered, until it begins to stick and brown. Stir in the remaining ingredients, bring the mixture to a boil, cover the pan, and simmer the mixture over low heat for about 1 1/2 hours, or until the lentils and cabbage are soft and most of the moisture is absorbed. Serve the stew hot.

Serves 4 to 6

THICK LENTIL-SPLIT PEA-BARLEY STEW

1 cup dry lentils
3/4 cup dry split peas
3/4 cup dry barley
8 cups water
2 bay leaves
1/4 teaspoon ground black or white pepper
2 large garlic cloves, minced
1/2 large onion, chopped
2 celery stalks, sliced crosswise
1/2 cup chopped parsley
1 cup tomato purée
2 teaspoons reduced-salt soy sauce or Bragg
   Liquid Aminos
1 teaspoon Vegit

In a large, covered pot bring all the ingredients to a boil. Lower the heat, and simmer the stew, covered, for about 2 1/2 hours, stirring occasionally.

Serve the stew hot. If you reheat it, add a little water to keep the stew from sticking or burning.

Serves 8

QUICK THICK LIMA BEAN-BARLEY-RICE STEW

This hearty, healthy stew takes very little time to prepare. It cooks in about 45 minutes, and is perfect for lunch or dinner on a cold day.

1 2/3 cups (1 16-ounce can) tomato purée
8 cups water
3 cups fresh or frozen lima beans
3/4 cup barley
3/4 cup uncooked brown rice
2 tablespoons reduced-salt soy sauce or Bragg
   Liquid Aminos
1/4 teaspoon ground white or black pepper
1 medium onion, coarsely chopped
1 medium red or green bell pepper, coarsely
   chopped
2 large celery stalks, sliced crosswise
2 medium carrots, sliced crosswise

In a large covered soup pot bring all the ingredients to a boil. Lower the heat, and simmer the stew, covered, for 40 minutes, or until the stew is thick and the vegetables are tender. Serve the stew hot.

Serves 8 to 10

Sweet and Tangy White Beans

These slightly tangy beans make a perfect side dish with vegetarian burgers or wieners.

2 1/4 cups large white beans
8 cups water
4 cups water
1/2 cup tomato purée
3 tablespoons cider vinegar
2 tablespoons maple syrup
1 tablespoon reduced-salt soy sauce or Bragg Liquid Aminos

In a 4- to 5-quart covered saucepan, bring the beans to a boil in 8 cups water. Boil the beans for 10 minutes, remove the pan from the heat, and let the beans soak in the water until they are cool, or overnight.

Drain and rinse the beans, and return them to the pot. Stir in 4 cups water and remaining ingredients, bring the beans to a boil again, and lower the heat. Simmer the beans, covered, for about 1 hour, or until they are tender. Serve the beans hot.

Serves 8

Country-Style White Beans

1 pound (2 1/4 cups) small or large white beans
8 cups water
5 cups water
2 teaspoons reduced-salt soy sauce or Bragg Liquid Aminos
2 bay leaves
1/2 teaspoon ground black pepper
2 medium onions, minced
2 large garlic cloves
1 green bell pepper, chopped
3 medium tomatoes, coarsely chopped
1/2 teaspoon dried oregano
1/4 cup chopped parsley

In a 4- to 5-quart covered saucepan, bring the beans to a boil in 8 cups water. Boil the beans for 10 minutes, then remove the pan from the heat. Let the beans soak in the water until they are cool, or overnight.

Drain and rinse the beans, and return them to the pot. Add 5 cups water, the soy sauce or Bragg, the bay leaves and the black pepper. Bring the mixture to a boil, and lower the heat. Simmer the beans for about 1 1/2 hours, or until they are tender. Drain.

In a preheated medium nonstick frying pan, sauté the onions and garlic until the onions begin to stick. Stir in 2 tablespoons water, and cook until the onions are soft. Stir in the remaining ingredients, cook for 5 minutes, then stir this mixture into the cooked, drained beans. Heat beans before serving.

Serves 6 to 8

EGGPLANT-BELL PEPPER STEW

2 medium eggplants, sliced 1/2 inch thick,
    soaked in water for 15 minutes, and drained
1 large onion, chopped
4 large garlic cloves, minced
2 tablespoons water
1 cup chopped fresh tomatoes (or 3
    tablespoons tomato paste plus 1/2 cup
    water)
1 green bell pepper, sliced into thin strips
1 red bell pepper, sliced into thin strips
1 tablespoon chopped fresh oregano (or 1
    teaspoon dried)
1 tablespoon chopped fresh basil (or 1
    teaspoon dried)
1 1/2 teaspoons reduced-salt soy sauce or
    Bragg Liquid Aminos
1 1/2 teaspoon olive oil

Cook the eggplant slices on a preheated non-stick griddle or in a preheated nonstick frying pan, without oil, over medium heat until the slices are brown on both sides. Cut the slices into large bite-size pieces, and set the pieces aside.

In a 4- to 5-quart covered saucepan over medium heat, sauté the onion and garlic uncovered without oil until the onion begins to stick. Stir in 2 tablespoons water, and cook until the onion softens. Stir in the next seven ingredients. Bring the mixture to a boil, reduce the heat, and simmer the stew for 15 minutes.

Stir in the eggplant, and heat the stew, uncovered, until the eggplant is hot. Serve the stew hot or cold.

Serves 4 to 6

HIGH-ENERGY STEW

1 large onion, cut into bite-size pieces
4 large garlic cloves, minced
2 tablespoons water
2 cups boiling water
1 tablespoon reduced-salt soy sauce or Bragg
    Liquid Aminos
2 bay leaves
2 whole cloves
1/8 teaspoon ground black pepper
4 teaspoons paprika
8 slices High-Energy Protein Loaf or Spicy
    High-Energy Protein Loaf (pages 82 and 83),
    cut in half
2 large (or 4 small) boiling potatoes, peeled
    and cut into bite-size pieces
2 cups fresh or frozen peas
1 tablespoon cornstarch, dissolved in 2
    tablespoons water (optional)

In a 4- to 5-quart covered saucepan sauté the onion and garlic uncovered over medium heat until the onion begins to stick. Stir in 2 tablespoons water and cook until the pan becomes dry again. Stir in all the remaining ingredients except the peas. Bring the stew to a boil, lower the heat, and simmer the stew, covered, for about 35 minutes, or until the potatoes are tender. Stir the stew occasionally as it cooks. At this point you can let the stew cool for later reheating.

Stir in the peas, and heat the stew thoroughly. If you like, you can thicken the gravy with 1 tablespoon cornstarch dissolved in 2 tablespoons water. Serve the stew hot.

Serves 3 to 4

Best Tofu Enchilada Casserole

This marvelously flavored Mexican-style casserole is the perfect dish for a party or a potluck.

Sauce

5 cups water
2/3 cup (6-ounce can) tomato paste
1/2 to 1 jalapeño pepper, seeded and chopped
2 large garlic cloves, minced
1/2 large onion, minced
1 tablespoon dried oregano
2 teaspoons ground cumin
1 teaspoon ground coriander
2 teaspoons chili powder
1 teaspoon Vegit
2 teaspoons reduced-salt soy sauce or low-sodium Bragg Liquid Aminos

Filling

3 14-ounce packages regular tofu, rinsed and well drained
1 tablespoon Vegit
3 teaspoons ground cumin
3 teaspoons chili powder
3 teaspoons dried oregano
3/4 teaspoon ground coriander
1/2 large onion, minced
3/4 cup firmly packed cilantro leaves
3 tablespoons reduced-salt soy sauce or low-sodium Bragg Liquid Aminos
18 corn tortillas

To make the sauce, in a 4- to 5-quart saucepan mix together all the ingredients until they are blended. Bring the mixture to a boil, then lower the heat. Simmer the sauce, covered, for 25 minutes.

To make the filling, crumble the tofu in a large bowl, and stir in the next eight ingredients with a fork until the filling is well mixed.

Preheat the oven to 350°.

In a lightly oiled 9- by 13-inch ovenproof glass baking pan, spread 1 cup. Put 1 cup sauce in a shallow pie plate. Dip each tortilla in the sauce in the pie plate, then fill the tortilla with 1/3 cup of the filling mixture. Roll the enchiladas, and place them seam side down, side by side, over the sauce in the baking pan. When the first layer is full, layer the rest on top. Cover the enchiladas with the remaining sauce, and cover the casserole with foil. Bake the casserole for about 1 hour, and serve it hot.

Serves 8 to 10

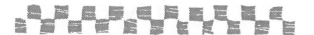

Fresh Cilantro Salsa

Serve this salsa with any Mexican entrée. It can keep in the refrigerator for up to one week.

2 large tomatoes, cut in quarters
2 green chili peppers, seeded and coarsely chopped
2 garlic cloves, coarsely chopped
1/4 cup chopped onion
1 cup firmly packed cilantro leaves, chopped
1 large green onion, chopped

Simmer the tomatoes, chilies, and garlic in a medium saucepan, uncovered, for 30 minutes. Let the mixture cool.

Stir the onion, cilantro, and green onion into the tomato-chili mixture. Serve the salsa immediately, or store in the refrigerator.

Yields 2 cups

Easy Guacamole

This guacamole makes a healthful topping for Mexican dishes, spread for toast or crackers, or dip for chips or vegetables.

2 avocados, chopped
1 tablespoon lemon juice
1/2 cup Fresh Spicy Salsa (page 65)

In a medium bowl, combine the avocados and lemon juice, then stir in the salsa. Cover the bowl and chill until serving time.

Serves 6

Fresh Spicy Salsa

This uncooked tomato salsa, which takes only minutes to prepare in a food processor, can add zest to most Mexican dishes.

2 medium tomatoes, coarsely chopped
1 jalapeño pepper, seeded and coarsely chopped
1/2 medium onion, coarsely chopped
1/2 cup firmly packed cilantro leaves, coarsely chopped
2 teaspoons cider vinegar

Combine all the ingredients. Chill the salsa before serving.

Yields 2 cups

Easy Mexican Sauce

1 2/3 cups (16-ounce can) tomato purée
3 cups water
1 teaspoon reduced-salt soy sauce or Bragg Liquid Aminos
1 teaspoon dried oregano
2 teaspoons paprika
About 1/2 teaspoon chili powder, to taste
1/2 medium onion, chopped
2 large garlic cloves, minced
1/2 large green bell pepper, chopped
Cayenne (optional)

Bring all ingredients to a boil in a 4- to 5-quart saucepan, then simmer, covered, for 30 minutes. Add cayenne to taste.

Yields 1 quart

Easy Enchilada Sauce

2/3 cup (1 6-ounce can) tomato paste
4 cups water
2 teaspoons chili powder
1 tablespoon onion powder
1 teaspoon garlic powder
2 teaspoons reduced-salt soy sauce or Bragg
   Liquid Aminos
Cayenne (optional)
1 tablespoon cornstarch
2 tablespoons water

In a saucepan, mix together the tomato paste, 2
cups water, and the seasonings. Stir in 2 cups
more water. Bring the mixture to a boil, lower
the heat, and simmer, covered, for 10 minutes.
Add cayenne to taste.

    Mix together the cornstarch and 2 tablespoons
water, and stir the mixture into the sauce. When
the sauce thickens slightly, remove the pan from
the heat.

Yields 4 1/2 cups

Tasty Refried Beans

You can use these tasty refried beans for burritos,
tostadas, tacos, and enchiladas. They freeze well.

4 cups dry pinto beans
8 cups water
8 cups water
2 cups chopped onions
4 garlic cloves, minced
1 large tomato, chopped
1/2 large red bell pepper
1 tablespoon chili powder
1 teaspoon dried oregano
2 teaspoons cider vinegar
1 tablespoon reduced-salt soy sauce or Bragg
   Liquid Aminos

Bring the beans and 8 cups water to a boil in a
large covered pot, and boil the beans for 10 minutes. Remove the pot from the heat, and soak
the beans in hot water until the water is cool, or
overnight.

    Drain and rinse the beans, then return them
to the pot. Add 8 cups water, bring the beans to
a boil, and reduce the heat. Cook the beans over
low heat, covered, for about 2 1/4 hours, or until
they are tender.

    In a large nonstick frying pan over medium
heat, sauté the onions, garlic, tomato, and bell
pepper, uncovered, without oil, until the vegetables begin to stick. Stir in the cooked beans
along with the remaining ingredients. Cook the
mixture over medium heat, stirring frequently
until it is a thick paste. Remove the pan from
the heat, and serve the beans hot.

Yields 8 1/2 cups

ZESTY CROCKPOT PINTO BEANS

This hearty, economical bean dish is great for people who work away from home all day. Left to soak during the day, the beans can cook through the night and the following day, so they're ready to eat when you arrive home. Serve the beans with brown rice and a salad.

3 cups dry pinto beans
8 cups water
1 large onion, chopped
2 celery stalks, chopped
1/2 red or green bell pepper, chopped
1 large tomato, chopped
2 bay leaves
1 tablespoon reduced-salt soy sauce or Bragg Liquid Aminos
1 teaspoon Vegit
4 cups boiling water

add last 15 minutes

Bring the beans and 8 cups water to a boil in a large pot, and boil the beans for 10 minutes. Let the beans soak in the water until they are cool, or overnight.

Drain and rinse the beans well, and put them into a crockpot. Stir in the remaining ingredients, cover the crockpot, and set the temperature on high. Cook the beans for at least 10 hours, preferably 12 to 16. Serve the beans hot.

Serves 8 to 10

SPICY CHILI BEANS

2 1/4 cups (1 pound) red beans
6 cups water
1 large onion, chopped
3 large garlic cloves, minced
1/2 large green bell pepper, chopped
1 teaspoon dried oregano
1 teaspoon ground cumin
→ 1 1/2 tablespoons chili powder
1 1/2 cups tomato purée
3 cups hot water
1 tablespoon reduced-salt soy sauce, or Bragg Liquid Aminos
1 teaspoon cider vinegar
1/4 cup chopped red onions, for garnish

Bring the beans and 6 cups water to a boil in a large pot, and boil the beans for 10 minutes. Remove the pot from the heat, and let the beans soak in the water until they are cool, or overnight.

Drain and rinse the beans well, and return them to the pot. Stir in the next ten ingredients, bring the mixture to a boil, and reduce the heat. Cook the beans, covered, over low heat for about 2 hours, or until they are tender. Stir occasionally to keep the beans from sticking.

Serve the beans sprinkled with chopped onion.

Serves 8

HEARTY CHILI BEANS

1 1/2 cups dry pinto beans
1 1/2 cups dry kidney beans
8 cups water
6 cups water
1 medium onion, chopped
6 garlic cloves, minced
1 1/2 tablespoons chili powder
1 1/2 teaspoons ground cumin
1 1/2 teaspoons dried oregano
2/3 cup (1 6-ounce can) tomato paste
1/2 cup diced green chili peppers (or 1
    4-ounce can diced green chili peppers)
2 tablespoons reduced-salt soy sauce or Bragg
    Liquid Aminos

Bring the beans and 8 cups water to a boil in a
large, covered pot. Cook the beans for 10 minutes, then remove the pot from the heat. Let the
beans soak in the water until they are cool, or
overnight.

Drain the beans, rinse them well, and return
them to the pot. Stir in 6 cups water and the
next five ingredients, bring the mixture to a boil,
and reduce the heat. Simmer the beans over low
heat, covered, for 1 hour.

Stir in the tomato paste, diced chili peppers,
and soy sauce or Bragg. Return the beans to a
boil, then lower the heat and continue simmering the beans, covered, for another 1 1/2 hours
or until the beans are tender. Stir the beans occasionally as they thicken. Serve the beans hot.

Serves 10

MILD CROCKPOT CHILI BEANS

This mildly spiced chili is the perfect meal to
come home to in cold or rainy weather. You can
add more chili powder and a little cayenne if
you like your chili spicier.

3 cups dry red kidney beans
12 cups water
5 cups water
1 large onion, chopped
4 large garlic cloves, minced
2 bay leaves
1 teaspoon dried oregano
1 tablespoon chili powder
1 tablespoon reduced-salt soy sauce or Bragg
    Liquid Aminos
1 cup tomato purée

Bring the beans and 12 cups water to a boil in a
large covered pot. Boil the beans, covered, for
10 minutes, then remove the pot from the heat.
Let the beans soak in the water until they are
cool, or overnight.

Drain the beans, rinse them well, and put
them into a 4-quart electric crockpot. Add 5 cups
water and the remaining ingredients, set the
crockpot on high, and cook the beans, covered,
for about 16 hours. Serve the beans hot.

Serves 8 to 12

Vegan Mexican-style Casserole

This casserole makes a flavorful party dish. Top each serving with Best Mexican Sauce and a dollop of Easy Guacamole.

Easy Mexican Sauce (page 65)
18 corn tortillas
3 cups Tasty Refried Beans (page 66), or lard-free commercial refried beans plus 2 teaspoons onion powder and 1 teaspoon garlic powder
1/2 medium onion, coarsely chopped
→ 1 jalapeño pepper, coarsely chopped
1/2 cup firmly packed cilantro leaves, coarsely chopped
1/2 red or green bell pepper, coarsely chopped
1 1/2 cups fresh or frozen corn kernels

Preheat the oven to 350°.

In a lightly oiled 9- by 13-inch ovenproof glass baking pan, spread 1 cup sauce. Lay six corn tortillas over the sauce. Pour 1/2 cup sauce evenly over the tortillas, then spread the beans on top. Cover the beans with six more tortillas, and spread 1/2 cup sauce over the tortillas.

Mix together the onion, jalapeño pepper, cilantro, and bell pepper (these can be chopped together in a food processor). Sprinkle this mixture evenly over the tortillas, then sprinkle the corn kernels on top. Cover with the last six tortillas, and pour 1 cup sauce over the top. Bake the casserole for 30 to 40 minutes, or until it is hot and bubbly.

Heat the remaining sauce to be spooned over each serving.

Serves 8 to 10

Mexican-style Tofu Casserole for Four

Serve this casserole with guacamole and salsa along with a tossed salad.

1 14-ounce package firm or regular tofu, rinsed and well drained
2 teaspoons onion powder
1 teaspoon garlic powder
1/2 teaspoon chili powder
2 teaspoons reduced-salt soy sauce or Bragg Liquid Aminos
2 cups Easy Mexican Sauce (page 65)
9 corn tortillas, cut in half
1/2 green bell pepper, coarsely chopped
1/2 small onion, coarsely chopped
→ 1/2 jalapeño pepper, coarsely chopped
1/2 cup firmly packed cilantro leaves, coarsely chopped
1 cup fresh or frozen corn kernels

In a medium bowl, crumble the tofu. Stir in the next four ingredients along with 1/2 cup of the sauce, and set the bowl aside.

Lightly oil a 10-inch ovenproof glass deep-dish pie plate. Spread 1/2 cup sauce in the bottom, and arrange six tortilla halves in a single layer over the sauce. Spread the tofu mixture over the tortillas, then lay six tortilla halves on top. Spread 1/2 cup sauce on the tortillas.

Mix together the bell pepper, onion, jalapeño pepper, and cilantro. Sprinkle this mixture over the tortilla layer, then sprinkle the corn evenly on top. Arrange the last six tortilla halves over the corn, and spread the last 1/2 cup sauce on the tortillas. Bake the casserole for about 50 to 55 minutes, and serve it hot.

Serves 4 to 6

SPICY VEGETARIAN TAMALES

These delicious tamales are surprisingly easy to prepare. A friend from Colombia showed us how to prepare the corn dough, roll it in corn husks, and cook the tamales. They taste great with either the bean or the tofu filling.

Filling #1
2 cups Tasty Refried Beans, Zesty Crockpot Pinto Beans, Spicy Chili Beans, or Hearty Chili Beans (pages 66, 67, or 68), or lard-free commercial refried beans or chili beans
1/2 small onion, chopped
2 pinches cayenne
2 1/2 teaspoons chili powder
2 teaspoons onion powder
1/2 teaspoon garlic powder
1/2 teaspoon dried oregano

Filling #2
Scrambled Tofu Ranchero (page 214)

Dough
2 1/2 cups *masa harina* or corn flour
2 1/2 cups water
2 1/2 tablespoons ~~safflower or canola oil~~ Soy Spread
1 tablespoon reduced-salt soy sauce or Bragg Liquid Aminos
1 teaspoon garlic powder
1/4 of an 8-ounce package dried corn husks

Soak the corn husks in cold water until they are softened. Separate and drain them.

Choose either Filling #1 or Filling #2. To make the bean filling, mix together all the ingredients in a medium bowl.

In another bowl, mix together the dough ingredients with a spoon until the dough is smooth.

To assemble the tamales, place one soaked corn husk (or two if they are small) in the palm of one hand. The width of the husk(s) should measure about 7 inches across, and the length of the husks should be about 10 inches. Drop two heaping tablespoons of the dough in the center of the husk(s). Then drop one heaping tablespoon of filling on top of the dough. Bring the sides of the husk(s) over the filling and dough, and turn down flaps on top and bottom, forming an envelope. Place another corn husk over the flaps and fold it over to keep the filling from coming out while the tamales are steaming.

Pour about 4 cups water into the bottom of a vegetable steamer or spaghetti cooker. Lay the tamales in two or three overlapping layers in the steamer basket. Cover the steamer and cook the tamales over medium-high heat until the water boils and steam forms. Then reduce the heat, and simmer the tamales for about 30 minutes. Serve them hot.

The tamales can also be reheated as needed in 1/4 cup water until they are hot and steamy.

Yields 12 tamales

Tofu Tamale Pie

Batter

1 cup cornmeal
3 cups water
1 tablespoon reduced-salt soy sauce or Bragg
  Liquid Aminos
1 tablespoon onion powder
1 teaspoon garlic powder

Filling

2 large garlic cloves
1 medium onion
1/2 green bell pepper
1/2 jalapeño pepper
2 tablespoons water
1 14-ounce package firm tofu, rinsed, well
  drained, and crumbled
3 tablespoons tomato paste
1/2 cup water
1 tablespoon reduced-salt soy sauce or Bragg
  Liquid Aminos
1/2 cup chopped fresh cilantro
Sprinkle of paprika

To make the batter, in a medium saucepan mix together the batter ingredients, and cook them over medium heat, stirring frequently until the batter is thick. Spread the batter evenly on the sides and bottom of a lightly oiled 9-inch oven-proof glass deep-dish pie plate, and set the plate aside.

Preheat oven to 400°.

To make the filling, sauté the vegetables in a medium nonstick frying pan, uncovered, over medium heat until the vegetables begin to stick. Stir in 2 tablespoons water, and cook until the vegetables soften. Stir in the remaining filling ingredients. Simmer the mixture uncovered, for 10 minutes.

Fill the cornmeal crust with the tofu mixture, and sprinkle paprika over the top. Bake the tamale pie for 20 minutes, and serve it hot.

Serves 3 to 4

Easy Black-Bean Tostadas

These healthy, mildly spiced tostadas can be prepared very quickly. If you like, add spicy hot sauce.

6 corn tortillas
3 cups Basic Black Beans (page 75)
1/3 cup chopped onion
1/2 cup chopped fresh cilantro
1 cup chopped tomatoes

Preheat the oven to 450°.

Lay six corn tortillas on a nonstick cookie sheet, and spread 1/2 cup beans on each tortilla. Bake the tostadas for 10 minutes.

Sprinkle the chopped onion, cilantro, and tomatoes over the tostadas, and serve.

Serves 3 to 6

Easy Tofu-Tamale Pie Casserole

Filling

2 14-ounce packages firm tofu, rinsed, drained well, and crumbled
3/4 cup Easy Enchilada Sauce (page 66)
2 teaspoons Vegit
2 teaspoons ground cumin
2 teaspoons chili powder
2 teaspoons dried oregano
1/2 teaspoon ground coriander
2 tablespoons reduced-salt soy sauce or Bragg Liquid Aminos
1/2 large onion, minced
1/2 cup firmly packed fresh cilantro leaves, minced

Batter

2 cups cornmeal
6 cups water
2 tablespoons reduced-salt soy sauce or Bragg Liquid Aminos
2 tablespoons onion powder
2 teaspoons garlic powder

To make the filling, in a medium bowl mix together the first nine ingredients. Stir in the cilantro, and set the bowl aside.

To make the batter, in a 3-quart saucepan mix together the batter ingredients. Cook over medium heat, stirring frequently, until the cornmeal thickens.

Preheat the oven to 350°.

To assemble the casserole, pour 1 cup sauce into the bottom of a lightly oiled 9- by 13-inch ovenproof glass baking dish. Drop half the bat-ter into the sauce by heaping serving-spoonfuls, distributing the batter evenly in the bottom of the baking dish. Spread the filling over the batter, then drop the rest of the batter evenly over the filling. Pour 1/2 cup sauce over the batter. Cover the casserole with foil, and bake for 30 minutes.

Remove the foil, and bake the casserole for another 25 to 30 minutes, or until it is set.

Before serving, heat the remaining sauce. Spoon some sauce over each serving.

Serves 8 to 10

ZESTY BEAN TAMALE PIE

2 cups Zesty Crockpot Pinto Beans or Tasty
   Refried Beans (pages 66 and 67) or lard-free
   commercial refried beans
→1 1/2 teaspoons chili powder
1/2 teaspoon garlic powder
→1/8 teaspoon cayenne
1 cup *masa harina* or corn flour
1 cup water
1 tablespoon safflower or canola oil
1 1/2 teaspoon reduced-salt soy sauce or
   Bragg Liquid Aminos
1 1/2 cups Quick and Easy Hot Enchilada
   Sauce
1 cup fresh or frozen corn kernels
1/2 cup chopped onions
1/2 cup chopped green bell pepper
1/2 cup chopped red bell pepper
1/3 cup chopped cilantro

Preheat the oven to 400°.

Put the beans in a medium bowl. Stir in the
chili powder, garlic powder, and cayenne, and
set the bowl aside.

In a small bowl, mix together with a fork the
masa harina or corn flour, the water, the oil, and
the soy sauce until the dough is smooth. Set the
bowl aside.

Lightly oil a 10-inch ovenproof glass deep-
dish pie plate, and pour 1/2 cup sauce into it.
Drop the dough, by tablespoons, evenly in the
bottom of the pie plate. Drop the beans evenly
over the dough. Pour 1/4 cup more sauce over
the beans, then sprinkle the corn kernels, onion, bell pepper, and cilantro over all. Cover the
plate with foil, and bake 15 minutes.

Remove the foil from the plate, and bake the
pie 15 minutes more. Spoon some of the remaining sauce over each serving.

Serves 6

QUICK AND EASY HOT ENCHILADA SAUCE

This hot, spicy sauce takes only minutes to prepare and cook. It can add zest to many Mexican
dishes.

3 cups water
1/2 cup tomato paste
→1/2 teaspoon cayenne (use less for a milder
   sauce)
1/4 teaspoon garlic powder
1 1/2 teaspoons onion powder
1 teaspoon dried oregano
1 teaspoon ground cumin
1/2 teaspoon ground coriander
→1 teaspoon chili powder
1/2 teaspoon Vegit
1 teaspoon reduced-salt soy sauce or Bragg
   Liquid Aminos

In a medium saucepan, mix all the ingredients
together. Bring the mixture to a boil, then lower
the heat, and simmer the sauce, covered, for 15
minutes.

Yields 3 cups

EASY SPANISH RICE

This dish takes only minutes to prepare and is a good use for leftover rice.

1 large onion, chopped
3 garlic cloves, minced
1/2 red or green bell pepper, chopped
2 tablespoons water
2 large ripe tomatoes, chopped (2 cups)
1 teaspoon reduced-salt soy sauce or Bragg Liquid Aminos
4 cups Basic Brown Rice (page 76)

In a large nonstick frying pan, sauté the onion, garlic, and bell pepper, uncovered, over medium heat without oil until the vegetables begin to stick. Stir in 2 tablespoons water, and continue cooking until onion is softened. Stir in the tomatoes and soy sauce or Bragg, and then the cooked rice. Reduce the heat to low, and cook, uncovered, stirring occasionally, until the rice is heated through. Serve the rice hot.

Serves 4

SPANISH RICE WITH FRESH CILANTRO

1 large onion, chopped
3 garlic cloves, minced
2 tablespoons water
2 cups chopped tomatoes
1 teaspoon reduced-salt soy sauce or Bragg Liquid Aminos
3 cups water
1 1/2 cups dry brown rice
1/3 cup chopped cilantro

In a large, covered nonstick frying pan, sauté the onion and garlic over medium heat, uncovered, without oil, until the onion begins to stick. Stir in 2 tablespoons water, and continue cooking until the onion is softened. Stir in the tomatoes, the soy sauce or Bragg, 3 cups water and the rice. Bring the mixture to a boil, then lower the heat, and simmer the rice, covered, for about 30 to 40 minutes, or until all the liquid is absorbed.

Stir in the chopped cilantro, and serve.

Serves 6

Spicy Spanish Rice

This spicy Spanish rice is flavored with chili powder, cumin, and fresh cilantro leaves. Adjust the spice quantities to suit your taste.

1 large onion, chopped
1/2 red or green bell pepper, chopped
3 garlic cloves, minced
2 tablespoons water
4 cups water
1 large tomato, chopped (1 cup)
1/2 cup tomato purée
2 cups dry brown rice
→ 1 teaspoon chili powder
1/2 teaspoon ground cumin
1 1/2 teaspoons reduced-salt soy sauce or
   Bragg Liquid Aminos
1/2 cup chopped cilantro

In a large nonstick, covered frying pan, sauté the onion, bell pepper, and garlic, uncovered, without oil, over medium heat until the vegetables begin to stick. Stir in 2 tablespoons water, and continue cooking until the vegetables are softened. Stir in the 4 cups water and the next six ingredients, bring the mixture to a boil, and lower the heat. Simmer the rice, covered, for 30 to 35 minutes, or until all the liquid is absorbed. Stir in the cilantro, and serve.

Serves 8

Basic Black Beans

This tasty bean dish is rich in protein, complex carbohydrates, and fiber. When eaten with rice and vegetables, it makes a complete meal.

1 pound dry black beans
8 cups water
5 cups water
2 medium onions, chopped
6 large garlic cloves, minced
2 tablespoons water
2 teaspoons cider vinegar
2 bay leaves
2 teaspoons reduced-salt soy sauce or Bragg
   Liquid Aminos
1/2 teaspoon dried oregano
→ 1 teaspoon chili powder
1/4 teaspoon ground cumin

Bring the beans and 8 cups water to a boil in a large, covered pot. Boil the beans for 10 minutes, then remove the pot from the heat. Let the beans soak in the water until they are cool, or overnight.

Drain the beans, rinse them well, and return them to the pot. Cook the beans, covered, in 5 cups water over low heat for 1 hour.

In a large, preheated nonstick frying pan, sauté the onions and garlic, uncovered, without oil, over medium heat until the onions begin to stick. Stir in 2 tablespoons water, and continue cooking until the onions soften. Add the sautéed onions and garlic to the beans along with the remaining ingredients. Cook the beans over low heat, covered, for about 1 hour, or until they are tender, stirring the beans occasionally as they cook. Serve them hot.

Serves 6

Basic Brown Rice

Preparing this brown rice is as easy as boiling water. Serve with Basic Black Beans (page 75).

2 cups brown rice
4 cups water
2 to 3 teaspoons reduced-salt soy sauce or
  Bragg Liquid Aminos

Bring the rice, water and soy sauce or Bragg to a boil in a 3-quart covered saucepan. Reduce the heat, and simmer the rice over low heat for about 30 minutes, or until the liquid is absorbed. To reheat leftovers, add 1/4 cup water, cover the pan, and simmer the rice over low heat until the rice is heated through. For two servings, use 1 cup uncooked brown rice to 2 cups water, and 3/4 teaspoon reduced-salt soy sauce. Serve the rice hot.

Serves 6 to 8

Holiday Brown-Rice Vegetable Casserole

This luscious, nutritious casserole can make any holiday more festive.

1 large onion, coarsely chopped
4 large garlic cloves, minced
6 celery stalks, coarsely chopped
4 large carrots, coarsely chopped
2 tablespoons water

1 cup water
2 small tomatoes, chopped
1 teaspoon dried oregano
1/2 teaspoon dried or ground sage
1/2 teaspoon dried or ground thyme
1/2 teaspoon ground white or black pepper
1/8 teaspoon cayenne
1 teaspoon celery seed
1 tablespoon reduced-salt soy sauce or Bragg
  Liquid Aminos
5 cups steamed brown rice
2 cups bread crumbs (toast bread and
  crumble)
1/4 cup raw sunflower seeds
1/2 cup chopped pecans
1/2 cup chopped almonds
1/2 cup chopped parsley
1 tablespoon cider vinegar
1 1/2 cups cooked, puréed banana squash
  (or 1 12-ounce package frozen cooked
  squash, thawed)
1/4 cup chopped almonds

Sauté the chopped onion, garlic, carrots and celery in a 4- to 5-quart saucepan, uncovered, over medium heat, without oil, until the vegetables begin to stick. Stir in 2 tablespoons water, and cook until the vegetables soften. Stir in 1 cup water and the next eight ingredients. Bring the mixture to a boil, then lower the heat, and simmer the mixture, covered, for 30 minutes.

Preheat the oven to 375°.

Remove the pan from the heat, and stir in the rice, bread crumbs, seeds, nuts, parsley, vinegar, and puréed squash. Put the mixture into a 2 1/2-quart ovenproof soufflé dish, and sprinkle chopped almonds on the top. Bake the casserole, uncovered, for about 30 minutes, or until it is a light golden brown on top. Serve it hot.

Serves 10 to 12

KASHA VARNISHKAS (HOLIDAY BUCKWHEAT GROATS WITH NOODLES)

This tasty, nourishing dish can be served as a side dish for a holiday meal, or as a main dish on any day. Buckwheat is the highest in protein of all the grains.

1 large onion, chopped
3 large garlic cloves, minced
1/2 large green bell pepper, chopped
2 tablespoons water
1/2 pound mushrooms, coarsely chopped
1 cup *kasha* (roasted buckwheat groats)
2 cups boiling water
1 tablespoon reduced-salt soy sauce or Bragg Liquid Aminos
8 ounces dry whole wheat noodles, cooked
1 tablespoon safflower or canola oil

In a 4- to 5-quart saucepan, sauté the onion, garlic, and bell pepper, uncovered, over medium heat, without oil, until the vegetables begin to stick. Stir in 2 tablespoons water and sauté until the vegetables soften. Stir in the mushrooms and *kasha*, and sauté over medium heat, uncovered, for 5 minutes. Stir in the boiling water and soy sauce or Bragg, cover the pan, and lower the heat. Cook the *kasha* for 12 minutes, or until all the liquid is absorbed.

Stir in the cooked noodles and oil, and continue cooking until the noodles are heated through. Serve hot.

Serves 6 to 8

TZIMMES (HOLIDAY CARROT SWEET POTATO PRUNE STEW)

This sweet stew from Eastern Europe is a special treat with any holiday meal. You can combine the ingredients a day in advance, and bake the *Tzimmes* just before serving.

2 pounds carrots, peeled and sliced (7 cups)
1 1/2 cups dried unsulphured pitted prunes
1/2 cup water
3 pounds sweet potatoes or yams, boiled or baked until soft, peeled, and cut into large bite-size pieces (3 cups)
Juice of 1 medium orange (1/4 cup)

In a 3-quart covered saucepan, bring the carrots, prunes, and water to a boil. Lower the heat, and simmer the mixture, covered, for about 30 minutes, or until the carrots are tender.

Preheat the oven to 350°.

In a large bowl, mix together the sweet potatoes and orange juice. Stir in the cooked carrots and prunes. Put the mixture into a 3-quart ovenproof casserole dish, bake it for about 30 minutes, or until the *Tzimmes* is hot, and serve.

Serves 8 to 10

ORANGE HALVES STUFFED WITH BANANA SQUASH PUDDING

These beautiful stuffed orange halves are a perfect addition to any holiday meal. You can prepare them a day in advance, and heat them before serving.

6 medium juice oranges
Double recipe Banana-Squash Pudding
Grated zest of 1/2 large orange
Sprinkle of cinnamon

Cut the oranges in half and juice them, leaving their skins intact, and saving the juice for another use.

Stir grated orange zest into the pudding. Fill each orange cup with about 1/2 cup pudding, or enough pudding to fill and extend 1/2 inch above the top of the orange cup. Place the stuffed orange halves in a 9- by 13-inch ovenproof glass baking dish. Sprinkle the cinnamon on top.

Half an hour before serving, take the dish out of the refrigerator. Preheat the oven to 400°. Bake the orange halves for 15 to 20 minutes, or until the filling is heated through. Serve the orange cups hot.

Serves 12

BANANA-SQUASH PUDDING

This sweetly spiced squash pudding is simple yet delicious.

3 pounds banana squash (or any sweet orange squash)
1 tablespoon cinnamon
1/2 teaspoon ground ginger
1/4 teaspoon ground cloves
1/2 teaspoon ground coriander
1 tablespoon maple syrup (optional)

Preheat the oven to 375°.

Place the halved squash, skin side down, in a 9- by 13-inch nonstick baking pan. Bake it for 30 minutes, then turn the squash over, and continue baking for another 30 to 45 minutes, or until the squash is just tender.

Remove the squash from the oven, and peel it. Purée the squash in a food processor or blender with the remaining ingredients until the mixture is smooth. Serve the squash pudding cold, or heat it at 400° for about 12 minutes before serving.

Yields about 3 cups

Holiday Baked Squash with Curried Brown Rice Stuffing

3 acorn squash
1 cup water
1 cup uncooked brown rice
2 cups water
2 tablespoons reduced-salt soy sauce or Bragg
    Liquid Aminos
1 medium onion, minced
2 tablespoons raw sunflower seeds
1/2 cup chopped pecans or walnuts
1/3 cup black raisins
1/4 teaspoon ground coriander
2 teaspoons curry powder
2 teaspoons cider vinegar
2 tablespoons frozen and thawed apple juice
    concentrate
1 teaspoon ground cinnamon

Preheat the oven to 375°.

Cut each squash in half, remove the seeds and lay the halves cut side down in a 9- by 13-inch baking pan. Pour 1 cup water into the bottom of the baking pan, and bake the squash in the oven for 30 to 40 minutes, or just until it is tender. Drain off the water. Leave the oven on.

While the squash bakes, cook the rice. In a 2-quart saucepan, mix together the rice, water, soy sauce or Bragg, and onion. Bring the mixture to a boil, lower the heat, and cook the rice, covered, for 30 minutes. Stir in the remaining ingredients, and cook over medium heat for 1 minute longer, uncovered, stirring constantly. Remove the pan from the heat.

Stuff the squash halves with the curried rice mixture. Return the pan to the oven, and bake the squash for 20 to 25 minutes.

Serve the squash hot. To reheat it, cover the pan with foil, and bake at 375° for about 20 minutes, or just until the squash is heated through.

Serves 6

Prakus (Holiday Sweet and Sour Cabbage Rolls)

This Polish dish of brown rice, lentils, and vegetables rolled in cabbage leaves makes a delicious holiday entrée, side dish, or buffet offering. The rolls can be made a day ahead and reheated before serving. The sauce must be prepared first to use in stuffing and for assembling this dish.

1 recipe Sweet and Sour Sauce or Easy Sweet and Sour Sauce (pages 81 or 85)
2 medium-large cabbages (about 2 pounds each), cored, but left whole
1 cup uncooked brown rice
1/3 cup dry brown lentils
2 1/3 cups water
1/2 medium onion, chopped
2 garlic cloves, minced
1/4 large green bell pepper, chopped
2 celery stalks, chopped
1 tablespoon low-salt soy sauce or Bragg Liquid Aminos
1 teaspoon cider vinegar
1/4 teaspoon ground black pepper
2 teaspoons Vegit
1/3 cup oat bran
1/2 cup chopped walnuts
1/3 cup Sweet and Sour Sauce or Easy Sweet and Sour Sauce

In 3 inches of boiling water, in a large, covered pot, steam a cabbage core side down, over medium heat for 10 minutes. Remove the cabbage from the water, and set it aside to cool. Repeat this process with the second cabbage.

In a 2-quart covered saucepan, bring the next eleven ingredients to a boil. Lower the heat, and simmer the mixture, covered, for about 30 minutes, or until the liquid is absorbed, but the mixture is still moist. Put the rice-and-lentil mixture into a medium bowl, and stir in the oat bran, the chopped walnuts, and 1/3 cup sweet and sour sauce.

Preheat the oven to 350°.

To assemble the cabbage rolls, pull apart the cabbage halves. Shred the small inner leaves and spread them in the bottom of two 9- by 13-inch ovenproof glass baking pans, or one large roasting pan. Pour 3/4 cup sweet and sour sauce over the shredded cabbage in each baking pan. Fill each of the larger cabbage leaves with about 1/4 cup stuffing, and roll up the leaf. If some leaves are too small to cover the filling, use two leaves for those rolls. Arrange the cabbage rolls on top of shredded cabbage, seam side down, with half the rolls in each pan. Pour the remaining sauce evenly over the cabbage rolls. Cover the dish with foil, pierce the foil in several places, and bake the rolls for about 3 hours. (If you're using two pans, place them on separate racks. Halfway through the baking time, move the baking pan on the upper rack to the lower rack, and vice versa.)

Serve the rolls hot. They taste even better when reheated. You can warm them in a 350° oven, covered, or, if you're reheating just a few, in a small, covered saucepan. Add a little water if the pan becomes too dry.

Yields 12 to 15 rolls

SWEET AND SOUR SAUCE

The lemon juice and apple juice give this tomato-based sauce a special, tangy taste. This sauce can be used in a variety of recipes.

1/2 large onion, chopped
2 garlic cloves, minced
2 tablespoons water
2 1/2 cups tomato purée
2 3/4 cups water
3/4 cup frozen or thawed apple juice
  concentrate
1/3 cup lemon juice
1 tablespoon reduced-salt soy sauce or Bragg
  Liquid Aminos
1/4 teaspoon ground black pepper
1/4 teaspoon ground ginger

In a 4- to 5-quart saucepan, sauté the onion and garlic, uncovered, over medium heat, without oil, until the onion begins to stick. Stir in 2 tablespoons water, and cook until the onion is softened. Stir in 2 3/4 cups water and the remaining ingredients, and bring the mixture to a boil. Lower the heat, and simmer the sauce, covered, for 20 minutes.

Yields 5 cups

Seitan

HIGH-ENERGY PROTEIN LOAF

The combination of soy flour and gluten flour in this loaf yields a very substantial amount of protein. Even though the loaf cooks for a long time, it doesn't take long to prepare. Protein-loaf slices can be used in many recipes and as a nutritious sandwich filling. The slices freeze well, and are easy to separate when wrapped separately.

Loaf

2 1/2 cups gluten flour (available in health-food stores)
2 cups soy flour (available in health-food stores)
1 1/2 tablespoons paprika
1 1/2 tablespoons onion powder
1 tablespoon garlic powder
1/2 teaspoon ground black pepper
1 1/2 teaspoons ground ginger
1 1/2 teaspoons curry powder
3 cups water
1/4 cup low-salt soy sauce or Bragg Liquid Aminos

Broth

2 quarts water
1 tablespoon reduced-salt soy sauce or Bragg Liquid Aminos
1 teaspoon cider vinegar
1 medium onion, quartered
6 whole garlic cloves
1/8 teaspoon ground black pepper
1 cup firmly packed fresh parsley leaves and stems
2 celery stalks, cut into thirds
1 1-inch slice gingerroot, minced

To make the loaf, in a large bowl mix together the dry ingredients. In a smaller bowl, stir together the water and soy sauce or Bragg, and mix the liquid into the dry ingredients with a fork until they are blended. Knead the dough in the bowl for a few minutes, and shape the dough into a loaf. Put the loaf in a 9- by 5-inch loaf pan, cover the pan, and refrigerate the loaf for at least 1 hour, or overnight.

Take the loaf out of the pan and put it in a 4- to 5-quart covered saucepan. Cook the loaf with all the broth ingredients, covered, over medium heat, for 20 minutes. Loosen the loaf from the bottom of the pan with a spatula, if it should stick. After 20 minutes, lower the heat, and simmer the loaf and vegetables, covered, for 2 hours. The loaf will float, swell, and almost fill the saucepan. Halfway through the cooking time, cut the loaf into quarters, and turn each quarter so those parts that were on top are submerged in the broth. Let the loaf pieces cool in the broth. Drain them, and discard broth. Cut each piece into 3/8- to 1/2-inch thick slices, or, if you prefer, leave them whole.

Thinner slices are best for sandwiches; thicker slices are better for breading and frying. Slices can be stored in the refrigerator for several days, or in the freezer, to be thawed as needed. When wrapping slices for the freezer, separate them with plastic wrap so you can remove one at a time.

You can serve protein-loaf slices cold as a sandwich filling, heated on a nonstick griddle or in a frying pan until brown on both sides, or broiled. Or warm them in a toaster oven, simmer them in broth or gravy, or sauté them with onions.

Yields about 36 slices

seitan

SPICY HIGH-ENERGY PROTEIN LOAF

This version of the High-Energy Protein Loaf is seasoned with more garlic, ginger, curry powder, and paprika.

Loaf
2 1/2 cups wheat gluten flour (available in health-food stores)
2 cups soy flour (available in health-food stores)
2 tablespoons paprika
1 tablespoon garlic powder
1/2 teaspoon ground black pepper
1 tablespoon curry powder
2 1/2 cups water
1/4 cup reduced-salt soy sauce or Bragg Liquid Aminos
1 large onion, minced (1 cup)
6 large garlic cloves, minced or crushed
1 2-inch slice fresh gingerroot, minced

Broth
2 quarts water
2 tablespoons reduced-salt soy sauce or Bragg Liquid Aminos
1 teaspoon cider vinegar
1 medium onion, quartered
6 whole garlic cloves
1/8 teaspoon ground black pepper
1 cup firmly packed fresh parsley and stems
2 celery stalks, cut into thirds
2 1-inch slices gingerroot, minced

To make the loaf, in a large bowl mix together the dry ingredients. In a small bowl, stir together the water, soy sauce or Bragg, onion, garlic, and ginger, stir this mixture into the dry ingredients with a fork until the dough is blended. Knead the dough in the bowl for a few minutes, and shape the dough into a loaf. Put it into a 9- by 5-inch loaf pan, cover the pan, and refrigerate the loaf for at least 1 hour, or overnight.

Remove the loaf from the pan and put it into a 4- to 5-quart covered saucepan, cook the loaf, covered, with all the broth ingredients, over medium heat, for 20 minutes.

Loosen the loaf from the bottom of the pan with a spatula, if it should stick. After 20 minutes, lower the heat, and simmer the loaf and vegetables, covered, for 2 hours. The loaf will float, swell, and almost fill the saucepan. Halfway through the cooking time, cut the loaf into quarters, and turn each quarter so those parts that were on top are submerged in the broth.

Let the loaf pieces cool in the broth. Drain them and discard broth. Cut each piece into 3/8- to 1/2-inch thick slices, or, if you prefer, leave them whole. For storing and serving suggestions, see the instructions for High-Energy Protein Loaf.

Yields about 36 slices

crunch *Jim*

Spicy High-Energy Slices *Seitan*

For a spicy high-protein sandwich serve these slices on whole-grain burger buns.

1/2 cup water
1 1/2 tablespoons tomato purée
1/4 teaspoon garlic powder
1 teaspoon onion powder
1/2 teaspoon chili powder
1/2 teaspoon cider vinegar
1/8 teaspoon cayenne
1 1/2 teaspoons frozen or thawed pineapple
    juice concentrate
4 to 6 slices High-Energy Protein Loaf or
    Spicy High-Energy Protein Loaf
    (pages 82 and 83)

In a small saucepan, combine the water and seasonings. Add the protein-loaf slices, and bring the sauce to a boil. Reduce the heat, and simmer the mixture, uncovered, for about 10 minutes, or until the sauce is reduced by half.

Serve the slices hot on whole-grain buns. Stack 2 or 3 on a bun, if desired. Spoon some of the sauce over the slices.

Serves 2

Broiled High-Energy Slices with Garlic and Ginger

Serve these slices with baked potatoes and a steamed vegetable.

4 garlic cloves, crushed
1 1-inch slice fresh gingerroot, grated
2 tablespoons reduced-salt soy sauce or Bragg
    Liquid Aminos
2 teaspoons cider vinegar
1 teaspoon safflower or canola oil (optional)
8 slices High-Energy Protein Loaf or
    Spicy High-Energy Protein Loaf
    (pages 82 and 83)

Preheat the broiler to 500°.

In a 9-inch glass pie plate, mix together the crushed garlic, gingerroot, soy sauce or Bragg, vinegar, and oil. Dip both sides of each slice in the mixture on both sides, and lay the slices in a foil-lined 10- by 15-inch baking pan. Pat any crushed garlic or grated ginger remaining in the pie plate onto the slices.

Broil the slices about 6 inches from the flame or electric coil, on one side only, for 8 minutes. Serve them at once.

Yields 8 slices; serves 4

SWEET AND SOUR HIGH-ENERGY SLICES

This is easy to prepare, if the loaf and sauce are made in advance. You can take the slices directly from the freezer; if you do, allow an extra 1/2-hour baking time.

1 1/2 cups Easy Sweet and Sour Sauce
1 1/2 tablespoons frozen and thawed pine apple juice concentrate
10 to 12 slices High-Energy Protein Loaf or Spicy High-Energy Protein, thawed (pages 82 and 83)
1/2 green bell pepper, sliced
1/2 medium onion, sliced

Preheat the oven to 350°.

Mix the sauce and pineapple juice together. Pour one-third of the mixture into a 1-quart ovenproof casserole dish. Layer half the protein-loaf slices and vegetables in the sauce. Pour one-third of the sauce over, add the remaining protein-loaf slices and vegetables, and top with the remaining sauce. Cover the dish with foil, and bake for about 45 minutes, or until the loaf slices and sauce are very hot.

Serves 2 to 3

EASY SWEET AND SOUR SAUCE

4 1/2 cups water
1 1/2 6-ounce cans tomato paste
1 tablespoon reduced-salt soy sauce or Bragg Liquid Aminos
1 tablespoon onion powder
1/4 teaspoon garlic powder
1/4 teaspoon ground black pepper
1 1/2 teaspoons cider vinegar
1/2 teaspoon ground ginger
1/3 cup lemon juice
2/3 cup frozen concentrated apple juice
3 tablespoons cornstarch
1/3 cup water

Bring the first 10 ingredients to a boil in a 4- to 5-quart covered saucepan. Reduce the heat, and simmer the sauce for 10 minutes.

Mix the cornstarch and water together, and stir this mixture into the sauce until the sauce thickens slightly.

Yields 5 cups

Broiled High-Energy Slices with Barbecued Flavor

3 tablespoons tomato paste
2 tablespoons frozen and thawed pineapple juice concentrate
2 teaspoons prepared mustard (preferably stone-ground)
2 tablespoons cider vinegar
2 teaspoons low-salt soy sauce or Bragg Liquid Aminos
1 1/2 teaspoons onion powder
1 teaspoon garlic powder
1 1/2 teaspoons chili powder
8 slices High-Energy Protein Loaf or Spicy High-Energy Protein Loaf (pages 82 and 83)

Preheat the broiler to 500°.

In a 9-inch glass pie plate, mix together all the ingredients except the protein-loaf slices. Dip both sides of each slice in the barbecue sauce, and lay the slices in a foil-lined 10- by 15-inch baking pan. Spoon any sauce left in the pie plate onto the slices.

Broil the slices about 6 inches from the flame or electric coil, on one side only, for 8 minutes. Serve them at once.

Yields 8 slices; serves 4

Saffron Rice Pilaf

This flavorful rice pilaf with vegetables is easy to prepare, and it goes well with a variety of dishes.

1 1/2 large onions, thinly sliced
3 large garlic cloves, minced
1 large green or red bell pepper, thinly sliced
1 large tomato, diced
2 cups uncooked long brown rice
3 cups boiling water
1 tablespoon reduced-salt soy sauce or Bragg Liquid Aminos
1/2 teaspoon ground saffron

In a preheated 4- to 5-quart saucepan, sauté the onion and garlic, covered, without oil, until the onions are soft. Stir in the bell pepper, tomato, and rice, and cook over medium heat for 5 minutes, stirring occasionally. Stir in the boiling water, soy sauce or Bragg and saffron. Bring the mixture to a boil, and simmer it over low heat, covered, for about 30 minutes, or until the liquid is absorbed.

Remove the pan from the heat. Remove the lid, place cheesecloth over the pot to absorb moisture, and replace the lid. Let the rice stand for about 15 minutes before serving.

Yields 8 cups

POLENTA TOPPED WITH VEGETABLES AND PINE NUTS

This colorful dish is a welcoming sight in cool weather.

1 cup cornmeal
3 cups cold water
1 tablespoon reduced-salt soy sauce or Bragg
    Liquid Aminos
1 tablespoon onion powder
1/2 teaspoon garlic powder
2 medium onions, thinly sliced
1/2 large green bell pepper, thinly sliced
2 celery stalks, thinly sliced crosswise
2 medium carrots, thinly sliced crosswise
3 large garlic cloves, minced
1 heaping tablespoon chopped fresh cilantro
    leaves
1 heaping tablespoon chopped fresh basil
    leaves
1 cup chopped fresh tomatoes
2 teaspoons reduced-salt soy sauce or Bragg
    Liquid Aminos
1/4 cup pine nuts

Preheat the oven to 350°. In a medium nonstick saucepan, mix together the first five ingredients. Bring this mixture to a boil, and cook it for 5 minutes over medium heat, stirring occasionally.

Spread the cornmeal mush in a lightly oiled 9-inch ovenproof glass deep-dish pie plate. Bake the polenta for 30 minutes.

While the polenta bakes, cook the vegetables.

In a large nonstick frying pan, sauté the onions, bell pepper, celery, carrots, garlic, and herbs, without oil, over medium heat. When the vegetables begin to stick, stir in the tomatoes and soy sauce or Bragg. Simmer the vegetables over low heat for 15 minutes.

When the polenta is ready, spread the sautéed vegetables evenly on top of the polenta, and top with the pine nuts. Serve at once.

Serves 3 to 4

Baked Tofu Slices with Garlic-Ginger Sauce

Marinade
4 large garlic cloves
1 1-inch slice gingerroot
1/3 cup cider vinegar
2/3 cup water
1 tablespoon dark molasses
2 teaspoons reduced-salt soy sauce or Bragg
   Liquid Aminos

2 14-ounce packages firm tofu, rinsed and
   well drained
1/2 medium onion, thinly sliced
2 tablespoons water
1 tablespoon cornstarch
2 tablespoons water

Blend the marinade ingredients in a food processor. Cut the tofu into 1/2-inch thick slices. Lay them in a 9- by 13-inch ovenproof glass baking dish, and pour the marinade over them. Marinate the tofu in the refrigerator for several hours, or overnight.

Preheat the oven to 400°.

In a small saucepan, cook the sliced onions in 2 tablespoons water until the onion is softened. Carefully drain the marinade from the tofu slices into the saucepan. Heat the marinade and onions over medium heat. Mix together the cornstarch and 2 tablespoons water, and add this mixture to the sauce. Continue to heat, stirring constantly, until the sauce thickens. Set the sauce aside.

Put the dish with the tofu slices into the oven, and bake for 15 minutes.

Pour the heated sauce over the tofu slices, and serve them immediately.

Serves 4 to 6

Steamed Buckwheat and Brown Rice

The combination has an appealing texture.

3/4 cup uncooked brown rice
3 cups water
3/4 cup *kasha* (roasted buckwheat groats),
   preferably medium granulation
2 teaspoons reduced-salt soy sauce or Bragg
   Liquid Aminos
2 teaspoons onion powder
1 teaspoon garlic powder

In a medium saucepan, bring the rice and water to a boil. Cook the rice, covered, for 15 minutes over medium heat. Stir in the remaining ingredients. Lower the heat, and simmer the mixture, covered, for 10 to 15 minutes, or until the liquid is absorbed.

Fluff the rice and buckwheat with a fork, and serve.

Serves 4 to 6

Easy Steamed Brown Rice with Celery, Onion, and Carrots

1 1/2 cups uncooked brown rice
3 cups water
1/2 medium onion, coarsely chopped
3 large celery stalks, diced
4 medium carrots, thinly sliced
2 to 3 teaspoons reduced-salt soy sauce or
  Bragg Liquid Aminos

In a 2-quart covered saucepan bring all the ingredients to a boil. Cook the rice and vegetables over medium heat, covered, for 20 to 25 minutes, or until holes begin to form in the top, indicating that all the liquid is absorbed.

Remove the pan from the heat, and let the rice steam in its own heat for 10 to 15 minutes before serving.

Serves 6

Easy Barley and Brown Rice

Barley and brown rice make a nourishing combination.

1/2 cup barley
1/2 cup dry brown rice
2 cups water
2 teaspoons reduced-salt soy sauce or Bragg
  Liquid Aminos
1 small onion, minced
2 garlic cloves, minced

In a medium covered saucepan, bring all the ingredients to a boil. Lower the heat, and simmer the mixture, covered, for about 30 minutes, or until all the liquid is absorbed.

Remove the pan from the heat, and let the barley and rice steam, covered, for another 10 to 15 minutes before serving.

Serves 2 to 4

Tofu with Vegetables and Cashews

1 14-ounce package firm tofu, rinsed, well
  drained, and crumbled
1 tablespoon reduced-salt soy sauce or Bragg
  Liquid Aminos
1 teaspoon dark molasses
1/2 teaspoon cider vinegar
1 1-inch slice gingerroot, grated
2 large garlic cloves, minced
3 cups thinly sliced celery
1/4 pound snow peas
1 large red bell pepper, sliced into thin strips
4 green onions, cut into 1/2-inch lengths
1/2 cup cashew pieces

Mix together the tofu, soy sauce or Bragg, molasses, vinegar, and grated ginger, and set the mixture aside. Over medium heat, sauté the remaining ingredients in a 4- to 5-quart preheated saucepan, uncovered, without oil, for 5 minutes, stirring occasionally. Stir in the tofu mixture, and continue sautéing for another 5 to 8 minutes, or until the tofu and vegetables are hot, but the vegetables are still crisp.

Serve the mixture at once over Easy Barley and Brown Rice.

Serves 2 to 3

Easy Sautéed Tofu and Vegetables

This dish is as good reheated as it is when it is fresh-made.

2 14-ounce packages firm tofu, rinsed and
  well drained
2 tablespoons reduced-salt soy sauce or Bragg
  Liquid Aminos
2 teaspoons dark molasses
1 tablespoon onion powder
1 teaspoon garlic powder
1/2 large onion, coarsely chopped
4 large garlic cloves, coarsely chopped
1 1-inch slice fresh gingerroot, coarsely
  chopped
1 bunch green onions, quartered
1/2 green bell pepper, sliced
1/2 red bell pepper, sliced
2 large broccoli stalks
2 1/2 cups sliced celery, thinly sliced
1 cup water
1 teaspoon cider vinegar
2 tablespoons cornstarch
2 teaspoons reduced-salt soy sauce or Bragg
  Liquid Aminos
2 teaspoons dark molasses

Cut apart the broccoli florets. Peel the stems, and slice them 1/4 inch thick.

Cut the tofu into 1-inch cubes. In a medium bowl, gently mix together the tofu cubes with the soy sauce or Bragg, molasses, onion powder, and garlic powder. Set the bowl aside.

Sauté the onions, garlic, and gingerroot, without oil, in a preheated 4- to 5-quart saucepan over medium heat. When the onion begins to stick, stir in the green onions, bell pepper, broccoli, and celery, and cook over medium heat for 5 minutes, stirring occasionally. Do not overcook the vegetables; they should be crisp. Stir in the tofu along with the last five ingredients. Heat the mixture, gently stirring until the sauce thickens. Serve the tofu and vegetables hot.

Serves 4 to 6

Asian-style Sweet and Sour Tofu with Pineapple and Bell Peppers

The tangy taste of the sauce complements the chewy texture of the tofu.

2 14-ounce packages firm tofu
1 tablespoon reduced-salt soy sauce or Bragg Liquid Aminos
2 teaspoons cider vinegar
1 tablespoon onion powder
1/2 teaspoon garlic powder
1/4 teaspoon ground coriander
1 cup fresh or canned pineapple chunks
1 large green bell pepper, cut into bite-size pieces
1/4 large onion, sliced

Sauce
3 tablespoons cider vinegar
2 tablespoons maple syrup
3 tablespoons water
1 teaspoon cornstarch

Freeze the tofu in unopened packages for at least one day before preparing this recipe. Allow the tofu to thaw overnight, then rinse and drain it, pressing out as much liquid as possible. Cut the tofu into 1- by 1-inch cubes, and place the cubes in a medium bowl. Gently mix in the next five ingredients, and marinate the tofu for at least 15 minutes.

Put the tofu cubes on a 10- by 15-inch non-stick baking pan. Broil the tofu cubes 6 inches from the flame or electric coil for about 10 minutes, or until the tofu begins to brown. Remove the tofu with a spatula.

While the tofu cooks, sauté the pineapple, green pepper, and onion over medium heat in a large nonstick frying pan until the pan becomes dry. Remove the pan from the heat, and add the tofu.

In a small saucepan, mix together the sauce ingredients. Cook them over medium heat, stirring frequently, until the sauce comes to a boil. Gently stir the sauce into the tofu and vegetables.

Before serving, warm the tofu and vegetables over medium heat just until they are well heated through. Serve them hot over steamed brown rice.

Serves 3 to 4

Broccoli-Bell Pepper Sauté

No oil is needed here in frying the vegetables.

3 large broccoli stalks
1/4 cup water plus 2 tablespoons water
2 tablespoons cider vinegar
1 teaspoon dark molasses
1 teaspoon reduced-salt soy sauce or Bragg
  Liquid Aminos
1 tablespoon cornstarch
1/2 medium onion, coarsely chopped
3 large garlic cloves, coarsely chopped
1 1-inch slice gingerroot, coarsely chopped
1 1/2 large red bell peppers, cut into 1/2-inch
  lengthwise slices
1 bunch green onions, cut into sixths

Cut apart the broccoli florets, peel the stems, and slice them 1/4 inch thick.

In a small bowl, mix together 1/4 cup water and the next four ingredients. Set the mixture aside.

Preheat a 4- to 5-quart saucepan or large frying pan, and sauté the onion, garlic and gingerroot, without oil, over medium heat until the pan becomes dry. Stir in 2 tablespoons water, and sauté until the onion is soft. Stir the broccoli, peppers, and green onions, and stir-fry over medium heat for 3 to 5 minutes, or until the vegetables are barely tender. Stir in the cornstarch mixture, and continue to stir over the heat until the sauce thickens. Serve the vegetables at once.

Serves 4

Easy Steamed Vegetables

These steamed vegetables, served over brown rice and perhaps topped with a little reduced-salt soy sauce or Bragg Liquid Aminos, make a very satisfying meal.

1/2 cup water
1 teaspoon Vegit
1 tablespoon reduced-salt soy sauce or Bragg
  Liquid Aminos
6 medium-large carrots (about 1 1/4 pounds),
  cut into 1/2-inch diagonal slices
3 zucchini, cut into 1/2-inch diagonal slices
1 medium cabbage (about 1 1/2 pounds), cut
  into 1/2-inch strips or wedges, with the core
  included

In a 4- to 5-quart covered saucepan, bring the water, Vegit, soy sauce or Bragg, and sliced carrots to a boil. Cook the carrots over medium heat, covered, for 5 minutes. Stir in the zucchini, and put the cabbage on top of these vegetables (it will fill the saucepan). Cook the vegetables over medium heat, covered, for 5 minutes, or just until the cabbage begins to wilt and shrink a little. Stir the vegetables, and serve them at once, or remove the pan from the heat and reheat the vegetables just before serving.

Serves 4

SAUTÉED TOFU AND BELL PEPPERS WITH GARLIC AND GINGER

1 14-ounce package firm tofu, rinsed and well drained
2 teaspoons onion powder
1/2 teaspoon garlic powder
1 teaspoon dark molasses
2 teaspoons reduced-salt soy sauce or Bragg Liquid Aminos
1/2 medium onion, coarsely chopped
3 large garlic cloves, coarsely chopped
1 1-inch slice gingerroot, peeled
1 large red bell pepper, sliced in thin strips
4 celery stalks, thinly sliced diagonally
1 cup water
1 tablespoon reduced-salt soy sauce or Bragg Liquid Aminos
1 1/2 tablespoons cornstarch
1 teaspoon dark molasses

Cut the tofu into 1-inch cubes. In a medium bowl, mix the tofu cubes with the onion powder, garlic powder, molasses, and soy sauce or Bragg. Set the bowl aside.

In a preheated 3-quart saucepan, over medium heat, sauté the onion, garlic, and gingerroot uncovered, without oil, until the onion begins to stick. Stir in the bell pepper and celery, and cook over medium heat for 5 minutes. Stir in the tofu mixture along with the remaining ingredients. Stir over the heat until the sauce thickens, then serve at once.

Serves 2 to 4

GARLIC-GINGER-TOFU DINNER SLICES

Serve these delicious tofu slices with steamed vegetables and Nutty Steamed Brown Rice or Steamed Brown Rice.

2 14-ounce packages regular tofu, rinsed well and drained
2 large garlic cloves, minced
1/4 cup chopped red bell pepper
1 1-inch slice gingerroot, grated
1/2 cup chopped onion
2 tablespoons water
3 tablespoons cider vinegar
1 tablespoon dark molasses
1 tablespoon reduced-salt soy sauce or Bragg Liquid Aminos

Preheat the oven to 450°.

Cut the tofu into 1/2-inch slices. Lay the slices in a 9- by 13-inch ovenproof glass baking dish.

In a nonstick frying pan, sauté the garlic, bell pepper, gingerroot, and onion, without oil, over medium heat until the vegetables begin to stick. Stir in 2 tablespoons water, and cook until the vegetables soften. Stir in the vinegar, molasses, and soy sauce or Bragg, and heat for 1 minute. Pour the sauce over the tofu slices in the baking dish, and bake uncovered for about 20 minutes. Serve the tofu hot.

Serves 4

DELUXE CHINESE-STYLE VEGETABLES WITH TOFU

2 14-ounce packages firm tofu, rinsed and
   well drained
2 tablespoons reduced-salt soy sauce or Bragg
   Liquid Aminos
2 teaspoons dark molasses
1 tablespoon onion powder
1 teaspoon garlic powder
1/2 large onion, coarsely chopped
4 large garlic cloves, coarsely chopped
1 1-inch slice gingerroot, coarsely chopped
1 bunch green onions, quartered
1 large bell pepper, sliced in thin strips
2 1/2 cups celery, thinly sliced diagonally
1 tablespoon reduced-salt soy sauce or Bragg
   Liquid Aminos
2 teaspoons dark molasses
6 large white mushrooms, cut into 4 slices
1/4 pound snow peas
3/4 pound bean sprouts
1 cup water
1 teaspoon cider vinegar
3 tablespoons cornstarch

Cut the tofu into 1-inch cubes. In a medium
bowl, gently mix the tofu cubes together with
two tablespoons soy sauce or Bragg, two tablespoons molasses, the onion powder, and the
garlic powder. Set the bowl aside.

   In a preheated 4- to 5-quart saucepan over
medium heat, sauté the onion, garlic, and gingerroot without oil. When the onion begins to
stick, stir in the green onions, bell pepper, and
celery, and cook over medium heat, stirring oc-

casionally, for 5 minutes. Vegetables should remain crisp. Stir in the tofu, 1 tablespoon soy
sauce or Bragg, 2 teaspoons molasses, and the
last six ingredients. Heat the mixture, gently stirring occasionally, until the sauce has thickened.
Serve immediately.

Serves 4 to 6

Sautéed Cabbage, Tofu, and Vegetables

Cabbage is featured in this Asian-style dish. Serve it over steamed brown rice.

2 14-ounce packages firm tofu, rinsed and well drained
2 tablespoons reduced-salt soy sauce or Bragg Liquid Aminos
2 teaspoons dark molasses
1 tablespoon onion powder
1 teaspoon garlic powder
1 teaspoon cider vinegar
1 medium onion, coarsely chopped
6 large garlic cloves, coarsely chopped
1 2-inch slice gingerroot, coarsely chopped
2 large green onions, sliced in 1-inch lengths
1 large green bell pepper, cut into bite-size pieces
4 celery stalks, sliced
1/2 large head green cabbage, cut into bite-size pieces
1 cup water
1 teaspoon cider vinegar
3 tablespoons cornstarch
2 teaspoons reduced-salt soy sauce or Bragg Liquid Aminos
2 teaspoons dark molasses

Cut the tofu into 1-inch cubes. In a medium bowl, gently mix the tofu cubes together with 2 tablespoons soy sauce or Bragg, two teaspoons molasses, the onion powder, the garlic powder, and cider vinegar. Set the bowl aside.

Sauté the onion, garlic, and gingerroot, without oil, in a preheated 4- to 5-quart saucepan over medium heat. When the onion begins to stick, stir in the green onions, bell pepper, and celery, and cook over medium heat for 5 minutes, stirring occasionally. The vegetables should remain crisp.

Stir in the cabbage, the water, the cider vinegar, the cornstarch, 2 teaspoons soy sauce or Bragg, and 2 teaspoons molasses. Lay the marinated tofu on top of the vegetables, cover the pan, and steam the mixture over medium heat for about 10 minutes, or until all ingredients are well heated through. Serve at once.

Serves 4 to 6

Steamed Vegetables with Easy Peanut Sauce

1 cup reserved broth from steamed vegetables (or add water to equal 1 cup)
1 tablespoon reduced-salt soy sauce or Bragg Liquid Aminos
2 tablespoons peanut butter
2 teaspoons rice vinegar or cider vinegar
1 large clove garlic, crushed
1 teaspoon cornstarch
Easy Steamed Vegetables (page 92)

In a small bowl, whisk together the first six ingredients until they are blended. Heat the sauce in a small nonstick saucepan over medium heat, stirring constantly until sauce thickens.

Stir the peanut sauce into the steamed vegetables. Heat the mixture briefly, and serve.

Serves 4

Flavorful Fried Rice

This delightful combination of brown rice, vegetables, and protein-loaf strips yields a nutritious and tasty entrée or side dish.

1 1/2 cups dry brown rice
3 cups water
2 teaspoons reduced-salt soy sauce or Bragg Liquid Aminos
4 slices High-Energy Protein Loaf (page 82)
3 tablespoons cider vinegar
2 tablespoons maple syrup
1 teaspoon reduced-salt soy sauce or Bragg Liquid Aminos
1 teaspoon paprika
1/2 teaspoon coriander
1 teaspoon garlic powder
4 celery stalks, coarsely chopped
4 small carrots, coarsely chopped
1/2 large green bell pepper, coarsely chopped
1 medium onion, coarsely chopped

In a medium covered saucepan, bring the rice, water, and soy sauce or Bragg to a boil. Cook the mixture over medium heat, covered, for 15 to 20 minutes, or until all the liquid is absorbed. Remove the pan from the heat, and let the rice steam, covered, until it is ready to use.

Cut the loaf slices into thin, narrow strips and place the strips in a glass pie plate. In a small bowl, mix together the next six ingredients, and pour the mixture over the strips. Marinate the strips in a pie plate while preparing the vegetables.

Preheat a large nonstick frying pan over medium heat. Sauté the vegetables and marinated protein-loaf strips, stirring occasionally, until the vegetables are hot.

Stir in the steamed rice, and cook until all ingredients are well heated through. Serve the rice hot.

Serves 6

Nutty Steamed Brown Rice

This method of cooking rice gives it a nutty texture.

2 cups uncooked brown rice
4 cups water
2 teaspoons reduced-salt soy sauce or Bragg Liquid Aminos

In a 2-quart covered saucepan, bring the rice, water, and soy sauce or Bragg to a boil over medium heat. Continue cooking the rice over medium heat, uncovered, for 15 minutes.

Remove the pan from the heat, cover it, and allow the rice to steam for another 15 minutes.

Serves 6

Steamed Brown Rice

1 1/2 cups uncooked brown rice, rinsed
3 cups water
1 teaspoon reduced-salt soy sauce or Bragg Liquid Aminos

Bring the rice, water, and soy sauce or Bragg to a boil in a medium covered saucepan. Cook the rice over medium heat, covered, until the liquid is absorbed, about 30 minutes. Gently fluff the rice with a fork, and serve.

Serves 3 to 4

Ginger-Red Bell Pepper-Tofu Sauté

1 14-ounce package regular or firm tofu
2 teaspoons reduced-salt soy sauce or Bragg Liquid Aminos
2 teaspoons onion powder
1/2 teaspoon garlic powder
1/2 medium onion, halved again and cut into 1/4-inch slices
1 large red bell pepper, sliced thin
1 1-inch slice gingerroot, grated
3 large garlic cloves, minced
1/2 medium tomato, chopped

Cut the tofu into 1- by 2-inch pieces. In a medium bowl, gently toss the tofu with the next three ingredients, and set the bowl aside.

In a medium covered saucepan over medium heat, sauté the onion, bell pepper, ginger, garlic, and tomato without oil, for 5 minutes. Gently stir in the tofu, cover the pan, and steam the mixture over low heat for 5 minutes.

Serve the tofu and vegetables hot over rice.

Serves 2

Easy Tofu and Veggies for Two

Once the tofu is drained, this dish takes only minutes to prepare.

1 14-ounce package regular or firm tofu,
    rinsed and well drained
2 teaspoons reduced-salt soy sauce or Bragg
    Liquid Aminos
1 teaspoon dark molasses
2 teaspoons onion powder
1/2 teaspoon garlic powder
1 cup water
2 tablespoons cornstarch
1 teaspoon dark molasses
1 tablespoon reduced-salt soy sauce or Bragg
    Liquid Aminos
1 teaspoon cider vinegar
1 large broccoli stalk
4 green onions, cut into 1-inch lengths
3 large garlic cloves, minced
4 celery stalks, thinly sliced diagonally
    (2 cups)

Cut the tofu into 1- by 2-inch pieces. In a medium bowl, gently toss the tofu with the next four ingredients.

In a small bowl, mix together the water, cornstarch, molasses, soy sauce or Bragg, and vinegar.

Cut the broccoli florets lengthwise into bite-size pieces. Peel the broccoli stems, and slice them 1/4 inch thick.

In a large preheated saucepan, stir the vegetables over medium heat, without oil, for 3 minutes. Gently stir in the tofu cubes along with the water-cornstarch mixture, and heat until the sauce thickens.

Serve the tofu and vegetables over Steamed Brown Rice.

Serves 2

Oven-Barbecued Tofu on Skewers

The tofu in this recipe must be frozen at least one day ahead of time, then thawed before broiling. You will need eight skewers.

2 14-ounce packages firm tofu
1/4 cup whole wheat or brown rice flour
1 tablespoon onion powder
1 teaspoon garlic powder
1 teaspoon chili powder
1 tablespoon paprika
1/8 teaspoon ground black pepper
1 teaspoon Vegit
1/2 large onion, cut into four wedges, and separated into layers
1 large red bell pepper, cut into 1- by 1-inch pieces
Spicy Barbecue Sauce (page 100)

Freeze the tofu in unopened packages for at least one day before preparing this recipe.

Allow the tofu to thaw overnight, then rinse and drain it. Cut the tofu into 1 1/2- by 1-inch pieces.

In a bowl, mix the flour with the next six ingredients. Roll the tofu pieces in this mixture until they are coated.

Line a 10- by 15- by 1/2-inch baking pan with foil. Set the oven or broiler rack 6 inches from the flame or electric coil. Preheat the oven or broiler.

Assemble the tofu and vegetables for broiling: Poke the skewer through one piece of tofu, lengthwise, and move this piece toward the other end of the skewer. Follow with one piece of onion and one piece of bell pepper. Repeat this pattern twice more, ending with a fourth piece of tofu. Then repeat the entire process with the remaining seven skewers.

Lay the skewered tofu and vegetables in the foil-lined baking pan. Baste the tofu and vegetables with half of the barbecue sauce. Broil the tofu on one side for 10 minutes.

Remove the baking pan from the oven or broiler. Turn the skewered tofu over, and baste this side with the remaining barbecue sauce. Return the baking pan to the oven or broiler, and broil for about 10 minutes longer. Do not allow the tofu to burn.

Serve the skewers over brown rice, or remove tofu and vegetables from skewers first, and serve them over the rice.

Serves 4 to 6

OVEN-BARBECUED TOFU "STEAKS"

These delicious, chewy "steaks" go well with steamed brown rice or a baked potato, and steamed vegetables. The tofu must be frozen at least one day ahead of time, then thawed before broiling.

2 14-ounce packages firm tofu
1/4 cup whole wheat or brown rice flour
1 tablespoon onion powder
1 teaspoon garlic powder
1 teaspoon chili powder
1 tablespoon paprika
1/8 teaspoon ground black pepper
1 teaspoon Vegit
Spicy Barbecue Sauce

Freeze the tofu in unopened packages for at least one day before preparing this recipe.

Allow the tofu to thaw overnight, then rinse and drain it. Cut each block of tofu through the middle lengthwise. You now have four "steaks."

In a shallow pie plate, mix the flour with the next six ingredients. Coat each tofu steak well on both sides and on the edges. Lay the steaks on a nonstick baking sheet.

Set oven or broiler rack 6 inches from the flame or electric coil. Preheat the oven or broiler. Broil the coated tofu on one side for 10 minutes.

Remove the baking sheet from the oven. Turn the tofu over, and spoon this side with barbecue sauce. Return the tofu to the oven, and broil it for about 10 minutes longer. Do not allow the tofu to burn. Serve the tofu hot.

Serves 2 to 4

SPICY BARBECUE SAUCE

Use this spicy sauce for basting broiled Oven-Barbecued Tofu on Skewers or as a dipping sauce.

1/2 cup water
1/4 cup tomato paste
2 teaspoons prepared mustard (preferably stone-ground)
3 tablespoons cider vinegar
3 tablespoons frozen and thawed pineapple juice concentrate
2 teaspoons reduced-salt soy sauce or Bragg Liquid Aminos
2 teaspoons onion powder
1 teaspoon garlic powder
2 teaspoons chili powder

In a medium bowl, mix all the ingredients together with a whisk until they are blended.

In a medium covered saucepan, bring the mixture to a boil over medium heat. Then lower the heat, and simmer the sauce for 5 minutes.

Yields 3/4 cup

Mushroom-Broccoli-Tofu Sauté

Delicately flavored with ginger and garlic, this oil-free Asian-style entrée is wholesome and delicious. Serve it with a double batch of Steamed Brown Rice (page 97).

2 14-ounce packages firm tofu, rinsed and well drained
4 teaspoons reduced-salt soy sauce or Bragg Liquid Aminos
2 teaspoons dark molasses
4 teaspoons onion powder
1 teaspoon garlic powder
1 cup water
2 tablespoons cornstarch
1 teaspoon dark molasses
1 tablespoon reduced-salt soy sauce or Bragg Liquid Aminos
1 teaspoon cider vinegar
2 broccoli stalks
6 large garlic cloves, minced
1 2-inch slice gingerroot, grated
6 green onions, quartered
1/2 green or red bell pepper, cut into bite-size pieces
3/4 pound white mushrooms, sliced

Cut the tofu into 1- by 2-inch cubes. In a medium bowl, gently toss the tofu with 1 tablespoon plus 1 teaspoon soy sauce or Bragg, 2 teaspoons molasses, and the onion and garlic powders.

In a small bowl, mix together the water, the cornstarch, 1 teaspoon molasses, 1 tablespoon soy sauce or Bragg, and the vinegar.

Cut the broccoli florets lengthwise into bite-size pieces. Peel the broccoli stems, and slice them 1/4 inch thick.

Preheat a 4- to 5-quart nonstick saucepan over medium heat. Sauté garlic, ginger, green onions, bell pepper, and broccoli, without oil, for 5 minutes. Stir in the tofu cubes, mushrooms, and water-cornstarch mixture. Heat, stirring occasionally, until the sauce thickens.

Serve the tofu and vegetables over rice.

Serves 4 to 6

Bell Peppers Stuffed with Tofu and Walnuts

This easy-to-prepare dish, topped with Easy Marinara Sauce, makes a fine meal on a cold day.

Stuffing
2 cups cooked brown rice
1 14-ounce package regular tofu, rinsed, well
    drained, and crumbled
1/4 teaspoon ground black or white pepper
2 teaspoons curry powder
1 teaspoon Vegit
1 cup minced walnuts
1/2 cup chopped parsley
1 tablespoon reduced-salt soy sauce or Bragg
    Liquid Aminos
4 green onions, chopped
2 large garlic cloves, minced

4 large green bell peppers, tops and seeds
    removed
1 cup water
1 small tomato, sliced
1 cup water

To make the stuffing, in a large bowl mix together the first ten ingredients.

In a large covered pot, cook the bell peppers in 2 inches of boiling water over medium heat for 10 minutes.

While the peppers cook, preheat the oven to 400°.

Drain the peppers. Fill them with the stuffing, and place a slice of tomato on top of each stuffed pepper. Stand the peppers in a 9-inch ovenproof glass deep-dish pie plate, and pour 1 cup of water into the plate. Cook the peppers in the oven for 35 to 40 minutes, or until the stuffing is well heated through and beginning to brown on top.

Serve the peppers hot, topped with Easy Marinara Sauce.

Serves 4 to 6

Easy Marinara Sauce

This versatile sauce can be used in many recipes.

1/2 large onion, chopped
2 large garlic cloves, minced
2 tablespoons water
1/2 teaspoon dried basil
1/2 teaspoon dried oregano
1 2/3 cups (1 16-ounce can) tomato purée
1/2 teaspoon frozen or thawed apple juice
    concentrate
1/2 teaspoon cider vinegar
1 cup water
1 tablespoon olive oil

Sauté the onion and garlic in a 4- to 5-quart covered saucepan, without oil, until the onion begins to stick. Stir in 2 tablespoons water, and cook until the onion softens. Stir in the remaining ingredients, bring the mixture to a boil, and lower the heat. Simmer the sauce, covered, for 20 minutes.

Yields 2 3/4 cups

Bell Peppers Stuffed with Lentils, Rice, Vegetables, and Pine Nuts

6 medium-large red or green bell peppers, halved lengthwise and seeded
1 cup uncooked brown rice
1/3 cup dry brown lentils
2 1/3 cups water
1/2 medium onion, chopped
3 garlic cloves, minced
1/4 large green bell pepper, chopped
2 celery stalks, chopped
2 medium carrots, thinly sliced rounds
1 medium tomato, chopped (3/4 cup)
1 tablespoon reduced-salt soy sauce or Bragg Liquid Aminos
1 teaspoon cider vinegar
1/8 teaspoon ground black pepper
2 teaspoons Vegit
3 tablespoons pine nuts or sunflower seeds

In a large covered pot over medium heat, cook the peppers in 2 inches of boiling water for 10 minutes. Drain the peppers, and let them cool.

In a 2-quart covered saucepan, bring all the remaining ingredients except the pine nuts or sunflower seeds to a boil. Lower the heat, and simmer the mixture for about 30 minutes, or until the liquid is absorbed but the rice is still moist.

Preheat the oven to 375°.

Stir the pine nuts or sunflower seeds into the stuffing mixture. Fill the pepper halves with the stuffing, and set them close together in a 9- by 13-inch ovenproof glass baking dish. Cover the dish loosely with foil, and bake the stuffed pep-

pers for 30 minutes. Remove the foil, and bake the peppers uncovered for another 10 to 15 minutes. Serve the peppers hot.

Serves 6 as an entrée, 12 as a side dish

Turkish Stuffed Eggplant and Bell Peppers

You can stuff the eggplant and peppers in advance and chill them until shortly before dinner time.

1 medium eggplant, stemmed and halved lengthwise
3 green or red bell peppers, tops and seeds removed
1/2 medium onion, thinly sliced
1 large clove garlic
2 medium tomatoes, cut into bite-size pieces
1/4 green or red bell pepper, cut into small bite-size pieces
4 teaspoons reduced-salt soy sauce or Bragg Liquid Aminos
1 teaspoon cider vinegar
1/2 cup uncooked long brown rice
3/4 cup boiling water
1/8 teaspoon ground saffron
3 tablespoons pine nuts

With a sharp knife, hollow out the eggplant halves by cutting 1/2 inch from the outer edges, taking care not to cut the peel. Scoop out the pulp with a spoon. Soak the eggplant pulp and shells in cold water for 10 minutes.

Drain the pulp and shells. Cut the pulp into small cubes. In a 4- to 5-quart covered saucepan, bring the eggplant shells and the 3 bell peppers to a boil in 1 cup water. Steam them, covered, over low heat for 8 minutes.

Drain the eggplant shells and peppers. Place them in a 9- by 13-inch ovenproof glass baking dish.

In a 4- to 5-quart covered saucepan, sauté the onion and garlic over medium heat until the pan becomes dry. Stir in the chopped eggplant along with the next eight ingredients. Bring the mixture to a boil, then lower the heat and cook for about 30 minutes, or until the liquid is absorbed.

Remove the pan from the heat, and let the rice and vegetables steam for 15 minutes.

Preheat the oven to 375°.

Stuff the eggplant shells and peppers with the rice-vegetable mixture, and cover the baking dish with foil. Bake the stuffed vegetables for 35 minutes, then remove the foil, and bake them for 10 minutes more, or until the stuffing is well heated through.

Serves 4 to 6

Easy Veggie Tofu Cutlets

Enjoy these high-protein cutlets with Easy Brown Rice Flour Gravy.

1 14-ounce firm tofu, rinsed and well drained
1 tablespoon reduced-salt soy sauce or Bragg Liquid Aminos
2 large garlic cloves, coarsely chopped
1/4 medium onion, coarsely chopped
1/2 large carrot, coarsely chopped
1 celery stalk, coarsely chopped
1/4 green or red bell pepper, coarsely chopped
1/2 cup chopped walnut
2 cups bread crumbs (toast bread and crumble)
3 tablespoons tahini

Preheat the oven to 400°.

Crumble the tofu in a medium bowl, and stir in the soy sauce or Bragg. Stir in the chopped vegetables, the walnuts, the bread crumbs, and the tahini. Shape the mixture into eight oval cutlets, 1/2 inch thick, and place the cutlets on a nonstick baking sheet. Bake them for 30 minutes, or until they are a light golden brown. Serve the cutlets immediately.

Serves 6 to 8

Easy Brown Rice Flour Gravy

This low-fat gravy takes only minutes.

2 cups cold water
3 tablespoons brown rice flour
1/8 teaspoon ground black pepper
1 tablespoon reduced-salt soy sauce or Bragg Liquid Aminos
1 teaspoon safflower or canola oil
1 teaspoon onion powder
Pinch dried oregano

Heat all the ingredients together in a small saucepan over medium heat, stirring occasionally, until the gravy thickens. Cook the gravy for a few minutes longer, then serve it at once.

Serves 4

Lentil-Nut Loaf

Enjoy this high-protein entrée with Mushroom-Onion-Garlic Gravy, baked potatoes, and vegetables.

1 1/2 cups dry brown lentils
3 cups water
1 tablespoon reduced-salt soy sauce or Bragg
    Liquid Aminos
2 cups cooked brown rice
1 cup finely chopped walnuts
1 tablespoon sesame seeds
1 tablespoon sunflower seeds
1 teaspoon curry powder
1 teaspoon chili powder
1 teaspoon Vegit
1 tablespoon onion powder
3 large garlic cloves, crushed or minced
1 tablespoon reduced-salt soy sauce or Bragg
    Liquid Aminos
1/4 teaspoon ground black pepper
1/2 teaspoon cider vinegar
1 cup oat bran

In a 3-quart covered saucepan, bring the lentils, the water, and 1 tablespoon soy sauce or Bragg to a boil. Reduce the heat and cook the lentils, covered, for 30 minutes, or until they are tender.

Preheat the oven to 375°.

Put the cooked lentils, and any liquid remaining in the saucepan, into a large bowl. Add 1 tablespoon soy sauce or Bragg and the remaining ingredients, and mix well. In a 9- by 13-inch nonstick baking pan, shape the lentil-nut mixture into an oval loaf about 3 inches thick. Bake the loaf 50 to 60 minutes, or until it is dark brown and crusty on the outside.

Cut the loaf into slices or wedges, and serve it with Mushroom-Onion-Garlic Gravy.

Serves 8 to 10

Mushroom-Onion-Garlic Gravy

This low-fat gravy can be served over mashed or baked potatoes, as well as Lentil-Nut Loaf.

1 medium onion, minced
4 large garlic cloves, minced
2 tablespoons water
1/2 pound white mushrooms, minced
1/8 teaspoon ground black pepper
Uncooked ingredients for Easy Brown Rice
    Flour Gravy (page 105)

Over medium heat, sauté the onion and garlic, uncovered, in a large, preheated nonstick frying pan until the onion sticks and begins to brown. Stir in 2 tablespoons water, and sauté until the onion softens. Stir in the mushrooms and black pepper. Cook the mixture over medium heat until the pan becomes dry.

Stir the ingredients for Easy Brown Rice Flour Gravy into the sautéed onion, garlic, and mushrooms. Cook the mixture over medium heat, stirring occasionally, until the gravy thickens. Cook the gravy for a few minutes longer, then serve it at once.

Serves 6

High-Protein Lentil Vegetable Loaf

Soy flour provides extra protein in this loaf of lentils, seeds, oat bran, and vegetables. Serve the loaf with Mushroom-Cashew Sauce or your favorite condiments.

1 cup dry brown lentils
3 1/2 cups water
1 tablespoon onion powder
1 teaspoon garlic powder
1/2 teaspoon celery seed
1/4 teaspoon ground black pepper
2 teaspoons Vegit
1 tablespoon reduced-salt soy sauce or Bragg
   Liquid Aminos
2 medium carrots, coarsely chopped
2 celery stalks, coarsely chopped
1/4 large red bell pepper, coarsely chopped
4 large garlic cloves, coarsely chopped
2 tablespoons sunflower seeds
1 tablespoon sesame seeds
1/3 cup soy flour
1 1/2 cups oat bran
2 teaspoons reduced-salt soy sauce or Bragg
   Liquid Aminos

In a 3-quart covered saucepan, bring the first seven ingredients and 1 tablespoon soy sauce or Bragg to a boil. Turn the heat to very low, and simmer the lentils for about 40 minutes, or until they are tender.

Preheat the oven to 375°.

Put the lentils, and any liquid still remaining in the saucepan, into a medium bowl. Stir in the vegetables, the seeds, the soy flour, the oat bran, and 2 teaspoons soy sauce or Bragg. Mound the lentil mixture in the center of a 9- by 9-inch non-stick baking pan, to form a round loaf about 7 inches in diameter. Bake the loaf for 1 hour, and serve it hot.

Serves 8

Mushroom Cashew Sauce

This delicately flavored sauce can be served over Lentil Vegetable Loaf, brown rice, or baked potatoes.

1 large onion, minced
1 large garlic clove, minced
1/2 pound mushrooms, coarsely chopped
1/2 cup raw cashew pieces
2 1/2 cups water
2 tablespoons cornstarch
3 tablespoons soy flour
Pinch cayenne
1/4 teaspoon dried basil
1/4 teaspoon dried oregano
1/4 teaspoon dried thyme
1 tablespoon reduced-salt soy sauce or Bragg
   Liquid Aminos

In a 3-quart saucepan, over medium heat, sauté the onion and garlic, uncovered, without oil, stirring occasionally, until the onion begins to stick. Stir in the chopped mushrooms, and sauté over medium heat, stirring occasionally, until the pan becomes dry again. Stir in the remaining ingredients, and bring the mixture to a boil, stirring frequently while the sauce thickens. If you like, purée the gravy in a blender before serving.

Yields 3 3/4 cups

Breaded Veggie "Wiener Schnitzel"

Low-fat, breaded and grilled protein-loaf slices are a vegetarian version of Wiener Schnitzel.

1/2 cup whole wheat flour or brown rice flour
3 tablespoons water
1 1/2 teaspoons cider vinegar
2 tablespoons prepared mustard
1 tablespoon reduced-salt soy sauce or Bragg
    Liquid Aminos
3/4 teaspoon garlic powder
1 tablespoon Vegit
1 1/2 teaspoons curry powder
1 1/2 cups soft bread crumbs, from wheat or
    non-wheat bread
12 1/2-inch slices High-Energy Protein Loaf or
    Spicy High-Energy Protein Loaf
    (pages 82 and 83)

Put the flour in a flat plate. In a pie plate, mix together the next seven ingredients with a fork. Put the bread crumbs in another flat plate.

To coat the protein-loaf slices, rub flour on both sides of the slices with your fingers, dip the slices in the mustard mixture in the pie plate, then coat the slices with bread crumbs. If you like, chill the breaded slices until just before serving time.

Fry the breaded slices in a preheated non-stick frying pan or on a preheated nonstick griddle until the slices are brown on both sides.

Serves 6 to 8

Tasty Lentil-Nut Burgers

Enjoy these wheat-free patties on whole grain burger buns or wheat-free bread with any of the trimmings. The fried or baked burgers freeze well, but wrap them separately.

1 1/2 cups dry brown lentils
3 cups water
1 tablespoon reduced-salt soy sauce or Bragg
    Liquid Aminos
2/3 cup minced walnuts
2 tablespoons sesame seeds
2 teaspoons curry powder
2 teaspoons chili powder
1 tablespoon onion powder
1 teaspoon garlic powder
1/4 teaspoon ground black pepper
1 tablespoon reduced-salt soy sauce or Bragg
    Liquid Aminos
1/2 cup water
1 cup oat bran

In a 3-quart covered saucepan bring the lentils, water, and soy sauce or Bragg to a boil. Reduce the heat to low, and simmer the lentils, covered, over medium heat for about 30 minutes, or until the liquid is absorbed.

Put the cooked lentils into a large bowl. Stir in the remaining ingredients, and mix well.

Shape the lentil mixture into twelve patties. Fry the patties in a nonstick frying pan, without oil, until they are brown on both sides, or bake them at 375° on a nonstick baking sheet for about 30 minutes, turning them over halfway through the baking.

Serves 8 to 12

Oven-Baked Garbanzo Bean Burgers

These delicious burgers have a taste similar to falafel balls. Serve them on whole-grain burger buns with mustard, chili sauce, lettuce, and sliced tomatoes. The fried or baked burgers freeze well, but wrap each one separately.

4 cups cooked, drained garbanzo beans
1/2 cup broth from garbanzo beans (or 1/2 cup water)
4 large garlic cloves
1/2 medium onion
2/3 cup minced parsley leaves
2 tablespoons lemon juice
1/2 cup sesame seeds
1 tablespoon reduced-salt soy sauce or Bragg Liquid Aminos
1/8 teaspoon cayenne
1/4 cup brown rice flour or oat bran

Preheat the oven to 375°.

In a food processor (in batches, if necessary) coarsely chop the beans with the broth, garlic, and onion. Put the chopped beans into a large bowl. Stir in the remaining ingredients. Shape the mixture into ten patties. Bake them on a nonstick baking sheet for about 25 minutes, or until they are firm to the touch and light brown. Serve the patties hot.

Serves 8 to 10

Bean-Barley-Oat Bran Burgers

These burgers are simple to prepare using left-over Hearty Crockpot Bean-Barley Stew. The baked burgers freeze well, but wrap them separately.

3 cups Hearty Crockpot Bean-Barley Stew (page 60)
2 teaspoons reduced-salt soy sauce or Bragg Liquid Aminos
2 teaspoons Vegit
1 cup oat bran
2 tablespoons sunflower seeds

In a medium bowl, stir all the ingredients together until they are well blended. Shape the mixture into eight balls, and press the balls into patties on a nonstick baking sheet. Bake the patties for 20 to 25 minutes, or until they are firm. Serve the burgers hot.

Serves 6 to 8

Garbanzo Bean Veggie Burgers

These vegetable-laden, high-protein burgers taste delicious on whole-grain buns. The baked burgers freeze well, but wrap them separately.

1 1/4 cups dry garbanzo beans
4 cups water
4 cups water
1 large onion, minced
3 large garlic cloves, minced
2 tablespoons water
1 medium carrot, minced
1 celery stalk, minced
1/2 green bell pepper, minced
1/4 teaspoon dried basil
1/4 teaspoon dried oregano
2 1/2 tablespoons reduced-salt soy sauce or
    Bragg Liquid Aminos
2 tablespoons tahini
1 cup cooked rice

In a 4- to 5-quart covered saucepan, bring the beans to a boil in 4 cups water. Cook the beans, covered, over medium heat for 10 minutes. Remove the pan from the heat, and let the beans soak in the water until the water is cool, or overnight.

Drain and rinse the soaked beans. Simmer them, covered, in 4 cups water for about 2 hours, or until they are tender.

Preheat the oven to 400°.

Drain the beans. In a food processor, finely chop them. Put the beans into a large bowl.

In a preheated large nonstick frying pan, sauté the onion and garlic, uncovered, without oil. When the onion sticks, stir in 2 tablespoons water, and cook until the onion is softened. Stir in the carrot, celery, and bell pepper, and sauté over medium heat until the vegetables are tender.

Add the sautéed vegetables to the garbanzo beans in the bowl, along with the remaining ingredients. Mix well with a fork. Shape the mixture into eight to ten burgers. Lay the burgers on two nonstick baking sheets. Bake for 20 minutes on separate racks, or one sheet at a time. Turn the burgers over, and bake them for another 20 minutes. Serve the burgers hot.

Serves 10

GARBANZO BEAN-
GARLIC BURGERS

These garlicky burgers made from sprouted beans freeze well. They can be reheated in an oven or toaster oven directly from the freezer. Wrap the patties separately before freezing so they won't stick together.

4 cups Crunchy Sprouted Garbanzo Beans
1 cup water
1/4 cup lemon juice
1 tablespoon reduced-salt soy sauce or Bragg
   Liquid Aminos
6 large garlic cloves, minced
1 bunch parsley, coarsely chopped
1 medium onion, coarsely chopped
1 small green bell pepper, coarsely chopped
2 cups oat bran
1 cup whole wheat flour, oat flour, or corn
   flour

Preheat oven to 400°.

   In a food processor or blender, coarsely chop the garbanzo beans with the water. Put the chopped beans into a large bowl. Stir in first the lemon juice and soy sauce or Bragg, then the chopped vegetables, and finally the oat bran and flour. Shape the mixture into eighteen patties, and bake the patties on nonstick baking sheets, in batches, for 12 to 15 minutes. Serve the burgers hot.

Serves 12 to 16

CRUNCHY SPROUTED
GARBANZO BEANS

These crunchy beans can be used in salads, or as nutritious snacks.

1 pound dry garbanzo beans
6 cups distilled or purified water

In a medium bowl, soak the beans in the water for 24 hours at room temperature until they sprout.

   Rinse them well, and store in the refrigerator until you are ready to use them.

Yields 5 1/2 cups

Easy High-Protein Lentil-Soy Burgers

These wheat-free burgers can be fried or baked and frozen for use at any time. You can quickly reheat the frozen burgers in the oven, in a toaster oven, or in a frying pan.

1 cup dry brown lentils
3 1/2 cups water
1 tablespoon onion powder
2 teaspoons garlic powder
1/2 teaspoon celery seed
1/4 teaspoon ground black pepper
1 tablespoon Vegit
1 tablespoon curry powder
1 tablespoon reduced-salt soy sauce or Bragg
   Liquid Aminos
2 tablespoons sunflower seeds
1/3 cup soy flour
1 cup oat bran

Bring the first nine ingredients to a boil in a 3-quart covered saucepan. Lower the heat, and simmer the lentils, covered, for about 40 minutes, or until they are tender.

Put the cooked lentils into a large bowl, and stir in the remaining ingredients. Preheat a large nonstick griddle or frying pan.

Drop the lentil mixture by small serving spoons (about 1/3 cup at a time) onto the griddle or pan, and flatten and shape the patties with the spoon. Fry the patties until they are brown on both sides. (The patties can also be baked, on two nonstick baking sheets at 400° for 20 to 25 minutes, or until they are firm and medium brown on top and bottom.) Serve the patties hot.

Serves 6 to 8

Split Pea Veggie Nut Burgers

These wholesome patties are a balanced meal in themselves.

1 cup dry split peas
1 cup uncooked brown rice
2 bay leaves
4 cups water
1/2 medium onion, coarsely chopped
1/2 green bell pepper, coarsely chopped
2 garlic cloves, coarsely chopped
1 carrot, coarsely chopped
1 cup pecans or walnuts, coarsely chopped
1/3 cup sunflower seeds
1 cup oat bran
1/4 teaspoon ground white or black pepper
1 tablespoon reduced-salt soy sauce or Bragg
   Liquid Aminos
1 teaspoon Vegit

Preheat the oven to 425°.

In a 3-quart covered saucepan, bring the split peas, rice, bay leaves, and water to a boil. Lower the heat, and simmer the mixture, covered, for 35 to 45 minutes, or until the split peas are tender, but not soft.

Coarsely chop the split peas and rice in a food processor or blender, in batches, and put the mixture into a large bowl. Stir in the remaining ingredients. Shape the mixture into twelve patties, lay the patties on two nonstick baking sheets, and bake them for 15 minutes, or until patties are light brown and firm to the touch. Serve the burgers hot.

Serves 8 to 10

Easy Lentil-Rice Veggie Burgers

These mildly spiced veggie burgers contain protein from the lentils and fiber from the rice and oat bran. Serve them on whole-grain buns.

1 cup dry lentils
1 1/2 cups uncooked brown rice
5 cups water
1 large onion, quartered
6 large, whole garlic cloves
2 bay leaves
1 tablespoon reduced-salt soy sauce or Bragg Liquid Aminos
1/2 cup parsley, coarsely chopped
3 large celery stalks, coarsely chopped
3 medium carrots, coarsely chopped
1 teaspoon dried oregano
2 teaspoons curry powder
2 teaspoons ground cumin
1/4 teaspoon ground white or black pepper
1 tablespoon reduced-salt soy sauce or Bragg Liquid Aminos
1/4 cup sunflower seeds
2 cups oat bran

In a 4- to 5-quart covered saucepan, bring the first seven ingredients to a boil. Lower the heat, and simmer the mixture, covered, for 30 to 40 minutes, or until the liquid is absorbed.

Remove the bay leaves from the pan. Purée half the lentil-rice mixture, including the onion and garlic, in a food processor, and return the purée to the saucepan. Stir in the vegetables, seasonings, and sunflower seeds, then stir in the oat bran. Shape the mixture into eighteen patties, 1/2 inch thick and 4 inches in diameter.

Preheat the oven to 400°.

Bake the patties for about 25 minutes, or until the patties are firm to the touch and brown around the edges. Serve the burgers hot.

Serves 12 to 16

Oven-Browned Red Potatoes and Onions

These great-tasting potatoes can be served for breakfast, brunch, lunch, or dinner.

6 medium red potatoes (2 pounds), scrubbed and unpeeled
1 large red onion, halved and sliced
2 tablespoons water
1/4 teaspoon ground black pepper
1 tablespoon reduced-salt soy sauce or Bragg Liquid Aminos

In a 4- to 5-quart covered saucepan, bring the potatoes to a boil in enough water to cover them well. Simmer them, covered, for 25 minutes (they need not be tender). Rinse the potatoes in cold water, and cut them into eighths, leaving the skins on. Put them into a large mixing bowl.

Preheat the oven to 425°.

In a preheated nonstick frying pan over medium heat, sauté the sliced onion until it begins to stick. Add 2 tablespoons water, and continue sautéing until the onion softens. Stir the sautéed onion into the potatoes, along with the pepper and soy sauce or Bragg. Spread the potatoes and onion on a 10- by 15-inch nonstick baking pan. Bake them for about 35 minutes, or until the potatoes are a dark golden brown. Serve the potatoes and onion at once.

Serves 6

OVEN-BAKED POTATO CHIPS

These are easy to make and a real treat. Serve them with any of the burgers.

4 medium potatoes, scrubbed and unpeeled
1 tablespoon onion powder
1/2 teaspoon garlic powder

Preheat the oven to 500°.

Slice the potatoes 1/4 inch thick. In a medium bowl, toss the sliced potatoes with the onion and garlic powder. Spread the potatoes in a 10- by 15-inch baking pan, and bake for 20 minutes. It is not necessary to turn them over.

If you'd like the chips to be crisper, set them under the broiler for a few minutes. Serve the chips at once.

Serves 3 to 4

FAT-FREE HASHBROWNS WITH ONIONS

These potatoes taste delicious, although they're cooked without any oil. Serve them with catsup, if you like. They are a treat at breakfast.

3 large potatoes, peeled, halved and thinly sliced
1/2 large onion, thinly sliced
1/4 teaspoon ground black pepper
1 tablespoon reduced-salt soy sauce or Bragg Liquid Aminos

In a large bowl, mix together the potatoes, onion, pepper, and soy sauce or Bragg. Heat a large covered nonstick frying pan. Sauté the potatoes and onion over medium heat, covered, stirring frequently. Whenever the potatoes and onions begin to stick, stir in 2 to 4 tablespoons water. You may need to do this several times. Continue cooking until the potatoes and onion are tender and a light golden brown. Serve the potatoes and onion hot.

Serves 3 to 4

EASY POTATO PANCAKES

These low-fat pancakes take only minutes to prepare if you mince the potatoes and onion in a food processor. Served with applesauce, potato pancakes make a great side dish with many entrées.

4 medium-large boiling potatoes, scrubbed and grated or minced (5 cups)
1 large onion, minced
2 tablespoons cornstarch
1 tablespoon reduced-salt soy sauce or Bragg Liquid Aminos
1/8 teaspoon ground black pepper
2 teaspoons safflower or canola oil

In a large bowl, mix together the potatoes and onion. Stir in the cornstarch, soy sauce or Bragg, pepper, and oil. Heat a nonstick griddle or large nonstick frying pan. Drop the potato mixture by tablespoonfuls onto the griddle or pan, and shape the mixture with a fork into round pancakes. Fry the pancakes, turning once, until they are brown on both sides. Serve them hot.

Yields 24 pancakes

Healthful Whole-Grain
Breads and Muffins

Imagine the aroma of healthful, delicious breads and muffins baking in your oven, and you and your loved ones sitting down and enjoying all the whole-grain goodness. You might choose among sandwich or dinner breads made of whole-grain wheat, corn, rye, or oats; breads flavored with seeds, nuts, or onions; and breakfast or tea breads sweetened with yams, pumpkin, raisins, bananas, or banana squash. You might try a special bread like Crunchy Toasted Cornbread, Paratha (Whole Wheat Indian Bread), or Wheat-Free Corn Rye Bread.

You might also choose among marvelous muffins, biscuits and scones, flavored with bananas, blueberries, pears, apples, lemons, oranges, currants, yams, banana squash, carrots, poppy seeds, spices, and oat bran.

Recipes for all these varieties of breads and muffins are here in this chapter. Our recipes call for only natural ingredients. All the breads and muffins are low in fat and salt, and free of cholesterol and sugar, and many are wheat-free. The recipes contain no animal products, including honey. You can enjoy eating these marvelous baked goods knowing they are good for you and for your loved ones.

For best results in your baking, carefully read the advice in the introduction of this cookbook.

WHOLE WHEAT SEED BREAD

This bread is easy to prepare. The dough needs to rise only once.

1 3/4 cups lukewarm water
1 envelope active dry yeast
1 tablespoon dark molasses
1 tablespoon reduced-salt soy sauce or Bragg Liquid Aminos
2 tablespoons safflower or canola oil *Soy Spread*
2 cups whole wheat flour
1 tablespoon sesame seeds
1 tablespoon sunflower seeds
1 tablespoon onion powder
2 tablespoons soy flour
2 to 2 1/2 cups whole wheat flour

In a large bowl, stir the yeast into the warm water. Stir in the molasses, soy sauce or Bragg, and oil, then stir in the next five ingredients, and mix well. Gradually stir in enough whole wheat flour to form a kneadable dough. Knead the dough on a floured board for 10 minutes, then shape the dough into a loaf. Put the loaf in a lightly oiled 9- by 5-inch nonstick loaf pan. Let dough rise in a warm place until it has doubled in bulk. Place the loaf in a cold oven, set the oven temperature to 350°, and bake the bread for about 35 minutes, or until the crust is light brown. Remove the bread from the pan, and let it cool before slicing with a sharp serrated knife.

Yields 1 loaf

WHEAT-FREE SCOTCH OAT-RYE BREAD

This sweet yeast bread is wheat-free. It slices well and makes delicious sandwiches and toast.

1 cup rolled oats
3/4 cup boiling water
1/4 cup dark molasses
1 tablespoon safflower or canola oil *Soy Spread*
1 teaspoon reduced-salt soy sauce or Bragg
    Liquid Aminos
1/2 cup lukewarm water
1 envelope active dry yeast
1 cup rye flour
1 cup oat flour

In a large bowl, combine the oats and boiling water. Stir in the molasses, oil, and soy sauce or Bragg.

In a small bowl, dissolve the yeast in the warm water, and add this mixture to the oats. In another bowl, mix together the rye and oat flours, and add them to the oats and yeast mixture while stirring with a fork. Cover the bowl, and let the batter rise in a warm place until it has doubled in bulk.

Spread the batter evenly in a lightly oiled 9-by 5-inch loaf pan. Let the batter again rise in a warm place until it has doubled in bulk. Preheat the oven to 375°.

Bake the bread for about 45 minutes, or until it tests done when you insert a cake tester.

Yields 1 loaf

EASY WHEAT-FREE OAT LOAF *Quick*

This onion-flavored, unsweetened dough takes only minutes to prepare. When the bread is cool, you can slice it and store it in the refrigerator or freezer.

1 2/3 cups water
2 teaspoons cider vinegar
2 teaspoons reduced-salt soy sauce or Bragg
    Liquid Aminos
1 tablespoon safflower or canola oil *Soy spread*
2 1/2 cups oat flour
1/2 cup rolled oats
1 cup oat bran
1 1/2 tablespoons onion powder
1 teaspoon baking soda
1 tablespoon cream of tartar
2 tablespoons minced onions (dehydrated,
    found in spice sections of supermarkets) or
    sesame seeds

Preheat the oven to 375°.

In a large bowl, stir together the water, vinegar, soy sauce or Bragg, and oil until they are well blended. In a medium bowl, mix together the next six ingredients and 2 tablespoons instant minced onions or sesame seeds, and add this mixture to the wet ingredients while stirring with a fork. In a lightly oiled 9- by 5-inch loaf pan, shape the dough into a loaf about 7 inches long. Smooth the top with moistened hands, and sprinkle 1/2 tablespoon minced onions or sesame seeds on top. Bake the loaf for about 40 minutes, or just until the bread tests done when you insert a cake tester. Let cool before removing from the pan.

Yields 1 loaf

WHEAT-FREE CORN-RYE-OAT BRAN BREAD WITH CARAWAY SEEDS

This hearty, wheat-free multigrain bread makes delicious toast.

1 envelope active dry yeast
1 3/4 cups lukewarm water
1 tablespoon dark molasses
1 tablespoon reduced-salt soy sauce or Bragg Liquid Aminos
2 tablespoons safflower or canola oil *Soy Spread*
2 cups rye flour
2 tablespoons caraway seeds
1 tablespoon sesame seeds
1 tablespoon onion powder
2 tablespoons soy flour
1 1/2 cups *masa harina* or corn flour
2 cups finely ground oats (about 2 1/2 to 3 cups rolled oats, finely ground in a food processor)

In a large bowl, stir the yeast into warm water until the yeast has dissolved. Stir in the molasses, soy sauce or Bragg, and oil, then stir in the next five ingredients. Stir until the mixture is smooth.

In a medium bowl, mix together the *masa harina* or the corn flour, and ground oats. With a fork, gradually stir this mixture into the large bowl, forming a kneadable, firm dough. Knead the dough on a floured board for 10 minutes, then shape the dough into a round loaf. Place the loaf in a 9-inch round baking pan. Let the dough rise in a warm place for about 1 hour (the dough will not rise very much).

Place the risen loaf in a cold oven, set the oven temperature to 350°, and bake the bread for about 50 minutes, or until the crust is light brown. Remove the bread from the pan, and let it cool before slicing with a sharp serrated knife.

Yields 1 loaf

Braided Whole Wheat Sabbath Loaves

This recipe makes two lovely large loaves to grace your sabbath meal. The potato gives the dough its moisture and fine texture.

1 medium-large potato, scrubbed, cut into
  eighths, cooked until tender, and drained (1
  cup)
1/2 cup water
3 packages active dry yeast
1/2 cup lukewarm water
1 1/2 teaspoons maple syrup
1 cup water
1/4 cup maple syrup
1/4 cup ~~safflower or canola oil~~ *Soy Spread*
2 tablespoons reduced-salt soy sauce or Bragg
  Liquid Aminos
4 cups whole wheat flour
3 cups whole wheat pastry flour
1 teaspoon safflower or canola oil, mixed
  with 1 tablespoon water
2 tablespoons sesame seeds

Purée the cooked potato with 1/2 cup water in a food processor or blender. In a large bowl, dissolve the yeast in 1/2 cup warm water. Stir in 1 1/2 teaspoons maple syrup, then the puréed potatoes, then 1 cup water, 1/4 cup maple syrup, 1/4 cup oil, and the soy sauce or Bragg. While stirring with a fork, add the whole wheat flour, then the whole wheat pastry flour. Knead the dough on a floured board for 15 minutes. Let the dough rise in a warm place until it has doubled in bulk.

Divide the dough in half. Set one half aside. Cut the other half into four parts. Shape three of the parts into three long ropes about 12 inches long. Braid these ropes, pinching both ends of the braid. Lay the braid in one side of a 10- by 15-inch nonstick baking pan. Cut the fourth part into three sections, shape each section into a rope about 8 inches long, and braid these ropes. Moisten the bottom of this braid and the top of the longer one with a little water. Lay the smaller braid on top of the larger. Repeat this process with the other half of the dough, and place the second loaf in the pan alongside the first loaf. Brush the tops and sides of the loaves with the oil and water mixture, then sprinkle half the sesame seeds on each loaf. Let the loaves rise in a warm place until they have doubled in bulk, then place them in cold oven, set the oven temperature to 350°, and bake the loaves for 40 minutes, or until they are a light golden brown.

Yields 2 loaves

Braided Whole Wheat Cashew-Onion Loaf

1 cup lukewarm water
1 1/2 envelopes active dry yeast
1 tablespoon maple syrup
1/4 cup broken cashews
1/2 cup water
1 3/4 cups whole wheat flour
1 1/2 tablespoons onion powder
1/8 teaspoon ground black pepper
1 1/2 teaspoons reduced-salt soy sauce or
    Bragg Liquid Aminos
1 cup whole wheat pastry flour
1 teaspoon onion powder, mixed with 1
    tablespoon water
1 tablespoon sesame or poppy seeds
    (optional)

In a large bowl of an electric mixer, mix together the warm water, yeast, and maple syrup. In a food processor or blender, grind the broken cashews with 1/2 cup water until the mixture is well blended. Stir the cashew mixture along with the next four ingredients into the mixer bowl. Beat on low speed for 8 minutes. By hand, fold 3/4 cup whole wheat pastry flour into the dough. Cover the dough, and let it rise in a warm place until it has doubled in bulk.

Punch the dough down. On a floured board, knead the dough 10 minutes, using the additional 1/4 cup flour as needed. Then cut the dough into thirds, and shape the pieces into three thick ropes each 12 inches long. Braid the three ropes into a loaf, pinching the ends. Set the loaf in a lightly oiled 9- by 5-inch loaf pan. Brush the top of the loaf with the onion pow-der-water mixture, and sprinkle seeds, if you like, on top. Let the dough again rise in a warm place until it has doubled in bulk.

Preheat the oven to 350°. Bake the dough for about 30 minutes, or until it is a light golden brown.

Yields 1 loaf

Sour Onion Corn-Rye Bread

This hearty bread slices well.

3/4 cup cornmeal
2 tablespoons onion powder
3/4 cup boiling water
1 envelope active dry yeast
3/4 cup lukewarm water
1 cup water
2 tablespoons cider vinegar
2 tablespoons safflower or canola oil
2 tablespoons maple syrup
2 teaspoons reduced-salt soy sauce or Bragg
  Liquid Aminos
2 cups rye flour
3 1/2 cups whole wheat flour
Sprinkle of onion powder or minced onions
  (dehydrated, found in spice section)

In a large bowl, mix the cornmeal and onion powder with the boiling water. In a small bowl, dissolve the yeast in the warm water. Stir the yeast mixture and the next five ingredients into the cornmeal. With a fork, stir in the rye flour and then add the whole wheat flour, kneading to form a soft dough. Knead the dough in the bowl for about 10 minutes, then cover the bowl. Let the dough rise in a warm place until it has doubled in bulk.

Punch the dough down, knead it again briefly, then lay it in a lightly oiled 9- by 5-inch loaf pan. Sprinkle the top with onion powder or minced onions, and let the dough rise for a third time until it has doubled in bulk.

Preheat oven to 400°.

Bake the loaf for 10 minutes, then reduce the oven temperature to 350°, and bake the loaf for about 50 minutes longer, or until it is dark brown on top.

Remove the loaf from the pan, and allow it to cool before slicing.

Yields 1 loaf

Coiled Sweet Whole Wheat Yam Bread

This bread is easy to prepare. The dough rises in the refrigerator, to be baked at your convenience.

2 envelopes active dry yeast
1/2 cup lukewarm water
3 tablespoons maple syrup
2 tablespoons ~~safflower or canola oil~~ *Soy Spread*
1/4 teaspoon sea salt
1 cup whole wheat flour
1 1/2 cups mashed cooked yams
1/2 cup coarsely chopped walnuts (optional)
1/2 cup whole wheat flour
2 cups whole wheat pastry flour

In a large bowl, dissolve the yeast in the warm water. Stir in the maple syrup, oil, and salt, then 1 cup whole wheat flour. Whisk the mixture until it is well blended. With a fork, stir in the mashed yams and the chopped walnuts, if desired. Mix together the remaining 1/2 cup whole wheat flour and the whole wheat pastry flour. Stir the flour into the dough with a fork, then knead the dough in the bowl for 6 minutes, turning the bowl often. Cover the bowl, and chill the dough in the refrigerator for 2 hours, or longer if you like.

Lightly oil two 8-inch round baking pans, and divide the dough in two. Roll each part into a 24-inch-long rope. Coil one rope in each baking pan, from the center outward. Let the dough rise in a warm place until it has doubled in bulk.

Place the baking pans in a cold oven, and set the oven temperature to 375°. Bake the loaves for about 35 minutes, or until they are a dark golden brown.

Remove the loaves from the pans, and let them cool before slicing.

Yields 2 loaves

OAT BRAN-PUMPKIN BREAD

Quick (handwritten)

This bread is wheat-free. Enjoy it with your favorite fruit juice-sweetened jam.

3/4 cup frozen and thawed apple juice
    concentrate
1 tablespoon ~~safflower or canola oil~~ *Soy Spread* (handwritten)
2 cups puréed pumpkin
2 teaspoons vanilla extract
1 cup oat flour or finely ground oatmeal
1 2/3 cups oat bran
2 tablespoons cornstarch
1 1/2 teaspoons baking soda
1 teaspoon baking powder
1 tablespoon ground cinnamon
1/2 teaspoon ground ginger
1/4 teaspoon ground cloves
1/2 teaspoon ground nutmeg
3/4 cup black raisins

In a large bowl, mix together the apple juice, oil, pumpkin, and vanilla until they are well blended. In another bowl, stir together the next nine ingredients. Add them to the wet ingredients all at once, mixing just until the batter is smooth. Fold in the raisins. Spread the batter evenly in a lightly oiled 9- by 5-inch nonstick loaf pan, and bake the bread for about 50 to 60 minutes, or until bread is light golden brown.

Let the bread cool in pan before slicing it.

Yields 1 loaf

BRAIDED WHOLE WHEAT-YAM-RAISIN BREAD

This beautiful bread is perfect for a party or celebration. The dough rises in the refrigerator, to be baked at your convenience.

2 envelopes active dry yeast
1/2 cup lukewarm water
1 teaspoon maple syrup
2 tablespoons ~~safflower or canola oil~~ *Soy Spread* (handwritten)
1/2 teaspoon sea salt
1 1/2 cups whole wheat flour
1/2 cup black raisins
1 3/4 cups mashed, cooked yams
2 cups whole wheat pastry flour

In a large bowl, dissolve the yeast in the warm water. Stir in the maple syrup, oil, and salt, then 1 cup of the whole wheat flour. Whisk the ingredients until they are well blended. With a fork, stir in the raisins and mashed yams, then the remaining 1/2 cup whole wheat flour. Knead in the pastry flour. Continue kneading, turning the bowl often, for 8 minutes, or until the dough is soft and elastic. Cover the dough, and chill it in the refrigerator for 2 to 8 hours.

Divide the dough into three parts. Roll each part into a long rope, and braid the ropes into a loaf, pinching the ends of the braid. Place the loaf on a lightly oiled nonstick baking sheet and let the dough rise until it has doubled in bulk. Place the baking sheet in a cold oven, set the oven temperature to 375°, and bake the loaf for about 25 minutes, or until it is a dark golden brown.

Remove the loaf from the pan, and let it cool before slicing.

Yields 1 loaf

Banana Squash-Raisin-Nut Bread

Enjoy this moist, delicious bread with your favorite nut butter and jam.

1 cup lukewarm water
1 1/2 envelopes active dry yeast
1 cup cooked banana squash, puréed
   (or 1 cup frozen cooked squash, thawed)
2 tablespoons maple syrup
2 tablespoons safflower or canola oil *Soy Spread*
1 tablespoon reduced-salt soy sauce or low-
   sodium Bragg Liquid Aminos
1 1/2 cups whole wheat flour
1 tablespoon ground cinnamon
1/2 cup chopped almonds, walnuts, or pecans
1/2 cup black raisins
Grated zest of 1 large orange
2 1/2 cups whole wheat flour

In a large bowl, mix together the warm water and yeast until the yeast has dissolved. Stir in the next four ingredients, and blend well. In a small bowl, mix together 1 1/2 cups whole wheat flour and the cinnamon. Add this mixture to the wet ingredients, mixing well with a whisk. With a fork, stir in the nuts, raisins, and orange zest, then the remaining 2 1/2 cups flour. Knead the dough in the bowl for 10 minutes; it will be soft and sticky. Shape the dough into a loaf, and place the loaf in a lightly oiled 9- by 5-inch nonstick loaf pan. Smooth the top with moistened fingers. Let the dough rise in a warm place until it has doubled in bulk.

Bake the loaf for about 45 minutes, or just until the top is a dark golden brown.

Remove the bread from the pan, and let it cool before slicing.

Yields 1 loaf

Easy Banana Bread *Quick*

1 2/3 cups mashed bananas (about 4 medium bananas)
1 cup frozen and thawed apple juice concentrate
1 teaspoon vanilla extract
1 tablespoon safflower or canola oil *Soy Spread*
2 1/4 cups whole wheat flour
1 teaspoon baking soda
2 teaspoons baking powder
2 tablespoons cornstarch
1/2 teaspoon ground coriander
1 tablespoon ground cinnamon
1/2 cup coarsely chopped walnuts

Preheat the oven to 350°.

In a large bowl, mix together the mashed bananas, apple juice, vanilla and oil. Combine the next six ingredients, and add them, all at once, to the banana mixture, stirring just until the ingredients are blended. Fold in the nuts. Spread the batter evenly in a 9- by 5-inch non-stick loaf pan. Bake the bread for about 55 minutes, or until it is golden brown on top. Let the bread cool somewhat before removing from pans.

Slice the bread, and serve it warm.

Yields 1 loaf

Brown Rice Flour Banana Bread *Quick*

This wholesome wheat-free bread is sweetened only with bananas.

2 1/3 cups mashed ripe bananas (about 7
    medium bananas)
2 tablespoons ~~safflower or canola oil~~ *Soy Spread*
1 tablespoon lemon juice
2 1/2 cups brown rice flour
1 tablespoon <u>baking powder</u>
1 tablespoon ground cinnamon
1 tablespoon cornstarch
→1/2 cup chopped walnuts

In a large bowl, stir together the mashed bananas, oil, and lemon juice. In another bowl, combine the remaining ingredients, and add them to the banana mixture all at once, mixing only until the ingredients are blended. Spread the batter evenly in a 9- by 5-inch lightly oiled loaf pan, and bake the bread for 55 minutes, or until it tests done. Let the bread cool in the pan before removing. Let the bread cool completely before slicing.

Yields 1 loaf

Wholesome Cornbread *Quick*

This nutritious cornbread is sweetened with sweet potatoes and a little maple syrup. It tastes delicious on its own or with jam.

2/3 cup mashed sweet potatoes, baked until
    soft, and peeled
1 1/4 cups water
1 tablespoon ~~safflower or canola oil~~ *Soy Spread*
1/2 teaspoon reduced-salt soy sauce or Bragg
    Liquid Aminos
2 tablespoons maple syrup
1 cup whole wheat flour
1 cup cornmeal
2 tablespoons cornstarch
2 teaspoons baking powder
2 teaspoons baking soda

Preheat the oven to 400°.

In a food processor or blender, blend the sweet potatoes and water until the mixture is smooth. Put the mixture into a large bowl. Add the oil, soy sauce or Bragg, and maple syrup, and stir until the ingredients are well blended. In another bowl, mix together the remaining five dry ingredients, and stir them into the wet ingredients with a spoon.

Spread the batter in a lightly oiled 9- by 5-inch nonstick loaf pan. Bake the bread for 35 minutes, or until it is golden brown on top. Serve hot.

Yields 1 loaf

Sweet Potato Cornbread

This wheat-free cornbread is sweetened only with sweet potatoes. It is delicious with fruit juice-sweetened jam for breakfast, but it can be served with any meal.

1 cup mashed cooked sweet potatoes
1 1/4 cups water
1 tablespoon safflower or canola oil
1 teaspoon reduced-salt soy sauce or Bragg Liquid Aminos
1 cup oat flour or finely ground rolled oats
1 cup cornmeal
2 tablespoons cornstarch
2 teaspoons baking powder
2 teaspoons baking soda

Preheat the oven to 400°.

In a food processor or blender, blend the sweet potatoes and water until the mixture is smooth. Put the mixture into a large bowl. Add the oil and soy sauce or Bragg and stir until the ingredients are blended. In another bowl, mix together the remaining ingredients. While stirring with a spoon, add the dry ingredients to the wet. Spread the batter in a lightly oiled 9- by 9-inch nonstick baking pan. Bake the bread for 30 minutes, or until it just begins to brown on the top. (Do not overbake, or the cornbread will be too dry.)

Cut the cornbread into large slices, and serve it warm.

Yields 9 to 12 pieces

Wheat-Free Banana-Squash Cornbread

Sweetened with banana squash and maple syrup, this cornbread is wholesome and delicious.

1 cup puréed banana squash (or other sweet orange winter squash)
3 tablespoons maple syrup
2 tablespoons safflower or canola oil
1 cup water
1 cup brown rice flour
1 cup *masa harina* or corn flour
2 tablespoons cornstarch
2 teaspoons baking powder
2 teaspoons baking soda

Preheat the oven to 400°.

In a large bowl, beat together the puréed squash, maple syrup, oil, and water until the mixture is smooth. In another bowl, mix together the next five ingredients, and add them to the wet ingredients all at once. Stir only until the batter is well blended.

Spread the batter evenly in a lightly oiled 9- by 9-inch nonstick baking pan. Bake the cornbread for about 25 minutes, or until it is a light golden brown on top.

Cut the cornbread into twelve pieces, and serve it warm.

Serves 12

Paratha
(Whole Wheat Indian Bread)

Serve this bread with any Indian dish. It tastes especially good with mango chutney.

2 1/2 cups whole wheat flour
2 1/2 cups whole wheat pastry flour
1 tablespoon onion powder
2 tablespoons sesame seeds
2 1/4 cups water
2 tablespoons oil
1 tablespoon oil

In a large bowl, mix together the whole wheat flour, whole wheat pastry flour, onion powder, and sesame seeds. In a medium bowl, mix together the water and 2 tablespoons oil. Stir the water-oil mixture into the dry ingredients with a fork until dough forms. Knead the dough for 10 minutes on a lightly floured board, then divide the dough into twelve parts. Roll each piece of dough into a ball, and flatten the ball with your hand on a lightly floured board. Using a rolling pin, roll the flattened balls into 6-inch rounds.

Place the remaining 1 tablespoon oil in a small bowl or cup. Tenderize the dough this way: Dip the fingertips of one hand into the oil, rub the top of each dough round with oil, then score the dough at right angles by pressing fingers down firmly across it leaving slight indentations. Next fold the dough into fourths, and roll the dough out again into a 6-inch round. With your hands, stretch the dough into a 9-inch round. Cook each round in a preheated nonstick frying pan, without oil, until brown spots appear on the underside. Turn the Paratha over, and cook it on the other side until brown spots appear. Repeat with the remaining pieces of dough. Serve hot.

Yields 12

Oval Whole Wheat Italian Loaves

Flavored with oregano, onion, garlic, and olive oil, this wholesome bread is perfect with salads and Italian entrées.

3 cups whole wheat flour
1 envelope active dry yeast
1 tablespoon onion powder
1/2 teaspoon garlic powder
2 teaspoons dried oregano
1 1/3 cups very warm water
1 1/2 tablespoons olive oil
2 teaspoons reduced-salt soy sauce or Bragg Liquid Aminos
Sprinkles of onion powder, garlic powder, and dried oregano

Put the first five ingredients into a large bowl. With a fork, stir in the warm water, olive oil, and soy sauce or Bragg. The dough will be very soft. Knead the dough in the bowl for 8 to 10 minutes, then cover the dough, and let it rise in a warm place until it has doubled in bulk.

Divide the dough in half, and, with moistened hands, form it into two balls. Let the dough rest, covered, for 10 minutes.

Sprinkle a little flour in a 10- by 15-inch non-stick baking pan. With moistened hands, stretch and shape each ball of dough into a flat oval loaf about 6 1/2 by 9 1/2 inches. Put the loaves in a baking pan, and sprinkle the tops generously with onion powder, garlic powder, and oregano. With a sharp knife, cut eight slits, 1/4 inch deep, from the center of each loaf outward. Let the dough again rise in a warm place until the loaves are doubled in bulk.

Place the loaves in a cold oven, set the oven temperature to 375°, and bake the loaves for about 25 minutes, or until they are a light golden brown.

Yields 2 loaves

Sweet Corn Muffins

These nutritious muffins are easy to make. They can be frozen and reheated.

1 cup fresh or frozen corn kernels
1 cup water
2 tablespoons safflower or canola oil
1/4 cup maple syrup
1/2 teaspoon reduced-salt soy sauce or Bragg Liquid Aminos
1 cup whole wheat flour
1 cup cornmeal
2 tablespoons cornstarch
2 teaspoons baking powder
2 teaspoons baking soda

Preheat the oven to 375°.

In a food processor or blender, blend the corn kernels and water. Put this mixture into a large bowl. Add the oil, maple syrup, and soy sauce or Bragg, and stir until the ingredients are blended. In another bowl, mix together the remaining ingredients. Add the dry to the wet ingredients, and stir with a spoon until they are combined.

Divide the batter among twelve paper-lined muffin cups, and bake for 12 to 15 minutes, or until the muffins test done when you insert a cake tester.

Yields 12 muffins

BANANA-BLUEBERRY-
OAT BRAN MUFFINS

What a treat these fruity muffins are. They freeze well; heat them before serving.

2 cups puréed bananas (about 4 medium bananas)
1 1/2 cups frozen and thawed apple juice concentrate
3/4 cup water
2 tablespoons safflower or canola oil
1 teaspoon vanilla extract
1 1/2 cups whole wheat flour
2 teaspoons baking soda
1 teaspoon baking powder
1 tablespoon cornstarch
1 tablespoon ground cinnamon
2 1/2 cups oat bran
1/2 cup rolled oats
1/2 cup chopped walnuts
1 cup fresh or frozen blueberries

Preheat the oven to 400°.

In a large bowl beat the puréed bananas, apple juice, water, oil, and vanilla until they are blended. In another bowl, mix together flour, baking soda, baking powder, cornstarch, and cinnamon. Add the dry ingredients to the wet all at once, mixing only until the batter is smooth. Add the remaining ingredients, and stir only until they are blended in.

Divide the batter among eighteen paper-lined muffin cups. Bake the muffins for 25 to 30 minutes, or until they are brown. Let the muffins cool before removing the paper linings.

Yields 18 muffins

BANANA-WHEAT BRAN-
RAISIN MUFFINS

These fiber-rich muffins are easy to prepare, and they freeze well.

2 1/2 cups unprocessed Miller's wheat bran
2 cups boiling water
1 cup puréed bananas (about 2 1/2 medium bananas)
1 cup frozen and thawed apple juice concentrate
1 tablespoon safflower or canola oil
1 1/2 cups whole wheat flour
1/2 cup soy flour
2 teaspoons baking soda
2 teaspoons baking powder
1 tablespoon ground cinnamon
1 1/2 teaspoons nutmeg
1/4 cup cornstarch or potato starch
1/2 cup chopped walnuts
1/2 cup black raisins

Preheat the oven to 400°.

In a large bowl, stir the bran and boiling water together. Stir in the banana purée, apple juice and oil. In another bowl, mix together the next seven ingredients. Add them all at once to the banana mixture, stirring just until the ingredients are blended. Fold in the nuts and raisins.

Divide the batter among twelve nonstick muffin cups, and bake the muffins for about 25 minutes, or until they test done when you insert a cake tester.

Let the muffins cool in their cups before removing them.

Yields 12 muffins

CAROB-OAT BRAN MUFFINS

Sweetened with pineapple juice and molasses, and enriched with soy milk and carob, these muffins taste especially delicious with berry jam.

1 1/3 cups soy milk
1 cup frozen and thawed pineapple juice
   concentrate
1 teaspoon cider vinegar
2 teaspoons dark molasses
1 teaspoon vanilla extract
1 tablespoon safflower or canola oil
1 3/4 cups whole wheat flour
1/4 cup carob powder
2 teaspoons baking soda
1 1/2 cups oat bran

Preheat the oven to 350°.

   In a large bowl, beat the first six ingredients with a whisk until they are well blended. In another bowl, mix together the whole wheat flour, carob powder, and baking soda. Add the dry ingredients to the soy milk-pineapple juice mixture all at once, stirring only until the batter is smooth. Fold in oat bran.

   Divide the batter among twelve nonstick muffin cups, and bake the muffins for 20 to 25 minutes, or just until a cake tester comes out clean. Let the muffins cool in their cups before removing them.

Yields 12 muffins

BANANA-SQUASH PASSOVER ROLLS

These tasty rolls can be enjoyed throughout the Passover holiday. Passover cake meal, made from finely ground matzo, is available in many supermarkets. This is used during the holiday as a substitute for flour. Non-Jews would also enjoy these rolls.

1 cup mashed cooked banana squash
2 tablespoons safflower or canola oil
2/3 cups water
Grated zest of 1 lemon
1 cup Passover cake meal
2/3 cup potato starch
1 teaspoon baking soda
2 tablespoons onion powder
1 teaspoon ground cinnamon

Preheat the oven to 400°.

   Mix the squash, oil, water, and grated lemon zest in a large bowl. In another bowl, mix together the remaining ingredients. Add the dry ingredients all at once to the squash mixture, mixing only until the dough is smooth.

   Roll the dough into eighteen balls. With moistened hands, put the balls of dough on a nonstick baking sheet, and flatten their tops with your hand. Bake the rolls about 25 minutes, or until the rolls are a light golden brown.

Yields 18 rolls

OAT BRAN-BANANA MUFFINS

These muffins freeze well; reheat them before serving.

1 1/2 cups black raisins
2/3 cup water
2 cups puréed bananas (about 4 medium)
1 1/3 cups frozen and thawed apple juice
    concentrate
1 cup water
1 teaspoon cider vinegar
1 teaspoon vanilla extract
2 cups whole wheat flour
2 teaspoons baking soda
1 teaspoon baking powder
2 tablespoons cornstarch
1 tablespoon ground cinnamon
1 1/2 teaspoon ground nutmeg
1 teaspoon ground coriander
2 cups oat bran

In a medium saucepan, cook the raisins in the water, uncovered, over low heat for 15 minutes, or until the liquid is gone. Blend the raisins in a food processor or blender.

Preheat the oven to 350°.

In a large bowl, mix together the puréed raisins, puréed bananas, apple juice, water, vinegar, and vanilla. In a medium bowl, mix together the next seven ingredients. Add them all at once to the raisin-banana mixture, stirring only until the batter is smooth. Fold in the oat bran.

Divide the batter among twenty-four lightly oiled nonstick muffin cups. Bake the muffins 30 to 35 minutes, or a cake tester comes out clean.

Yields 24 muffins

BANANA-RAISIN-PEAR-OAT BRAN MUFFINS

These fruity muffins are sweetened with bananas and studded with raisins and pear pieces.

1 2/3 cups puréed bananas (about 4 medium
    bananas)
1/2 cup water
3/4 cup frozen and thawed apple juice
    concentrate
2 tablespoons safflower or canola oil
2 teaspoons vanilla extract
1 1/2 cups whole wheat flour
2 teaspoons baking soda
1 teaspoon baking powder
1 tablespoon ground cinnamon
1 teaspoon ground nutmeg
1 large pear, peeled and cut into bite-size
    pieces
2/3 cup black raisins
2 cups oat bran

Preheat the oven to 375°.

In a large bowl, beat the puréed bananas, water, apple juice, oil, and vanilla with a whisk until they are well blended. In another bowl, mix together the next five ingredients. Add them all at once to the banana mixture, mixing only until the batter is smooth. Stir in pear pieces, raisins and oat bran.

Divide the batter evenly among eighteen lightly oiled or paper-lined muffin cups, and bake the muffins for about 20 minutes, or just until a cake tester comes out clean.

Let the muffins cool in their cups before removing them.

Yields 18 muffins

WHOLE WHEAT-BANANA-PINEAPPLE MUFFINS

These fruit-and-nut-filled muffins contain no oil.

2 cups mashed bananas (about 5 medium bananas)
1 1/4 cups frozen concentrated pineapple juice
1 1/2 teaspoons vanilla extract
1/3 cup water
3 1/4 cups whole wheat flour
3 tablespoons cornstarch
1 tablespoon baking powder
1 1/2 teaspoons baking soda
1 1/2 tablespoons ground cinnamon
1 teaspoon coriander
1/2 cup chopped walnuts
3/4 cup black raisins

Preheat the oven to 375°.

In a large bowl, beat together the mashed bananas, pineapple juice, vanilla, and water. In another bowl, mix together the next six ingredients, and stir them, half at a time, into the banana mixture, mixing only until the batter is smooth. Fold in the nuts and raisins.

Divide the batter among eighteen muffin cups. Bake the muffins for about 20 minutes, or just until they are a light golden brown and a cake tester comes out clean.

Let the muffins cool in their cups before removing them.

Yields 18 muffins

WHEAT-FREE BANANA-RAISIN-NUT SCONES

Within 30 minutes time you can be enjoying these healthful, delicious scones.

1 cup puréed bananas (about 2 1/2 bananas)
1 cup water
1 tablespoon safflower or canola oil
1 teaspoon lemon juice
Grated zest of 1/2 orange or lemon
1 1/2 cups brown rice flour
1 1/2 teaspoons baking powder
1 1/2 teaspoons cream of tartar
2/3 cup black raisins
1/3 cup chopped walnuts

Preheat the oven to 450°.

Purée the bananas in a blender or food processor, and put the purée in a large bowl. Add the water, oil, lemon juice, and orange or lemon zest, and stir until the ingredients are blended. In another bowl, mix together the remaining ingredients, and add them all at once to the banana mixture, while stirring with a fork.

Using a large serving spoon, drop the batter into eight mounds on a 10- by 15-inch nonstick baking pan or sheet. Bake the scones for 18 to 20 minutes, or until they are golden brown. Serve the scones warm.

Yields 8 scones

CARROT SPICE BISCUITS

Enjoy these biscuits piping hot with your favorite fruit juice-sweetened jam.

3 large carrots (1/2 pound), sliced into sixths
1 cup water
Grated zest of 1 lemon
1 tablespoon safflower or canola oil
2 cups whole wheat flour
1 1/2 teaspoons baking soda
1 tablespoon cream of tartar
1 teaspoon ground cinnamon
1/2 teaspoon ground ginger
1/4 teaspoon ground cloves

Preheat the oven to 450°.

In a medium covered saucepan, bring the carrots and water to a boil. Lower the heat, and simmer the carrots, covered, for 15 minutes, or until the carrots are tender.

Remove the carrots with a slotted spoon, reserving the liquid. Purée the carrots in a food processor or blender, with 1/2 cup reserved liquid. Put the puréed carrots, grated lemon zest, and oil into a large bowl. In another bowl, mix together the remaining ingredients, and add them all at once to the carrot mixture, mixing only until the ingredients hold together as a soft dough.

On a lightly floured board, press the dough into a circle 3/4 inch thick. Cut out biscuits with a 2 1/2-inch biscuit cutter or a small drinking glass, and arrange the biscuits on a nonstick baking sheet. Bake the biscuits for 12 minutes, or until the are light brown on top.

Serve the biscuits hot.

Yields 12 biscuits

WHEAT-FREE BAKING-POWDER BISCUITS

1 cup mashed cooked sweet potatoes
3/4 cup water
1 tablespoon safflower or canola oil
1 teaspoon reduced-salt soy sauce or Bragg Liquid Aminos
2 cups brown rice flour
1 tablespoon baking powder
1 cup oat bran

Preheat the oven to 450°.

In a food processor or blender, purée the sweet potatoes with the water. Put the purée into a medium bowl. Stir in the oil and soy sauce or Bragg. In another bowl, mix together the rice flour and baking powder, and add them all at once, while mixing with a fork, to the sweet potato mixture. Add the oat bran, and stir only until the ingredients are well blended.

Roll or pat the soft dough into a 3/4-inch-thick round. Cut out biscuits with a 2 1/2-inch biscuit cutter or a small drinking glass. Place the biscuits on a nonstick baking sheet, and bake them for 12 to 15 minutes, or until they are light brown on top.

Serve the biscuits hot.

Yields 10 to 12 biscuits

Easy Onion-Poppy Seed Scones

These delicious scones can be served as dinner rolls. They take only minutes to prepare.

1 1/2 cups water
1/4 cup soy flour
2 teaspoons cider vinegar
1/2 medium onion, minced
2 tablespoons safflower or canola oil
3 1/2 cups whole wheat flour
2 tablespoons cream of tartar
1 tablespoon baking soda
1/4 cup poppy seeds

Preheat the oven to 450°.

Combine the first five ingredients. In another bowl, mix together the flour, cream of tartar, baking soda, and poppy seeds, and add half this mixture to the water-soy flour mixture. Stir only until the ingredients are blended. Add the remaining half of the ingredients, and stir only until the flour is blended in.

Divide the dough into twelve equal pieces. Roll each piece into a ball, and place the balls on a nonstick baking sheet. Press the tops of the balls down slightly, so that the scones are about 1 1/2 inches high by 3 inches across. Bake them for 20 minutes, or until they are golden brown on top.

Serve the scones warm.

Yields 12 scones

Easy Baking-Powder Biscuits

You can make these simple biscuits very quickly.

1 cup water
2 tablespoons safflower or canola oil
1 tablespoon maple syrup
1/4 teaspoon sea salt
1 cup whole wheat flour
1 1/4 cups brown rice flour
1 tablespoon baking powder

Preheat the oven to 450°.

In a medium bowl, beat the first four ingredients with a fork until they are blended. In another bowl, mix together the whole wheat flour, brown-rice flour, and baking powder. Add the dry ingredients all at once to the liquid, while mixing with a fork. Stir only until the ingredients hold together as a dough.

On a floured board, press the dough down into a round, 3/4 inch thick. Cut out biscuits with a 2 1/2-inch biscuit cutter or small drinking glass. Place the biscuits on a nonstick baking sheet, and bake them for 12 to 15 minutes, or until they are golden brown.

Serve the biscuits hot.

Yields 10 biscuits

ONION-POPPY SEED-OAT BRAN MUFFINS

These onion-flavored poppy-seed muffins can be served as dinner rolls.

2 cups water
3/4 cup minced onion
2 teaspoons cider vinegar
2 tablespoons safflower or canola oil
1 3/4 cups whole wheat flour
1/4 cup soy flour
2 teaspoons baking powder
1 tablespoon cornstarch
1 1/2 cups oat bran
2 tablespoons poppy seeds

Preheat the oven to 350°.

In a large bowl, stir together the water, onion, vinegar, and oil until they are blended. In another bowl, mix together the flour, soy flour, baking powder and cornstarch. Add the dry ingredients all at once to the liquid, mixing only until the batter is smooth. Stir in the oat bran and poppy seeds.

Divide the batter among twelve lightly oiled nonstick muffin cups, and bake the muffins for 25 to 30 minutes, or until a cake tester comes out clean.

Serve the muffins hot.

Yields 12 muffins

BROWN RICE FLOUR-SWEET POTATO SCONES WITH RAISINS OR CURRANTS

Enjoy these citrus-flavored scones with fragrant herb tea.

2/3 cup mashed sweet potatoes, baked until soft and peeled (about 1 pound)
1 1/4 cups water
1 tablespoon safflower or canola oil
1 teaspoon lemon juice
Grated zest of 1 lemon
Grated zest of 1 orange
1 cup brown rice flour
1 1/2 teaspoons baking powder
1 1/2 teaspoons cream of tartar
2/3 cup black raisins or currants

Preheat the oven to 450°.

In a food processor or blender, blend the first six ingredients, and put the mixture into a medium bowl. In another bowl, mix together the rice flour, baking soda, cream of tartar, and raisins, and add the dry ingredients all at once, while mixing with a fork, to the sweet-potato mixture. Stir only until the ingredients are blended.

Drop the batter by heaping tablespoonfuls into eight mounds onto a 10- by 15-inch nonstick baking pan or sheet. Bake the scones for about 25 minutes, or until they are light golden brown on top.

Serve the scones hot.

Yields 8 scones.

WHEAT-FREE OAT BRAN-SWEET POTATO SCONES

These crunchy scones, high in fiber, are perfect for breakfast.

2/3 cup mashed, cooked sweet potatoes
1 1/4 cups water
1 teaspoon lemon juice
Grated zest of 1 lemon
Grated zest of 1 orange
1 tablespoon safflower or canola oil
1/2 cup oat flour
1 cup oat bran
1 1/2 teaspoons baking soda
1 1/2 teaspoons cream of tartar
1/2 cup chopped walnuts

Preheat the oven to 450°.

Blend the first six ingredients in a food processor or blender, and put the mixture into a medium mixing bowl. In another bowl, mix together the oat flour, oat bran, baking soda, cream of tartar, and walnuts, and add the dry ingredients all at once to the sweet-potato mixture, while stirring with a fork. Stir only until the ingredients are blended.

Drop the batter by heaping tablespoonfuls into twelve mounds on a 10- by 15-inch nonstick baking pan or sheet. Bake the scones for about 30 minutes, or until they are a dark golden brown on top.

Serve the scones hot.

Yields 12 scones

WHOLE WHEAT-ORANGE-SWEET POTATO SCONES

These healthful scones can be prepared and baked for breakfast in about half an hour.

2/3 cup mashed sweet potatoes
1 cup water
1 tablespoon safflower or canola oil
2 tablespoons frozen or thawed orange juice concentrate
1 cup whole wheat flour
1 teaspoon baking powder
2 teaspoons cream of tartar
1/2 teaspoon ground coriander
1/2 cup black raisins

Preheat the oven to 450°.

In a food processor or blender, blend the sweet potatoes, water, oil, and orange juice until the mixture is smooth. In another bowl, mix together the next five ingredients, and add them all at once to the sweet-potato purée, mixing only until the ingredients are blended.

Drop the batter by heaping tablespoonfuls into eight mounds on a 10- by 15-inch nonstick baking pan or sheet. Bake the muffins for 20 to 25 minutes, or until they are golden brown.

Serve the muffins hot.

Yields 8 muffins

UNSWEETENED WHEAT-FREE OAT BRAN SCONES

You'll enjoy these tasty scones as snacks at any time of the day.

1 1/2 cups boiling water
2 tablespoons onion powder
2 teaspoons reduced-salt soy sauce or Bragg Liquid Aminos, or 1/2 teaspoon sea salt
1/2 teaspoon ground cinnamon
1/8 teaspoon ground black or white pepper
2 tablespoons safflower or canola oil
1 1/2 cups brown rice flour
1 tablespoon baking soda
2 cups oat bran

Preheat the oven to 450°.

In a large bowl, beat the first six ingredients with a whisk. In another bowl, mix together the rice flour, baking soda, and oat bran. Add the dry ingredients, half at a time, to the liquid, mixing with a fork only until the mixture is blended.

Drop the batter into twelve mounds, 1 inch high by 3 inches across, on a nonstick baking sheet.

Bake the scones for about 20 minutes, or until they are a dark golden brown on top.

Serve the scones hot.

Yields 12 scones

WHEAT-FREE BANANA-APPLE-OAT BRAN MUFFINS

These muffins freeze well; reheat them before serving.

2 cups mashed ripe bananas (about 5 medium bananas)
1 cup frozen and thawed apple juice concentrate
2 tablespoons safflower or canola oil
1 1/4 cups finely ground rolled oats (about 2 cups rolled oats, ground in a food processor or blender)
2 teaspoons baking powder
2 teaspoons baking soda
1 tablespoon ground cinnamon
1/2 teaspoon ground coriander
2 cups oat bran
1/3 cup raw sunflower seeds
1 cup chopped walnuts
1 cup black raisins

Preheat the oven to 400°.

In a large bowl, beat the mashed bananas, apple juice, and oil with a whisk until the ingredients are blended. In another bowl, mix together the next five ingredients, and add them all at once to the banana mixture, mixing only until the batter is smooth. Stir in the oat bran, sunflower seeds, chopped walnuts, and raisins only until they are blended in.

Divide the batter among eighteen nonstick muffin cups, and bake the muffins for 15 to 18 minutes, or until a cake tester comes out clean.

Serve the muffins warm.

Yields 18 muffins

Fruit-Sweetened Wheat-Free Oat Bran Muffins

1 cup black raisins
2/3 cup water
2 tablespoons frozen or thawed orange juice concentrate
3/4 cup frozen or thawed apple juice concentrate
1/2 cup frozen or thawed pineapple juice concentrate
2 tablespoons safflower or canola oil
1 1/4 cups finely ground rolled oats (about 2 cups rolled oats, ground in a food processor or blender)
2 teaspoons baking powder
2 teaspoons baking soda
1 tablespoon ground cinnamon
1/2 teaspoon ground coriander
1/2 cup chopped walnuts
2 cups oat bran

In a small saucepan, simmer the raisins in the water over medium heat for 6 minutes. Purée the raisins in a food processor or blender, and put the mixture into a large bowl. Stir in the orange, apple, and pineapple juices, and the oil. In another bowl, mix the finely ground oats with the next five ingredients, and add the dry ingredients all at once to the raisin mixture, stirring only until the batter is smooth. Fold in the oat bran. Let the batter stand at room temperature for 30 minutes.

Preheat the oven to 400°.

Divide the batter among eighteen paper-lined muffin cups, and bake the muffins for 18 to 20 minutes, or until a cake tester comes out clean.

Let the muffins cool for 10 minutes before removing them from their paper linings.

Yields 18 muffins

Easy Wheat-Free Oat Bran Muffins

3 cups rolled oats
1 1/3 cups oat bran
2 tablespoons ground cinnamon
1 teaspoon ground nutmeg
2/3 cup black raisins
1 1/2 cups frozen and thawed apple juice concentrate
1/2 cup water
1 tablespoon safflower or canola oil

Preheat the oven to 375°.

In a large bowl, mix together the oats, oat bran, cinnamon, nutmeg, and raisins. In a small bowl, combine the apple juice, water and oil. With a fork, stir the juice mixture into the dry ingredients until the batter is blended.

Divide the batter among twelve lightly oiled nonstick muffin cups. Bake the muffins for 20 minutes.

Serve the muffins hot.

Yields 12

Delicious Cakes, Tortes and Pies

Imagine being able to bake luscious cakes, tortes, pies, and other desserts that are totally nutritious and good for you. These recipes can make this fantasy become a reality, and the range of choices is enormous. As you browse through this section, you'll find recipes for cakes like Pear-Raisin-Nut Cake, Banana-Walnut Cake with Banana-Blueberry Filling and Easy Blueberry Topping, Carob-Cherry-Date Cake with Easy Cherry Sauce, Lemon-Walnut Cake with Creamy Lemon-Walnut-Tofu Frosting, and even Passover Date and Walnut Pudding Cake.

Our torte recipes include Plum Torte with Brown Rice Flour-Almond Butter Crust, Date Brownie Torte with Bananas and Boysenberry Topping, and Fruit-Sweetened Almond Torte. Many of these tortes are wheat-free.

You'll also find here recipes for dozens of fruit pies, Fancy Wheat-Free Yam-Pecan Pie, Mocha Tofu Pie, tofu "cheese" pies, and Lemon Pudding Pie, among many others. Almost all of these pies are wheat-free.

Other desserts in this chapter include Easy Blueberry Cobbler, Peach Cereal Casserole, Date-Almond-Brown Rice Pudding with Easy Cashew Cream or Vanilla Cashew Cream, and Strawberry Tofu Mousse.

The ingredients used in all our dessert recipes are natural, low in fat and salt, free of cholesterol and sugar, and free of all animal products, including honey. These desserts are good for you; you can enjoy baking and eating them without any guilt or worry.

HOLIDAY BANANA-SQUASH FRUIT CAKE

Enjoy this moist fruitcake for the holidays, or at any time of the year.

2 cups mashed cooked banana squash, or
  other sweet orange winter squash
1/2 cup maple syrup
2 tablespoons safflower or canola oil
2 3/4 cups whole wheat pastry flour
2 teaspoons baking soda
1 teaspoon baking powder
1 tablespoon ground cinnamon
1 teaspoon ground nutmeg
1 teaspoon ground ginger
1 teaspoon ground coriander
1/4 teaspoon ground cloves
2 tablespoons cornstarch
2 cups black raisins
1 cup chopped walnuts
1 cup crushed fresh pineapple

Preheat the oven to 350°.

In a large bowl, beat together the squash, maple syrup, and oil until they are blended. In another bowl, mix together the next nine ingredients, and add them to the squash mixture. Stir until the ingredients are just blended. Stir in the raisins, nuts, and pineapple.

Spread the batter in two lightly oiled 9- by 5-inch nonstick loaf pans. Bake the cakes 40 minutes, or until a cake tester comes out clean. Let the cakes cool before removing them from the pans.

Yields 2 cakes

PEAR-RAISIN-NUT CAKE

1 pound black raisins
1/2 cup water
2 large ripe pears, peeled and puréed
  (1 1/2 cups)
1/2 cup frozen and thawed apple juice
  concentrate
1 tablespoon safflower or canola oil
2 teaspoons vanilla extract
2 1/2 cups whole wheat pastry flour
2 teaspoons baking soda
1 teaspoon baking powder
1 tablespoon ground cinnamon
1/2 teaspoon ground coriander
1 cup chopped walnuts

In a medium saucepan, simmer the raisins in the water for 10 minutes.

Preheat the oven to 375°.

Purée the raisins with the remaining water in a food processor or blender, and put the raisin purée into a large bowl. Add the puréed pears, apple juice, oil, and vanilla, and stir until the ingredients are blended. In another bowl, mix together the next five ingredients. Stir them into the raisin-pear mixture only until the batter is blended. Fold in the walnuts.

Spread the batter evenly in a 9- by 9-inch lightly oiled nonstick baking pan, and bake the cake for about 35 minutes, or until a cake tester comes out clean. Cool the cake in the pan before slicing.

Serves 9 to 12

YAM-RAISIN-SPICE CAKE

This moist cake makes a wholesome snack.

2 cups mashed cooked yams
1 large banana, sliced
1/4 cup frozen and thawed orange juice
  concentrate
1/2 cup frozen and thawed pineapple juice
  concentrate
2 tablespoons safflower or canola oil
3 cups whole wheat pastry flour
2 teaspoons baking soda
1 teaspoon baking powder
1 tablespoon ground cinnamon
1 teaspoon ground nutmeg
1/2 teaspoon ground cloves
1 teaspoon ground ginger
2 tablespoons cornstarch
1/2 cup black raisins

Preheat the oven to 350°.

In a food processor or blender, purée the yams and banana. Put the purée into a large bowl. Add the orange juice, pineapple juice, and oil, and stir until the ingredients are blended. In another bowl, mix together the next eight ingredients. Add them, half at a time, to the yam-banana mixture. Stir only until the ingredients are just blended. Stir in the raisins.

Spread the batter in a lightly oiled 10-inch tube pan. Bake the cake for 50 to 55 minutes, or just until a cake tester comes out clean.

Let the cake cool before removing it from the pan.

Serves 12

Banana-Walnut Cake with Blueberry-Banana Filling and Easy Blueberry Topping

What could be better than a delicious banana cake that is good for you? For an added treat, this one has a blueberry-banana filling and a blueberry topping.

Cake

2 1/2 cups puréed bananas (6 medium bananas)
3/4 cup frozen and thawed apple juice concentrate
2 tablespoons safflower or canola oil
1/4 cup water
2 teaspoons vanilla extract
3 cups whole wheat pastry flour
2 teaspoons baking soda
1 teaspoon baking powder
1 tablespoon ground cinnamon
1/2 teaspoon ground coriander
3/4 cup chopped walnuts

Topping

5 cups fresh or frozen (unthawed) blueberries
1 cup frozen and thawed apple juice concentrate
1/4 cup cornstarch

Filling

3 large bananas, quartered lengthwise, then sliced 1/4 inch thick (2 1/2 cups)
1 teaspoon lemon juice
1 1/2 cups blueberry topping

Preheat the oven to 375°.

In a large bowl, beat the first five ingredients with a whisk. In another bowl, mix together the flour, baking soda, baking powder, cinnamon, and coriander. Add these to the banana mixture, half at a time, and stir just until the batter is blended. Fold in the nuts. The batter will be thick.

Spread the batter evenly in a 9- by 9-inch non-stick baking pan. Bake the cake for about 35 minutes, or just until a cake tester comes out clean. Let the cake cool before removing it from the pan.

While the cake cools, make the topping. In a 3-quart saucepan, mix together blueberries, apple juice, and cornstarch. Cook the mixture over medium heat, stirring gently but constantly, until it thickens. Remove the pan from the heat. Set aside 1 1/2 cups for the filling.

When the cake and topping have cooled completely, make the filling. In a medium bowl, toss the bananas in the lemon juice. Stir in 1 1/2 cups of the blueberry topping.

Cut the cake horizontally into two layers. Cover it with the blueberry and banana filling. Place the second layer on top, cut-side down. Spread the blueberry topping over the cake.

Chill the cake well before serving.

Serves 9 to 12

Carob-Cherry-Date Cake

You and your loved ones can enjoy this cake, adorned with puréed cherries, without any guilt at all.

3/4 cup pitted dates
1/2 cup water
1 16-ounce package frozen dark sweet pitted cherries, partially thawed
1/3 cup frozen and thawed apple juice concentrate
2 tablespoons safflower or canola oil
1 teaspoon dark molasses
1 teaspoon almond extract
1 teaspoon vanilla extract
1/2 cup water
2/3 cup carob powder
2/3 cup boiling water
2 cups whole wheat pastry flour
2 teaspoons baking powder
1 teaspoon baking soda
1 tablespoon cornstarch

Sauce
2 cups frozen (unthawed) dark sweet pitted cherries
1/3 cup frozen and thawed apple juice concentrate
1/4 teaspoon ground coriander

In a medium saucepan, cook the dates in 1/2 cup water, uncovered, over medium heat for 8 minutes. Remove the pan from the heat.

Preheat the oven to 350°.

Purée all but 1 cup of the cherries, along with the cooked dates and any liquid remaining in the saucepan, in a food processor or blender. In a large mixing bowl beat the next six ingredients with a whisk until blended.

In a small bowl, stir together the carob powder and boiling water until the mixture is smooth, and stir this mixture into the ingredients in the large mixing bowl.

In another bowl, mix together the flour, baking powder, baking soda, and cornstarch, and add them all at once to the cherry-date-carob mixture. Stir only until the batter is smooth.

Spread the batter evenly in a lightly oiled 10-inch springform baking pan. Bake for 40 to 45 minutes, or just until a cake tester comes out clean. The cake should be moist when you remove it from the pan.

Let the cake cool before removing it from the pan.

While the cake bakes, make the sauce. Purée the cherries, apple juice and coriander in a food processor or blender.

Chill the cake until you're ready to serve.

Serve each slice of cake with some of the sauce spooned over it.

Serves 8 to 10

Moist Fig-Carob Fudge Cake

2 cups fresh, ripe black figs, stems removed
1/3 cup carob powder
1 teaspoon dark molasses
1 tablespoon safflower or canola oil
2 teaspoons vanilla extract
1 cup boiling water
1/3 cup maple syrup
1 1/2 cups whole wheat pastry flour
1 teaspoon baking powder
1 teaspoon baking soda
1 tablespoon cornstarch

Preheat the oven to 400°.

Purée the figs in a food processor or blender, and put the purée into a large bowl. Blend the next six ingredients in a food processor or blender, and stir the mixture into the puréed figs. Mix together the flour, baking powder, baking soda, and cornstarch. Add the dry ingredients all at once to the fig mixture, stirring only until the batter is blended.

Spread the batter evenly in a lightly oiled 9-inch round baking pan. Bake the cake for about 20 minutes, or just until a cake tester comes out clean. The cake should be moist when you remove it from the oven.

Let the cake cool before removing it from the pan.

Serves 6 to 8

Lemon-Walnut Cake with Creamy Lemon-Walnut-Tofu Frosting

You can assemble the cake quickly if you drain the tofu earlier in the day, or the day before. Creamy Lemon-Walnut-Tofu Frosting also makes a good cake or pie filling.

Cake

3/4 cup pitted dates
1/2 cup water
1/3 cup frozen and thawed orange juice concentrate
1/3 cup frozen and thawed pineapple juice concentrate
1/2 cup water
1/4 cup lemon juice
Grated zest of 1 lemon
2 tablespoons safflower or canola oil
1/4 teaspoon almond extract
2 cups whole wheat pastry flour
2 teaspoons baking soda
2 teaspoons baking powder
1 tablespoon cornstarch
3/4 cup chopped walnuts

Frosting

1 14-ounce package soft tofu, well rinsed
2 tablespoons frozen and thawed orange juice concentrate
1/3 cup frozen and thawed apple juice concentrate
2 tablespoons maple syrup
Grated zest of 1/2 lemon
1/2 teaspoon cider vinegar
1 tablespoon cornstarch

1 tablespoon water
2 tablespoons lemon juice
1/2 cup chopped walnuts

In a medium saucepan, cook the dates, in 1/2 cup water, uncovered, over medium heat for 8 minutes. In a food processor or blender, purée the dates and any liquid left in saucepan with the orange juice and pineapple juice. Put the mixture into a large bowl. Stir in 1/2 cup water and the next four ingredients.

In a medium bowl, mix together the flour, baking soda, baking powder, and cornstarch, and add the dry ingredients all at once to the date mixture, mixing only until the batter is smooth. Fold in the chopped walnuts.

Spread the batter evenly in a lightly oiled 10-inch springform baking pan. Bake the cake for 25 to 30 minutes, or just until a cake tester comes out clean.

Let the cake cook before removing it from the pan.

To make the frosting, cut a piece of cheesecloth large enough to hold the tofu. Place the tofu in the center, draw up the cheesecloth around the tofu, and tie the corners together. Squeeze as much liquid as possible from the tofu, then let the tofu, still tied in the cheesecloth, drain in a colander for at least 1 hour.

In a small saucepan, mix together the next five ingredients. Bring the mixture to a boil over medium heat, and let it simmer for 5 minutes. In a small cup mix the cornstarch and water together, and stir this mixture into the saucepan. Heat, stirring, until the fruit juices thicken.

In a food processor or blender, blend the tofu with the hot sauce and the lemon juice until the mixture is very smooth and creamy. Frost the top of the Lemon-Walnut Cake, and sprinkle the chopped walnuts on top.

Serves 10

CARROT-RAISIN-WALNUT CAKE

Frost this cake with Creamy Pineapple-Tofu Frosting, sprinkle the top with walnuts, and enjoy.

1 cup black raisins
1 cup water
2 cups mashed, cooked carrots (about 1 pound)
1/2 cup water
1/2 cup frozen and thawed pineapple juice concentrate
2 tablespoons safflower or canola oil
2 teaspoons vanilla extract
1 tablespoon maple syrup
2 cups whole wheat pastry flour
2 teaspoons baking powder
2 teaspoons baking soda
1 tablespoon ground cinnamon
1 tablespoon ground nutmeg
2 tablespoons cornstarch
3/4 cup chopped walnuts
Creamy Pineapple-Tofu Frosting (page 147)
1 cup chopped walnuts

Preheat the oven to 350°.

In a medium saucepan, cook the raisins in 1 cup water, uncovered, over medium heat for 8 minutes. In a food processor or blender, purée the raisins, and any liquid left in the saucepan, with the mashed carrots. Put the purée into a large bowl. Stir in 1/2 cup water and the next four ingredients.

In a medium bowl, mix together the flour, baking powder, baking soda, cinnamon, nutmeg, and cornstarch. Add the dry ingredients all at once to the raisin-carrot mixture, stirring only until the batter is blended. Fold in 3/4 cup chopped walnuts.

Spread the batter evenly in a lightly oiled 9-by 13-inch ovenproof glass baking pan. Bake the cake for 40 to 45 minutes, or just until a cake tester comes out clean. The cake should be moist when you remove it from the pan.

Let the cake cool before removing it from the dish. Place it on a cake plate, frost it with Creamy Pineapple-Tofu Frosting, and sprinkle the top with 1 cup chopped walnuts.

Serves 12 to 16

DATE-CARROT CAKE

A carrot cake without a lot of oil!

1 cup pitted dates
1/2 cup water
2 tablespoons safflower or canola oil
1/4 cup water
2 teaspoons vanilla extract
1 cup frozen and thawed apple juice
    concentrate
2 cups whole wheat flour
2 teaspoons baking soda
1 teaspoon baking powder
1 tablespoon ground cinnamon
2 teaspoons ground nutmeg
2 tablespoons cornstarch
3 cups firmly packed grated carrots
3/4 cup chopped walnuts
3/4 cup black raisins
Creamy Pineapple-Tofu Frosting

Preheat the oven to 350°.

In a medium saucepan, cook the dates in 1/2 cup water, uncovered, over medium heat for 8 minutes. Purée the dates, and any liquid remaining in the saucepan, in a food processor or blender. Put the puréed dates into a large bowl. Stir in the oil, 1/4 cup water, the vanilla, and the apple juice. Beat the mixture with a whisk until it is well blended.

In another bowl, mix together the flour, baking soda, baking powder, cinnamon, nutmeg, and cornstarch. Add the dry ingredients all at once to the date mixture, stirring only until the batter is well blended. Fold in the grated carrots, the walnuts and the raisins.

Spread the batter in a lightly oiled 9- by 9-inch nonstick baking pan. Bake the cake for about 45 minutes, or just until it is light brown.

Let the cake cool before removing it from the pan. When the cake has cooled completely, place it on a cake plate. Frost the top with Creamy Pineapple-Tofu Frosting.

Serves 12

CREAMY PINEAPPLE-TOFU FROSTING

Spread this maple syrup-sweetened frosting on Carrot-Raisin-Walnut Cake or Date-Carrot Cake.

1 14-ounce package soft tofu (well rinsed)
1/3 cup frozen and thawed pineapple juice
    concentrate
1/3 cup maple syrup
1/2 teaspoon cider vinegar
Grated zest of 1 orange
1 tablespoon cornstarch
1 tablespoon water

Cut a piece of cheesecloth large enough to hold the tofu. Place the tofu in the center, draw up the cheesecloth around the tofu, and tie the corners together. Squeeze as much liquid as possible from the tofu, then let the tofu, still tied in the cheesecloth, drain in a colander for 1 hour.

In a small saucepan, bring the pineapple juice, maple syrup, vinegar, and grated orange zest to a boil. Reduce the heat, and simmer for 5 minutes. In a small cup, mix together the cornstarch and water and stir into the saucepan. Continue simmering, stirring, until the syrup thickens.

Blend the drained tofu and the hot pineapple syrup to make a smooth frosting.

Yields 1 1/2 cups

Passover Date-Walnut Pudding Cake

This cake is good warm or cold. It is made with the finely crushed crumbs of matzo (unleavened crackers). Matzo meal is available in supermarkets around Passover.

1 1/2 cups pitted dates
1 cup water
1 cup mashed cooked banana squash
1/2 cup water
2 tablespoons safflower or canola oil
1 teaspoon vanilla extract
1/2 cup potato starch
1/2 cup matzo ground meal
2 teaspoons ground cinnamon
2 teaspoons baking soda
2/3 cup chopped walnuts

Preheat the oven to 350°.

In a medium saucepan, cook the dates in 1 cup water over medium heat for 5 minutes. In a food processor or blender, purée the dates, any liquid remaining in the pan, and the banana squash. Put the mixture into a large bowl, and stir in 1/2 cup water, the oil and the vanilla.

In a small bowl, combine the remaining ingredients. Add them to the date-squash mixture, and stir until the batter is smooth. It will be thick.

Spread the batter in a lightly oiled 9- by 9-inch baking pan. Bake the cake for about 35 minutes, or until a cake tester comes out clean.

Let the cake cool before removing it from the pan.

Serves 6 to 8

Apple-Pecan Torte

This wheat-free dessert will grace any table.

2 tablespoons fruit juice-sweetened apricot jam
1 1/2 recipes Brown Rice Flour-Nut Crust (page 157)
7 cups peeled, sliced apples (about 5 large apples)
3/4 cup frozen and thawed apple juice concentrate
1 tablespoon ground cinnamon
1/2 teaspoon ground coriander
1/2 cup pecan halves or chopped pecans

Preheat the oven to 400°.

Spread the jam evenly over the unbaked crust. Bake the crust for 10 minutes. Leave the oven on.

While the crust bakes, mix together in a 4- to 5-quart saucepan the sliced apples, apple juice, cinnamon, and coriander. Cook the mixture, covered, over medium heat for 7 minutes, stirring occasionally. Remove the lid, and cook for 5 minutes longer, or until the apple slices are tender and the juice is syrupy.

Arrange the apple slices in the prepared crust, and decorate the torte with the pecan halves or pieces around the edge and in the center. Bake the torte for 15 minutes.

Serves 8

APPLE DELIGHT TORTE

This torte is wheat-free.

1 1/2 recipes Brown Rice Flour-Nut Crust
  (page 157)
3 large Delicious or pippin apples, peeled,
  and sliced thick
1/4 cup frozen and thawed apple juice
  concentrate
1/4 cup frozen and thawed orange juice
  concentrate
1 teaspoon ground cinnamon

Preheat the oven to 400°.

Prepare the crust mixture according to the recipe. Pat the mixture in the bottom and 1/2 inch up sides of a 10-inch springform baking pan. Bake the crust for 12 to 15 minutes, or until it is brown around the edges. Set the crust aside to cool.

In a 4- to 5-quart saucepan, cook the apples, apple juice, orange juice, and cinnamon over medium heat, covered, for 20 minutes, stirring occasionally. Let the mixture cool.

Arrange apple slices in a circle around the edge of the crust, then in the center like the petals of a flower. Chill the torte well before serving.

Serves 8

WHEAT-FREE DATE-CAROB-WALNUT TORTE

2 1/2 cups pitted dates, packed down
1 cup water
2 tablespoons carob powder
1/2 teaspoon dark molasses
1/4 cup water
1 tablespoon cornstarch
1/2 teaspoon baking soda
1/2 teaspoon lemon juice
1/2 cup brown rice flour
1 cup coarsely chopped walnuts
1/4 cup black raisins
2 tablespoons chopped walnuts

In a medium saucepan, cook the dates in 1 cup water over medium heat, uncovered, for 10 minutes. Purée them in a food processor or blender, then blend in the carob powder and molasses. Put the date mixture into a large bowl. In a small bowl, mix together 1/4 cup water, the cornstarch, the baking soda, and the lemon juice, and stir this mixture into the date mixture. Add the rice flour and walnuts, and stir only until the batter is blended.

Sprinkle the black raisins in the bottom of a lightly oiled 9-inch round baking pan. Spread the torte batter on top of the raisins, then sprinkle the chopped walnuts on top. Bake the torte for 15 to 18 minutes.

Chill the torte well before slicing.

Serves 6

Plum Torte with Brown Rice Flour-Almond Butter Crust

This torte is lovely to look at, delicious to eat, and wheat-free. The crust needs no prebaking.

8 medium red plums, quartered and pitted
1/4 cup frozen and thawed apple juice
   concentrate
1/2 teaspoon ground coriander
Brown Rice Flour-Almond Butter Crust

Preheat the oven to 400°.

In a medium bowl, toss the plums with the apple juice and coriander. Arrange the plum quarters in circular fashion, skin side down, on top of the crust, and spoon the juice over the plums. Cover the pan with foil, and pierce the top of the foil in several places.

Bake the torte for 35 minutes, then remove the foil, and bake for 15 minutes longer. Chill before serving.

Serves 6

Brown Rice Flour-Almond Butter Crust

5 tablespoons frozen and thawed apple juice
   concentrate
3 tablespoons almond butter
1 cup brown rice flour
2 teaspoons ground cinnamon
1 teaspoon cream of tartar

In a medium bowl, beat together the apple juice and almond butter until they are blended. In another bowl, mix together the rice flour, cinnamon and cream of tartar. Add the dry ingredients to the apple juice-almond butter mixture, and stir with a fork until the dough is blended. Press the dough into the bottom of a 9-inch springform pan. Fill the pie, and bake it according to the pie recipe.

Yields 1 9-inch bottom pie crust

Date Brownie Torte
with Bananas and
Boysenberry Topping

Torte
1 cup pitted dates
3/4 cup water
1/3 cup carob powder
1/3 cup water
1 teaspoon vanilla extract
1 tablespoon safflower or canola oil
1 teaspoon dark molasses
3/4 cup whole wheat pastry flour
3/4 cup chopped walnuts
1 teaspoon baking soda
2 ripe bananas, sliced in 1/4-inch rounds

Topping
3 cups fresh or frozen boysenberries
1/2 cup frozen and thawed apple juice
  concentrate
3 tablespoons cornstarch
1/4 teaspoon ground coriander

Preheat the oven to 400°.

In a small saucepan, cook the dates in 3/4 cup water over medium heat for 8 minutes. Remove the pan from the heat, and stir in the carob powder. Purée the carob-date mixture in a food processor or blender, then put the purée into a large bowl. Stir in 1/3 cup water, the vanilla, the oil, and the molasses.

In another bowl, mix together the flour, walnuts, and baking soda. Add these all at once to the carob-date mixture, and stir only until the batter is blended.

Spread the batter in a lightly oiled 9-inch springform pan or round cake pan. Bake the torte for 10 minutes; it should be moist when you remove it from the oven.

Let the torte cool partially before removing it from the pan. Place it on a cake plate, and let it cool completely. Arrange the banana slices on top of the cooled torte.

In a medium saucepan, mix together the topping ingredients. Cook them over medium heat, stirring constantly, until the mixture thickens. Spread the topping over the bananas.

Chill the torte well before serving.

Serves 6 to 8

ALMOND MOCHA TORTE

This dense torte is sweetened with dates and flavored with carob and instant coffee substitute. It keeps well in the refrigerator.

1 1/2 cups pitted dates
1/2 cup water
3 tablespoon carob powder
1 teaspoon dark molasses
2 teaspoons instant coffee substitute
2 teaspoons vanilla extract
1 tablespoon safflower or canola oil
2/3 cup whole wheat pastry flour
1 teaspoon baking soda
1 cup chopped almonds
1/4 cup chopped raw almonds for top

Preheat the oven to 350°.

In a medium saucepan, cook the dates in the water, uncovered, over medium heat for 8 minutes. Remove the pan from the heat. Stir in the next five ingredients. Purée the date-carob mixture in a food processor or blender, then put the purée into a large bowl.

In a smaller bowl, mix together the flour, the baking soda, and 1 cup chopped almonds. Gently fold the dry ingredients into the date-carob mixture.

With moistened fingers, pat the dough down evenly in a lightly oiled 9-inch springform baking pan or a round cake pan. Sprinkle the remaining chopped almonds on top, and bake the torte for 20 minutes, or just until a cake tester comes out clean. The torte should be moist when you remove it from the oven.

Let the torte cool before removing it from the pan, and chill before serving.

Serves 8

FRUIT-SWEETENED ALMOND TORTE

This torte is easy to prepare and a delight to eat.

2/3 cup black raisins
1/3 cup water
1/4 cup frozen and thawed apple juice concentrate
1 cup banana slices, firmly packed
1/4 teaspoon almond extract
2 teaspoons vanilla extract
1 tablespoon safflower or canola oil
1 cup whole wheat pastry flour
1 teaspoon baking soda
1 1/4 cups chopped almonds
2 teaspoons ground cinnamon
1/2 teaspoon ground coriander

Preheat the oven to 350°.

In a medium saucepan, cook the raisins in the water, uncovered, over medium heat for 8 minutes. In a food processor or blender, purée the raisins, and any liquid remaining in the saucepan, with the next five ingredients. Put the purée into a large bowl.

In a smaller bowl, mix together the flour, baking soda, 1 cup chopped almonds, the cinnamon, and the coriander. Add the dry ingredients to the raisin-banana mixture, stirring with a fork only until the dough is blended.

Spread the dough evenly in a lightly oiled 9-inch springform pan or a round cake pan. Sprinkle the remaining 1/4 cup chopped almonds on top, and bake the torte for 22 minutes.

Let the cake cool before removing it from the pan, and chill before serving.

Serves 8

WHEAT-FREE CAROB-ALMOND TORTE

This fruit torte tastes delicious topped with fresh fruit, or as a bottom layer for Wheat-Free Almond-Pear Torte.

1 cup pitted dates
1/2 cup black raisins
1/2 cup water
1/2 cup water
3 tablespoons carob powder
1 teaspoon dark molasses
1/4 teaspoon almond extract
2 teaspoons vanilla extract
1 1/2 tablespoons safflower or canola oil
1 cup brown-rice flour
1 teaspoon baking powder
1/3 cup sliced almonds

Preheat the oven to 350°.

In a small saucepan, cook the dates and raisins in 1/2 cup water over medium heat for 8 minutes. In a food processor or blender, purée the dates and raisins with 1/2 cup water and the next five ingredients. Put the purée into a medium bowl.

In a small bowl, mix together the flour and baking powder, and add them all at once to the fruit purée while stirring with a fork. Stir just until the batter is blended. Spread the batter in a lightly oiled 10-inch springform pan. Sprinkle the sliced almonds on top. Bake the torte for 20 minutes.

Let the cake cool before removing it from the pan.

Serves 8

WHEAT-FREE ALMOND-PEAR TORTE

Wheat-Free Carob-Almond Torte
7 large ripe but still firm Bartlett or Comice pears, peeled, halved and cored
1/2 cup frozen and thawed pineapple juice concentrate
1/4 cup frozen and thawed apple juice concentrate
2 teaspoons ground cinnamon
1/4 teaspoon ground coriander
1 tablespoon cornstarch
1 tablespoon water
1/3 cup sliced almonds

Prepare Wheat-Free Carob-Almond Torte according to the recipe and leave the torte layer in the pan. While torte layer is baking, poach the pears in the pineapple juice, apple juice, cinnamon, and coriander, covered, in a 4- to 5-quart saucepan, for 10 minutes, or until the pears are tender. (Do not overcook the pears, or they will fall apart.) Remove the pears with a slotted spoon, and arrange ten pear halves, with rounded sides up, on top of the torte, around the edge with the wide parts of the pears toward the outside. Use the remaining four pear halves to fill in the center. Mix together the cornstarch and water, and stir this mixture into the syrupy juice left in the saucepan. Heat the mixture over medium heat, stirring, until the sauce has thickened. Spread the sauce evenly over the pears, and sprinkle the almonds on top. Bake the torte for 15 minutes.

Let the torte cool before removing it from the pan.

Serves 8

WHEAT-FREE DUTCH APPLE PIE

This apple pie has a rice-flour bottom crust and, instead of a top crust, a crunchy rice-flour topping. The assembled pie needs no baking.

12 cups thinly sliced Red Delicious or
  Golden Delicious apples, peel left on
  (about 6 large apples)
1 cup frozen and thawed apple juice
  concentrate
2 tablespoons ground cinnamon
1/4 teaspoon ground coriander
1 tablespoon cornstarch
Brown Rice Flour Crust prebaked for 12
  minutes (page 156)
Crunchy Brown Rice Flour Topping,
  prebaked (page 156)

In a 4- to 5-quart saucepan, mix together the apples, apple juice, cinnamon, coriander, and cornstarch. Cook the apple slices, covered, over medium heat, stirring occasionally, for about 20 minutes, or until the apple slices are tender. Do not allow the apples to become too soft or fall apart. Spread the apple filling in the prepared crust, and sprinkle the crunchy topping evenly on top.

  Serve the pie warm or cool.

Serves 6 to 8

TART SUMMER FRUIT COBBLER

This deliciously tart, wheat-free dessert is a special summer treat.

14 cups sliced summer fruits (mixed apricots,
  peaches, nectarines, plums)
1 cup frozen and thawed apple juice
  concentrate
1/4 cup cornstarch
1 teaspoon ground cinnamon
1 teaspoon vanilla extract
Double recipe Crunchy Brown Rice Flour-
  Nut Topping (page 158)

Preheat the oven to 375°.

  In a large bowl, mix together the first five ingredients. Spread the sliced fruit evenly in a 9- by 13-inch ovenproof glass baking pan. Sprinkle the topping evenly over the fruit, and bake the cobbler for about 45 minutes, or until the syrup from the fruit bubbles and the topping is brown.

  Serve the cobbler warm or chilled.

Serves 10

Wheat-Free Tart Dutch Apple Pie

Here's a recipe for those who prefer a tart apple pie.

9 cups peeled, sliced pippin apples or other
   tart green apples (about 5 large apples)
1 cup frozen and thawed apple juice
   concentrate
2 tablespoons maple syrup
2 tablespoons ground cinnamon
1/4 teaspoon ground coriander
Brown Rice Flour Crust prebaked for 12
   minutes (page 156)
Crunchy Brown Rice Flour Topping,
   unbaked (page 156)

Preheat the oven to 425°.

In a large bowl, toss together the sliced apples, apple juice, maple syrup, cinnamon, and coriander. Spread the sliced apples in the prepared crust, and pour the juice evenly over the apples. Crumble the topping dough evenly over the apple slices. Cover the pie plate with foil, and pierce the foil in several places with a sharp knife.

Bake the pie for about 50 minutes, or until the apples are tender.

Remove the foil, and bake the pie for 10 to 15 minutes longer, or until the topping is dark golden brown and crunchy.

Serve the pie warm or chilled.

Serves 6 to 8

Apricot Pie

Here's an easy dessert to enjoy during the apricot season.

5 1/2 cups apricots, halved if small, quartered
   if large
1 cup frozen and thawed apple juice
   concentrate
1/4 cup maple syrup
1/4 teaspoon ground coriander
2 tablespoons cornstarch
Brown Rice Flour Crust (page 156)
2 tablespoons chopped walnuts

Preheat the oven to 400°.

In a large saucepan, toss the first five ingredients together. Heat the apricot mixture, stirring occasionally, just until the juice boils and thickens slightly. Remove the pan from the heat. Pour the apricot mixture into the prepared crust, sprinkle the walnuts on top, and bake the pie for 10 minutes.

Let the pie cool, then chill it well before serving.

Serves 6 to 8

Brown Rice Flour Crust

Brown rice flour makes a delicious, crunchy crust that is very easy to prepare.

2/3 cup brown rice flour
1/2 teaspoon baking powder
1 teaspoon ground cinnamon
3 tablespoons frozen and thawed apple juice concentrate
1 tablespoon water
1 tablespoon safflower or canola oil

In a medium bowl, mix together the rice flour, baking powder, and cinnamon. In a small bowl, mix together the apple juice, water, and oil. Stir the juice mixture into the dry ingredients. Mix until the dough is blended.

Press the dough in the bottom and up the sides of a 10-inch ovenproof glass deep-dish pie plate. The dough will be sparse, and it may not completely cover the bottom of the dish. Bake the crust for 12 to 15 minutes, or as directed in the recipe.

Yields 1 10-inch bottom pie crust

Crunchy Brown Rice Flour Topping

This crunchy, sweet topping can be used for any fruit pie, fruit cobbler, or fruit casserole.

1/2 cup brown rice flour
1/4 teaspoon baking powder
3/4 teaspoon ground cinnamon
2 tablespoons frozen and thawed apple juice concentrate
1 tablespoon safflower or canola oil

In a medium bowl, mix together the rice flour, baking powder, and cinnamon. In a small bowl, mix together the apple juice and oil, and stir this mixture into the dry ingredients with a fork. Continue stirring just until the dough is blended.

The topping dough can be either prebaked and then sprinkled over the pie filling, or baked along with the pie. To prebake the topping dough, crumble the dough in a 9-inch round baking pan or pie plate, and bake the dough at 400° for 20 minutes, or until the topping is medium brown and crunchy. Sprinkle the topping over the prepared pie filling.

To bake the topping along with the pie, crumble the dough over the fruit, cover the pie with foil, and pierce the foil in several places. Bake according to the pie recipe. Remove the foil, and brown the topping for 10 to 15 minutes, or until it is medium brown and crunchy.

Yields topping for 1 pie

DELUXE DUTCH APPLE PIE

This apple pie has a crust enriched with chopped pecans or walnuts.

8 cups Red Delicious or Golden Delicious apples, peeled and sliced
1 1/3 cups frozen and thawed apple juice concentrate
2 tablespoons ground cinnamon
1/4 teaspoon ground coriander
1 tablespoon cornstarch
Brown Rice Flour-Nut Crust prebaked for 12 minutes
Crunchy Brown Rice Flour-Nut Topping, unbaked (page 158)

Preheat the oven to 425°.

In a large bowl, toss the apple slices with the apple juice, cinnamon, coriander, and cornstarch. Spread the apple slices evenly in the baked crust, and pour over them any juice left in the bowl.

Sprinkle the topping dough over the apple slices. Cover the pie with foil, crimping the edges. Pierce the foil in several places with a sharp knife, and bake the pie for about 50 minutes, or until the apples are tender. Remove the foil, and bake the pie for 10 to 15 minutes longer, or until the topping is dark golden brown and crunchy.

Serve the pie warm or cool.

Serves 6 to 8

BROWN RICE FLOUR-NUT CRUST

Walnuts or pecans give this wholesome pie crust crunchiness and flavor.

2/3 cup brown rice flour
1/3 cup minced pecans or walnuts
1 teaspoon ground cinnamon
2 tablespoons frozen and thawed apple juice concentrate
1 tablespoon safflower or canola oil

In a medium bowl, mix together the rice flour, nuts, and cinnamon. In a small bowl, mix the apple juice and oil, and stir this mixture into the dry ingredients with a fork. Continue to stir just until the dough is blended. Press the dough in the bottom and 1/2 inch up the sides of a 10-inch ovenproof glass deep-dish pie plate. The dough will be sparse; it may not completely cover the bottom of the dish. Bake the crust at 400° for 12 minutes, or as directed in the pie recipe.

Yields 1 10-inch bottom pie crust

CRUNCHY BROWN RICE FLOUR-NUT TOPPING

This topping can be used on fruit pies and cobblers.

1/2 cup brown rice flour
1/3 cup chopped pecans or walnuts
1 teaspoon ground cinnamon
2 tablespoons frozen and thawed apple juice
 concentrate
1/2 tablespoon safflower or canola oil

In a small bowl, mix together the brown rice flour, nuts, and cinnamon. In another small bowl, mix the apple juice and oil. Stir the apple juice mixture into the dry ingredients with a fork. Continue to stir until the dough is blended.

The topping dough can be baked along with the pie, or it can be prebaked, and then sprinkled over the pie filling. To prebake the dough, spread it evenly in the bottom of a 9-inch round nonstick baking pan, without pressing the dough down. Bake the topping at 400° for 15 minutes, then sprinkle it on top of a raw or poached fruit pie.

Yields topping for 1 10-inch pie

GLAZED POACHED APPLE PIE

This elegant dessert is flavored with pineapple juice and adorned with sliced almonds.

4 to 5 large green apples, peeled and
 quartered
1/2 cup frozen and thawed apple juice
 concentrate
1/4 cup frozen and thawed pineapple juice
 concentrate
2 teaspoons ground cinnamon
1 tablespoon cornstarch
Pineapple-Almond-Brown Rice Crust,
 prebaked (page 159)
1/4 cup sliced almonds

In a 4- to 5-quart covered saucepan, poach the apples in the apple juice, pineapple juice, cinnamon, and cornstarch for 10 minutes, stirring occasionally. Remove the pan from the heat, and allow the apples to steam covered for 12 minutes.

Preheat the oven to 400°.

Arrange the apples, rounded side up, close together in the prebaked pie crust. Spoon the sauce evenly over the apples, then sprinkle the almonds over. Bake the pie for 10 minutes.

Serve the pie warm or cool.

Serves 6

PINEAPPLE-ALMOND-BROWN RICE CRUST

This crust takes only minutes to prepare.

2/3 cup brown rice flour
1 teaspoon ground cinnamon
1/3 cup finely chopped almonds
3 tablespoons frozen and thawed pineapple
   juice concentrate
1 tablespoon safflower or canola oil

Preheat the oven to 400°.

In a medium bowl, mix together the flour, cinnamon, and chopped almonds. In a small bowl, beat the pineapple juice and oil together with a fork. Stir the juice-oil mixture into the dry ingredients with a fork; continue to stir until the dough is blended.

Pat the dough in the bottom and 1/2 inch up the side of a 10-inch ovenproof glass deep-dish pie plate. Bake the crust for 12 minutes.

Yields 1 10-inch bottom crust

DELUXE POACHED PEAR PIE

This wheat-free pie makes a special party treat. It can be made the day before serving.

Dough for Carob-Pecan-Brown Rice Flour
   Crust (page 167)
6 large firm green winter pears, peeled and
   quartered
2/3 cup frozen and thawed apple juice
   concentrate
1 teaspoon lemon juice
Grated zest of 1 lemon
1 tablespoon ground cinnamon
1 teaspoon ground coriander
2 tablespoons cornstarch
2 tablespoons water

Preheat the oven to 400°.

Pat half the dough in the bottom of a 10-inch ovenproof glass deep-dish pie plate. The dough will be sparse. Bake the crust for 12 to 15 minutes, or until it is medium brown. Leave the oven on. While the bottom crust bakes, poach the pears.

In a 4- to 5-quart covered saucepan, over medium heat, cook the pears, covered, in the apple juice, lemon juice, grated lemon zest, and spices, for 10 minutes. Remove the lid of the saucepan, and cook the pears for 5 minutes longer, stirring occasionally. Mix together the cornstarch and water, and gently stir this into the pears. Continue heating and stirring until the syrup thickens.

Arrange the pears on top of the baked crust, and pour the syrup from the saucepan over the pears. Crumble the remaining dough evenly over the pears. Bake the pie for 15 minutes, or until the top crust is brown. Chill the pie before serving.

Serves 8

SUMMER PEAR COBBLER

This cobbler can be served warm or cold.

6 medium firm Bartlett pears, unpeeled, quartered and cored
1/4 cup frozen and thawed apple juice concentrate
1/2 cup frozen and thawed pineapple juice concentrate
2 teaspoons ground cinnamon
1/4 teaspoon ground coriander
Crunchy Brown Rice Flour-Nut Topping, unbaked (page 158)

Preheat the oven to 400°.

Sauté pears in apple juice, pineapple juice, cinnamon, and coriander in a 10-inch nonstick frying pan, over medium heat, only until the pears are tender and the juice is thick and syrupy.

Arrange the pears in an ovenproof glass 9-inch deep-dish pie plate. Spoon the syrup, then crumble the topping dough, evenly over the pears. Bake the cobbler for about 15 minutes, or until the topping is dark golden brown and crunchy.

Serve the cobbler warm or cool.

Serves 6

POACHED PEAR PIE

The pineapple juice and coriander give the poached pears a delicious flavor.

5 firm green winter pears, peeled, halved, and cored
3/4 cup frozen and thawed pineapple juice concentrate
1/8 teaspoon ground coriander
3 tablespoons chopped almonds
Whole Wheat Almond Pineapple Crust (page 172)

Preheat the oven to 400°.

Bake the crust for 10 minutes. Remove it from the oven, but leave the oven on.

In a 4- to 5-quart saucepan, poach the pears, rounded side down, in the pineapple juice and coriander for 10 minutes over medium heat. Turn the pears over carefully, and poach them, uncovered, for 5 minutes longer, or until the syrup thickens.

Arrange eight poached pear halves on the baked crust, with their wider ends toward the outside and their rounded sides up. Cut the last two pear halves in half lengthwise, and arrange these pieces in the center of the pie, overlapping them if necessary. Spoon the syrup remaining in the pan evenly over the pears, and sprinkle the almonds on top. Bake the pie for 10 minutes, or until the almonds are toasted and the pears are light golden brown on top. Serve the pie chilled.

Serves 6

WHEAT-FREE POACHED PEAR-ALMOND PIE

This delicious wheat-free pie may become your favorite in pear season.

4 large firm green pears, peeled and sliced
  into sixteenths
1/2 cup frozen and thawed apple juice
  concentrate
1 teaspoon ground coriander
1 1/2 teaspoons ground cinnamon
1 1/2 tablespoons cornstarch
1 1/2 tablespoons water
Brown Rice Flour Crust (page 156)
1/2 cup sliced almonds

Preheat the oven to 350°.

In a 4- to 5-quart covered saucepan, poach the sliced pears in the apple juice and spices over medium heat, stirring occasionally, for about 12 minutes, or until the pears are tender.

Mix together the cornstarch and water, and stir this mixture into the pot. Stir constantly over medium heat until the juice thickens. Arrange the pears and juice in the prebaked pie crust, and sprinkle the sliced almonds evenly over the top. Bake the pie for about 10 minutes, or until the almonds are light golden brown.

Serves 6

EASY STRAWBERRY-BLUEBERRY PIE

2 boxes fresh strawberries, hulled and halved
  (about 4 cups)
2 cups fresh or frozen (unthawed) blueberries
1 cup frozen and thawed pineapple juice
  concentrate
1/3 cup cornstarch
1/4 teaspoon ground coriander
**Brown Rice Flour Crust, prebaked for 15
  minutes (page 156)**

In a 4- to 5-quart saucepan, mix together the berries, pineapple juice, cornstarch, and coriander until the ingredients are blended. Cook the mixture over medium heat, stirring frequently until it thickens and turns a dark red-purple. Remove the pan from the heat.

Fill the prepared crust with the berry filling, and chill the pie well before serving.

Serves 6

GLAZED FRESH STRAWBERRY PIE

In strawberry season, this lovely and refreshing pie is one you will want to make more than once.

3 baskets fresh strawberries, hulled (about 2 3/4 cups)
1/4 cup cornstarch
1 cup frozen and thawed apple juice concentrate
Brown Rice Flour-Nut Crust (page 157)

In a food processor or blender, purée 1 basket of strawberries with the cornstarch. Put the mixture into a 3-quart saucepan, and stir in the apple juice. Cook the purée over medium heat, stirring frequently, until the glaze comes to a full boil and becomes thick and shiny. Remove the pan from the heat, and let the mixture cool.

Put the remaining strawberries into a large bowl. Pour the glaze over them, and gently coat the strawberries with the glaze. Arrange the glazed strawberries in the prepared pie crust. Pour the remaining glaze evenly over the top, cover the pie loosely with plastic wrap, and chill it well before serving.

Serves 6

Note: For a darker red glaze, use 2 1/2 cups hulled strawberries and 1/4 cup fresh or frozen blueberries.

CRUSTLESS GELLED STRAWBERRY BANANA PIE

The agar (a kind of seaweed) in this low-calorie pie has natural gelling properties.

2 cups water
1/4 cup agar flakes
1/2 cup frozen (unthawed) apple juice concentrate
1/2 cup frozen (unthawed) pineapple juice concentrate, unthawed
2 baskets fresh strawberries, hulled and sliced lengthwise into thirds or fourths
1 medium banana, sliced 1/4 inch thick

In a small saucepan, bring the water and agar flakes to a boil, then lower the heat and simmer for 7 minutes, or until the agar flakes are dissolved. Stir in the frozen apple and pineapple juices.

Arrange the strawberry slices in a 9-inch glass deep-dish pie plate. Pour the agar mixture into the pie plate. Decorate the top of the pie with the banana slices. Cover the pie with plastic wrap, and chill it well before serving.

Serves 6

CRUSTLESS GELLED MIXED-FRUIT PIE

This beautiful pie can be made with any kind of fresh fruit, or with frozen fruit or berries.

2 cups water
1/4 cup agar flakes
1/2 cup frozen (unthawed) apple juice concentrate, unthawed
1/2 cup frozen (unthawed) pineapple juice concentrate, unthawed
1 medium banana, sliced 1/4-inch thick
1 cup fresh blueberries
1 cup fresh raspberries

In a small saucepan, bring the water and agar flakes to a boil. Lower the heat, and simmer the mixture, stirring occasionally, for 7 minutes, or until the agar flakes are dissolved. Remove the pan from the heat, and stir in the apple and pineapple juices.

Arrange the banana slices around the edge of a 9-inch glass deep-dish pie plate. Fill the center with blueberries and raspberries. Gently pour the agar-juice mixture over the fruit. Cover the plate loosely, and chill the pie until it is set.

Serves 6

CRUSTLESS GELLED BANANA-BLUEBERRY PIE

If you keep blueberries in your freezer, you can make this pie at any time of the year.

2 cups water
3 tablespoons agar flakes
1/2 cup frozen (unthawed) apple juice concentrate
1/2 cup frozen (unthawed) pineapple juice concentrate
3 medium bananas, sliced 1/4 inch thick
1 cup fresh or frozen blueberries

In a small saucepan, bring the water and agar flakes to a boil, then simmer them, stirring occasionally, for 7 minutes, or until the agar flakes are dissolved. Stir in the apple and pineapple juices.

In a 9-inch glass deep-dish pie plate, spread the banana slices evenly, and sprinkle the blueberries on top. Gently pour the agar-juice mixture evenly over the fruit. Chill the pie well before serving.

Serves 6

CRUSTLESS GELLED KIWI-BANANA PIE

Follow the recipe for Gelled Mixed-Fruit Pie, omitting the blueberries and raspberries, and adding in their place six peeled, sliced kiwis and another medium sliced banana.

GELLED FRESH PEACH PIE

This summer pie is lovely to look at. The crust stays crunchy.

Dough for Brown Rice Flour Crust (page 156)
1 tablespoon frozen and thawed apple juice concentrate
1/2 cup frozen and thawed apple juice concentrate
2 cups water
1/4 cup agar flakes
1/2 cup frozen and thawed pineapple juice concentrate, unthawed
4 large ripe peaches, thinly sliced with peels on

Preheat the oven to 400°.

With moistened fingers, press the pie crust dough in the bottom and 1/2 inch up the sides of a 10-inch glass deep-dish pie plate. Spread 1 tablespoon apple juice over the bottom of the crust to serve as a glaze. Bake the crust for 15 minutes, or until it is brown around the edges.

In a small saucepan, bring the apple juice, water, and agar flakes to a boil. Lower the heat, and simmer, stirring occasionally, for 5 to 7 minutes, until the agar flakes are dissolved. Stir in the frozen pineapple juice concentrate. Let the mixture cool until it begins to gel.

Spread the peaches evenly in the pie plate, and pour the agar-juice mixture over them, covering all the slices. Chill the pie well before serving.

Serves 6 to 8

EASY WHEAT-FREE PEACH PIE

This pie can be served warm or cold.

Dough for Brown Rice Flour-Nut Crust (page 157)
3 to 4 large ripe peaches or nectarines, sliced thinly with peels on
1/3 cup frozen and thawed apple juice concentrate
1/4 teaspoon ground coriander

Preheat the oven to 400°.

Pat three-quarters of the dough in the bottom of a 9-inch ovenproof glass deep-dish pie plate. In a medium bowl, toss the peaches with the apple juice and coriander. Spread the sliced peaches on top of the crust, and pour the juice over. Crumble the remaining crust dough, and sprinkle it evenly over the peaches.

Cover the pie with foil, and pierce the foil in several places. Bake the pie for about 30 minutes, or until the peaches are tender. Remove the foil, and bake the pie uncovered for 10 minutes longer.

Serve the pie warm or cool.

Serves 4

Easy Wheat-Free Apple-Pecan Pie

The "crust" for this pie is simply oat-bran cereal flakes. Use a fruit-sweetened, salt-free brand.

1 cup oat bran cereal flakes
8 cups thinly sliced apples (about 6 large apples)
1/2 cup frozen and thawed apple juice concentrate
1 tablespoon ground cinnamon
1/8 teaspoon ground nutmeg
1/2 teaspoon ground coriander
1/2 cup chopped pecans

Preheat the oven to 400°.

Spread the cereal flakes in the bottom of a 10-inch ovenproof glass deep-dish pie plate. In a large bowl, toss the apple slices in the apple juice and spices. Spread the apple slices on top of the cereal, and pour the juice over the apples. Sprinkle the chopped pecans evenly on top of the apple slices.

Cover the pie plate with foil, and pierce several holes in the foil with a sharp knife. Bake the pie for about 40 minutes, or until the apples are tender. Remove the foil, and bake the pie for 8 to 10 minutes longer.

Serve the pie warm or cool.

Serves 6 to 8

Crowd-Size Wheat-Free Apple Casserole

Here is a tasty, easily prepared dessert to serve for parties or to take to a potluck brunch or supper.

Dough for Brown Rice Flour-Nut Crust (page 157)
12 medium apples, thinly sliced with peels on
1 cup frozen and thawed apple juice concentrate
2 tablespoons ground cinnamon
1 teaspoon ground coriander
1 teaspoon lemon juice
Double recipe Crunchy Brown Rice Flour-Nut Topping (page 158)

Preheat the oven to 400°.

Pat the crust dough in the bottom of a 9- by 13-inch ovenproof glass baking dish. Bake the crust for 10 minutes. Leave the oven on.

Put the sliced apples into a large bowl. Stir in the remaining ingredients, and toss well. Spread the apples in the prebaked crust, and pour the juice over the apple slices. Sprinkle the topping evenly over the apples.

Cover the dish with foil, and pierce the foil in several places with a sharp knife. Bake the pie for about 1 hour, or until the apple slices are tender. Remove the foil, and bake the pie for 10 minutes longer.

Serve the pie warm or cool.

Serves 12

Wheat-Free Fancy Yam-Pecan Pie

This beautiful, wholesome pie would grace any holiday table.

Dough for Brown Rice Flour-Nut Crust (page 157)
3 cups mashed cooked yams
1/2 cup maple syrup
2 tablespoons cornstarch
2 teaspoons ground cinnamon
1/2 teaspoon ground coriander
1/2 cup chopped pecans
24 pecan halves
1 tablespoon maple syrup for top

Preheat the oven to 400°.

Prepare the crust using chopped pecans. Press the dough in the bottom and up the sides of a 9-inch ovenproof glass deep-dish pie plate. Bake the crust for 12 minutes. Reduce the oven temperature to 350°.

Whip the yams in a food processor or mixer until they are light and fluffy. Add 1/2 cup maple syrup, the cornstarch, and the spices, and blend until the mixture is smooth. Stir in the chopped pecans. Fill the prepared crust with the yam mixture. Decorate the top with pecan halves, and drizzle 1 tablespoon maple syrup evenly over the top. Bake the pie for 25 minutes, or until the filling is set but still soft.

Serve the pie warm, cool, or chilled.

Serves 6

Mocha Tofu Pie

This wheat-free dessert may well become a favorite of yours.

1 unbaked 10-inch Carob-Pecan-Brown Rice Flour Crust, prebaked for 15 minutes (page 167)
2 14-ounce packages soft tofu, rinsed and well drained
2/3 cup hot water
1/4 cup carob powder
2 tablespoons instant coffee substitute
1 teaspoon dark molasses
2 teaspoons vanilla extract
1/2 cup maple syrup
3 tablespoons cornstarch
1 teaspoon cider vinegar

Preheat the oven to 350°.

Partially bake the crust for 15 minutes. Reduce the oven temperature to 325°.

In a food processor or blender, blend the well-drained tofu until it is smooth and creamy. Put the tofu into a large bowl. Mix together the hot water, carob powder, and coffee substitute. Stir until the carob powder is dissolved. Blend the carob mixture in a food processor or blender with the five remaining ingredients, and add this mixture to the tofu. Stir until the ingredients are well blended.

Pour the tofu filling into the prebaked crust. Bake the pie for 35 minutes.

Let the pie cool, then chill it well before serving.

Serves 6 to 8

CAROB-PECAN-BROWN RICE FLOUR CRUST

This nutty, wheat-free crust is flavored with carob and vanilla.

3 tablespoons water
1 1/2 tablespoons safflower or canola oil
1/2 teaspoon vanilla extract
2 tablespoons maple syrup
1/2 teaspoon dark molasses
1 cup brown rice flour
1 tablespoon carob powder
1/4 cup chopped pecans

In a medium bowl, blend together the first five ingredients. Mix together the rice flour, carob powder, and pecans. Add the dry ingredients to the liquid, and stir with a fork until the dough is blended. Pat the dough in the bottom of a 9- or 10-inch ovenproof glass deep-dish pie plate. Bake the crust at 400° for 15 minutes, or according to the pie recipe.

Yields 1 9- or 10-inch bottom pie crust

CREAMY CAROB MOUSSE PIE

This rich-tasting, high-protein mousse pie makes a lovely dessert for any meal.

3 14-ounce packages soft tofu, well rinsed
1 unbaked 9-inch Carob-Pecan-Brown Rice
   Flour Crust, prebaked for 15 minutes
1/2 cup carob powder
1 1/4 cups maple syrup
1 teaspoon vanilla extract
1 teaspoon dark molasses
1/4 cup cornstarch

Preheat the oven to 400°.

Bake the crust for 15 minutes. Reduce the oven temperature to 325°.

Cut a piece of cheesecloth large enough to hold the tofu. Place the tofu in the center, and draw up the cheesecloth around the tofu. Tie the top, or secure with a rubber band. Squeeze as much liquid as possible from the tofu. Drain the tofu, still in the cheesecloth, in a colander for at least 1 hour.

In a food processor or blender, blend the tofu until it is smooth and creamy. Add the remaining ingredients, and blend again. Fill the pie shell with the mixture, and smooth the top. Bake the pie for 25 minutes.

Let the pie cool, then chill it well before serving.

Serves 6 to 8

Tofu "Cheese" Pie with Blueberry Glaze

This healthful, vegetarian version of cheesecake is very easy to prepare.

2 14-ounce packages soft tofu, well rinsed
2 tablespoons frozen and thawed apple juice concentrate
3 tablespoons frozen and thawed pineapple juice concentrate
1 tablespoon lemon juice
Grated zest of 1 lemon
1/2 cup maple syrup
3 tablespoons cornstarch
2 teaspoons vanilla extract
1/4 teaspoon almond extract
1 10-inch Oat-Pecan Crust, prebaked for 15 minutes
2 cups fresh or frozen (unthawed) blueberries
1/3 cup frozen and thawed apple juice concentrate
2 tablespoons cornstarch

Preheat the oven to 325°. Drain tofu well for at least 30 minutes.

In a food processor or blender, blend the tofu with the next eight ingredients, in batches, if necessary, until the mixture is smooth and creamy. Pour the mixture over the Oat-Pecan Crust, and bake the pie for 25 minutes.

Let the pie cool for about 15 minutes. Meanwhile prepare the glaze.

In a medium saucepan, mix together the blueberries, apple juice, and cornstarch. Cook them over medium heat, stirring frequently, until the mixture thickens. Stir gently to keep the berries

whole. Remove the pan from the heat, and gently spread the blueberry glaze over the pie.

Serves 6 to 8

Oat-Pecan Crust

This simple crust of ground oats and pecans takes only minutes to prepare.

1 cup rolled oats
1/4 cup pecans
1 tablespoon frozen and thawed pineapple juice concentrate
1 teaspoon ground cinnamon
1/4 teaspoon ground coriander

Preheat the oven to 325°.

Blend all the ingredients in a food processor or blender. Pat the dough into the bottom of a 9- or 10-inch ovenproof glass deep-dish pie plate. Bake the crust for 15 minutes.

Remove the crust from the oven, and fill the pie according to the recipe.

Yields 1 9- or 10-inch bottom pie crust

Lemon Tofu Pie

The crust of this pie is made of chopped granola.

2 14-ounce packages soft tofu, well drained

Crust

1 cup fruit juice-sweetened granola
1 tablespoon frozen and thawed orange juice concentrate
2 tablespoons water

3 tablespoons frozen and thawed orange juice concentrate
3 tablespoons lemon juice
Grated zest of 1 large lemon
1/2 cup maple syrup
3 tablespoons cornstarch
1 teaspoon cider vinegar

Drain the tofu in a colander for at least 30 minutes.

Preheat the oven to 325°.

Coarsely chop the granola, with the orange juice and water, in a food processor. Pat the dough in the bottom of a 9-inch ovenproof glass deep-dish pie plate. Bake the crust for about 15 minutes, or until the crust is set. Leave the oven on.

Press the tofu to release any remaining liquid. Blend the tofu and the remaining ingredients in a food processor until the mixture is smooth and creamy. Pour the mixture over the prepared crust, and bake the pie for 25 minutes.

Let the pie cool, then chill it well before serving.

Serves 6 to 8

Note: You can use 3 tablespoons fresh orange juice in place of frozen and thawed orange juice concentrate and water.

Lemon Pudding Pie

Serve this pie with Lemon Tofu Custard Sauce.

Unbaked 9-inch Whole Wheat-Pecan Crust (page 172)
1/3 cup frozen and thawed orange juice concentrate
2/3 cup frozen and thawed apple juice concentrate
1/3 cup cornstarch
1 1/4 cups cold water
1/3 cup lemon juice
Grated zest of 1 lemon
1 tablespoon safflower or canola oil

Preheat the oven to 400°.

Bake the crust for 15 minutes, or until it is brown around the edges.

In a medium saucepan, mix together the orange juice, apple juice, cornstarch, and cold water. Bring the mixture to a boil over medium heat, stirring constantly. Heat and stir the mixture until it thickens. Remove the pan from the heat and stir in lemon juice, grated zest, and oil. Pour the pudding into the prepared crust.

Let the pie cool, and chill it well before serving it with Lemon Tofu Custard Sauce spooned over each slice.

Serves 6

LEMON TOFU PIE
WITH LEMON GLAZE

This is the perfect dessert for lemon lovers, especially those who are allergic to wheat.

Dough for Brown Rice Flour Crust or Brown-Rice Flour-Nut Crust (pages 156 and 157)

Filling
1 14-ounce package soft tofu, rinsed and well drained
1 cup frozen and thawed apple juice concentrate
2 tablespoons cornstarch
2 tablespoons lemon juice
Grated zest of 1 lemon
1/4 teaspoon ground coriander
1/2 teaspoon cider vinegar

Glaze
2/3 cup frozen and thawed apple juice concentrate
1/3 cup water
1 tablespoon cornstarch
2 tablespoons lemon juice
Grated zest of 1/2 lemon

Preheat the oven to 400°.

Pat the dough in the bottom and 1 inch up the side of a 9-inch ovenproof glass deep-dish pie plate. Bake the crust for 15 minutes. Reduce the oven temperature to 325°.

In a food processor or blender, blend the filling ingredients until the mixture is very smooth. Fill the pie shell with the filling, and bake the pie for 25 minutes exactly.

When the pie is baked, make the glaze: In a medium saucepan, mix together the apple juice, water, and cornstarch. Cook the mixture over medium heat, stirring constantly, until it thickens and comes to a boil. Remove the pan from the heat, and stir in the lemon juice and zest. Spread the glaze over the pie while both pie and glaze are still warm.

Let the pie cool, then chill it well before serving.

Serves 4 to 6

LEMON TOFU CUSTARD SAUCE

Spoon this delicious sauce over Lemon Pudding Pie, fresh fruit, baked apples, or cake.

1 14-ounce package soft tofu, well rinsed
1 cup frozen and thawed pineapple juice concentrate
3 tablespoons cornstarch
1/4 cup water
1 cup sliced bananas (about 1 1/2 large bananas)
2 tablespoons lemon juice
Grated zest of 1 lemon

Drain the tofu in a colander for at least 30 minutes. Press it to release any remaining liquid, and set it aside.

Heat the pineapple juice, cornstarch, and water in a medium saucepan over medium heat, stirring occasionally, until the mixture thickens.

In a food processor or blender, blend the hot mixture with the drained tofu, sliced bananas, lemon juice, and grated lemon zest until the sauce is smooth and creamy.

Chill the sauce well before serving.

Serves 6 to 8

WHEAT-FREE CREAMY LEMON PIE

Dough for Brown Rice Flour Crust or
   Brown Rice Flour-Nut Crust (pages 156 and
   157)
2 14-ounce packages soft tofu, well rinsed
1/4 cup frozen and thawed orange juice
   concentrate
2/3 cup frozen and thawed apple juice
   concentrate
1/4 cup maple syrup
Grated zest of 1 large lemon
1 teaspoon cider vinegar
3 tablespoons cornstarch
3 tablespoons water
1/4 cup lemon juice

Preheat the oven to 400°.

Pat the dough in the the bottom of a 9-inch ovenproof glass deep-dish pie plate. Bake the crust for 15 minutes. Remove it from the oven, and set it aside.

Cut a piece of cheesecloth large enough to hold the tofu. Place the tofu in the center, draw up the cheesecloth around the tofu, and tie the corners together. Squeeze as much liquid as possible from the tofu, then drain the tofu, still tied in the cheesecloth, in a colander for 1 hour.

In a small saucepan, mix together the juices, maple syrup, lemon zest, and vinegar. Bring the mixture to a boil over medium heat, and let it simmer for 5 minutes. In a small cup, mix the cornstarch and water together. Stir this mixture into the saucepan. Heat the sauce, stirring, until it thickens.

In a food processor or blender, blend the tofu, the hot sauce, and the lemon juice until smooth and creamy. Spread it in the prepared crust.

Chill the pie well before serving.

Serves 6

DATE-SWEETENED TOFU "CHEESE" PIE

This pie is wheat-free.

2 14-ounce packages soft tofu
1 1/4 cups pitted dates
1 cup water
2 tablespoons lemon juice
Grated zest of 1 lemon
1/4 teaspoon almond extract
2 teaspoons vanilla extract
1/4 teaspoon ground nutmeg
3 tablespoons cornstarch
1 teaspoon cider vinegar
Oat-Pecan Crust (page 168)
Generous sprinkle of ground nutmeg

Press the tofu to release any remaining liquid, and set it aside.

Preheat the oven to 325°.

In a medium saucepan, cook the dates in the water, over medium heat, uncovered, for 10 minutes. Purée the mixture in a food processor or blender, and put the purée into a large bowl.

In a food processor or blender, blend the tofu, lemon juice, lemon zest, almond extract, vanilla extract, nutmeg, cornstarch, and vinegar until the mixture is smooth and creamy. Stir the mixture into the puréed dates.

Pour the tofu filling into the prepared crust, and sprinkle the top of the pie with nutmeg. Bake the pie for 25 minutes.

Chill the pie well before serving.

Serves 6

WHOLE WHEAT-PECAN CRUST

2/3 cup whole wheat pastry flour
1/2 teaspoon baking powder
1/3 cup minced pecans
1 1/2 teaspoons ground cinnamon
1/3 cup frozen and thawed apple juice
  concentrate
1 tablespoon safflower or canola oil

In a medium bowl, mix together the first four ingredients. In a small bowl, mix together the apple juice and oil, and stir this mixture into the dry ingredients with a fork. Stir until the dough is blended.

Pat the dough evenly in the bottom and 2 inches up the side of a 9- or 10-inch deep-dish ovenproof glass pie plate. (If the dough is sticky, moisten your hands.)

Bake the crust at 400° for about 10 minutes, until it is brown around the edges, or as directed in the pie recipe.

Yields 1 9- or 10-inch bottom pie crust

WHOLE WHEAT-ALMOND-PINEAPPLE CRUST

Follow the recipe for Whole Wheat-Pecan Crust, substituting minced almonds for the minced pecans, and frozen and thawed pineapple juice concentrate for the apple juice concentrate.

Yields 1 9- or 10-inch bottom pie crust

DATE-ALMOND-BROWN RICE PUDDING

Serve this old-fashioned dessert chilled with Easy Cashew Cream or Vanilla Cashew Cream.

1 cup pitted dates
1/2 cup chopped almonds, pecans, or walnuts
1/2 cup water
4 cups cooked brown rice
2 tablespoons cornstarch
1 teaspoon baking powder
1/3 cup frozen and thawed apple juice
  concentrate
1 1/2 cups water
1 tablespoon ground cinnamon
1 teaspoon ground coriander
2 teaspoons vanilla extract
1/2 cup black raisins

Preheat the oven to 375°.

In a food processor or blender, mince the dates and nuts in 1/2 cup water. Put the mixture into a large bowl. Add the remaining ingredients, and stir until until the batter is blended.

Bake the pudding in a 3-quart ovenproof soufflé dish for about 40 minutes, or until the pudding is set.

Let the pudding cool, then chill it well before serving. Spoon Easy Cashew Cream or Vanilla Cashew Cream over each helping.

Serves 10

EASY CASHEW CREAM

This cashew-date purée tastes delicious over Simply Delicious Baked Apples and Date-Almond-Brown Rice Pudding.

1/2 cup raw cashew pieces
2/3 cup cold water
4 pitted dates
8 ice cubes

In a food processor, blend the first three ingredients with four ice cubes, then add four more ice cubes and blend again.

Serve the sauce chilled.

Yields 1 1/3 cups

VANILLA CASHEW CREAM

Follow the recipe for Easy Cashew Cream, but blend in 2 tablespoons maple syrup in place of the dates, and add 1 teaspoon vanilla.

Serve the sauce chilled, with any fruit pie or cobbler.

Yields 1 1/2 cups

STRAWBERRY TOFU MOUSSE

This mousse can also be used as a cake filling and frosting.

1 basket fresh strawberries, hulled
1 14-ounce package tofu, rinsed and well drained
1 cup frozen and thawed apple juice concentrate
1/3 cup agar flakes (natural sea vegetable gelatin)
1/4 cup water
2 ice cubes

Reserve four large strawberries to garnish the mousse.

In a food processor or blender, blend the tofu with the remaining strawberries until the mixture is creamy and smooth. Put the mixture into a medium bowl.

In a small saucepan, mix together the apple juice, agar flakes, and water. Heat the mixture to boiling over medium heat, then reduce the heat to low, and simmer the mixture for 5 minutes. Remove the pan from the heat. Stir in the ice cubes until they are melted, then blend the agar-juice mixture into the tofu mixture. Put the mousse into a 1-quart soufflé dish or four individual dessert cups.

Chill the mousse well before serving. Slice the reserved strawberries, and garnish each serving with some of the slices.

Serves 4

CREAMY CAROB
MOUSSE PUDDING

This can also be used as a cake filling or frosting.

2 14-ounce packages soft tofu, well rinsed
1/4 cup carob powder
1/2 cup maple syrup
1/2 teaspoon vanilla extract
1/2 teaspoon cider vinegar
1 teaspoon molasses
1 teaspoon instant coffee substitute

Cut a piece of cheesecloth large enough to hold the tofu. Place the tofu in the center of the cheesecloth and draw up the cheesecloth around the tofu. Tie the top, and squeeze as much liquid from the tofu as possible. Drain the tofu, still in the cheesecloth, in a colander for at least 1 hour.

In a food processor or blender, blend the tofu until it is smooth and creamy. Add the remaining ingredients, and blend until the mixture is smooth. Pour the pudding into four small bowls or cups, and chill the pudding well before serving.

Serves 4

CAROB MOCHA MOUSSE
WITH SLICED ALMONDS

This mousse is sweetened with barley malt.

2 14-ounce packages soft tofu, well rinsed
1/4 cup carob powder
1/2 cup barley malt
2 teaspoons dark molasses
2 teaspoons instant coffee substitute
1 teaspoon almond extract
1/2 teaspoon cider vinegar
1/4 cup sliced almonds

Cut a piece of cheesecloth large enough to hold the tofu. Place the tofu in the center of the cheesecloth, and draw up the cheesecloth around the tofu. Tie the corners, and squeeze as much liquid from the tofu as possible. Drain the tofu, still in the cheesecloth, in a colander for at least 1 hour.

In a food processor or blender, blend the tofu until it is very smooth and creamy. Add the next six ingredients, and blend until the mixture is smooth.

Fill four stemmed dessert glasses with the thick mousse, and sprinkle 1 tablespoon sliced almonds over each serving.

Chill the mousse well before serving.

Serves 4

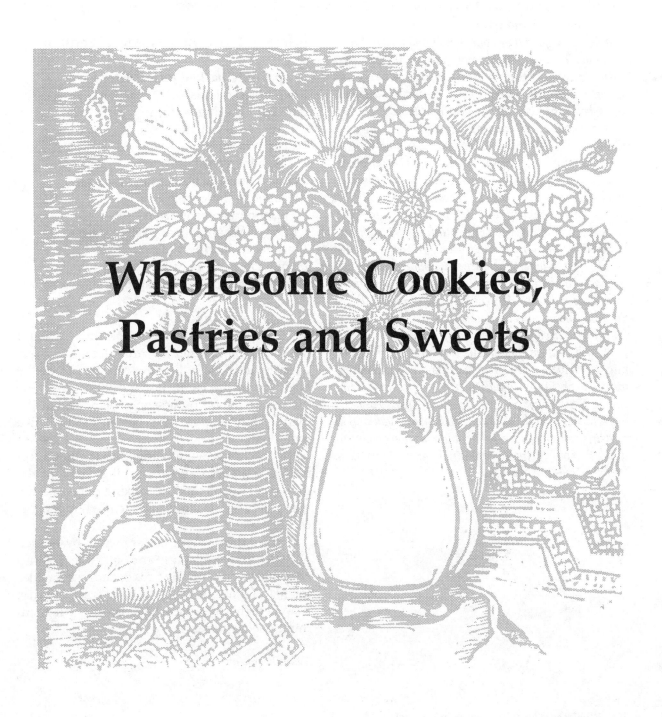

Wholesome Cookies, Pastries and Sweets

Wouldn't it be wonderful if cookies, pastries, and candies could be good for you? Well, they can be. In this chapter you will find recipes for home-baked goodies that you and your loved ones can enjoy without worrying about sugar, cholesterol, fat, or salt. The pure natural ingredients used in our cookies, pastries, and sweets will keep you feeling good, because eating these home-baked goods is eating healthful food.

Here you'll find cookies made with fruit—like Petite Date-Carob-Pecan Bars, Easy Granola-Banana Squares, and Gingerbread Raisin Bars—and others made with vegetables—such as Wheat-Free Unsweetened Carrot-Spice Cookies, Wheat-Free Squash-Oat Bran-Spice Cookies, and Brown Rice-Yam-Pecan Cookies. Brown rice flour or oatmeal takes the place of wheat flour in many of these cookie recipes.

For pastry-lovers, here are wholesome, mouth-watering recipes for such treats as Sweet Yam-Cinnamon-Raisin Buns, Apricot-Nut Mini Sweet Rolls, Swirled Orange-Pecan Pastries, and Prune-filled or Jam-filled Three-Cornered Pastries.

You'll find candy and other sweets here, too. You might try Date Carob Fudge Balls, Frozen Bananas with Carob Fudge Sauce, Date-Sunflower-Sesame Candy Squares, or Simply Delicious Baked Apples.

Whichever of these recipes you choose, you will be pleasing not only your palate, but also your body. As with all of our recipes, none contain animal products; many recipes are also wheat-free.

MOIST CAROB PECAN BROWNIES

1 cup firmly packed pitted dates
1 cup black raisins
1 1/2 cups boiling water
3/4 cup carob powder
2/3 cup soy milk
2 teaspoons vanilla extract
2 tablespoons safflower or canola oil
2 teaspoons dark molasses
1/2 teaspoon cider vinegar
1 1/2 cups whole wheat pastry flour
2 teaspoons baking soda
1/2 cup chopped pecans
1/4 cup chopped pecans for top

Preheat the oven to 400°.

In a medium saucepan, cook the dates and raisins in boiling water for 5 minutes, uncovered, over medium heat. Remove the pan from the heat, stir in the carob powder, and purée the mixture in a food processor or blender. Put the mixture into a large bowl. Stir in the next five ingredients.

In another bowl, mix together the flour and baking soda, and add them all at once to the date-raisin-carob mixture, mixing only until the batter is blended. Fold in 1/2 cup chopped pecans.

Spread the brownie batter in a 10- by 15-inch nonstick jelly roll pan, and sprinkle 1/4 cup chopped pecans on the top. Bake the brownies for 10 to 12 minutes or until layer is set, but dry.

When the brownies have cooled, cut them into 2-inch squares.

Yields 36 brownies

PETITE DATE-CAROB-PECAN BARS

These moist brownies are our favorite. Sometimes we eat them straight from the freezer.

4 cups firmly packed pitted dates
2 cups water
1 cup carob powder
3/4 cup water
1 tablespoon vanilla extract
2 tablespoons safflower or canola oil
2 teaspoons dark molasses
1 teaspoon cider vinegar
2 cups whole wheat pastry flour
2 teaspoons baking powder
1 teaspoon baking soda
2 teaspoons instant coffee substitute
2 tablespoons cornstarch
1 1/2 cups chopped pecans

Preheat the oven to 400°.

In a medium saucepan, bring the dates and water to a boil, uncovered. Lower the heat, and simmer the dates for 8 minutes. Remove the pan from the heat, and stir in the carob powder. Purée this mixture in a food processor or blender, and put it into a large mixing bowl. Stir in the next five ingredients.

In another bowl, mix together the flour, baking powder, soda, coffee substitute, and cornstarch. Fold in the nuts. Stir just until the batter is blended.

Spread the batter evenly in a 10- by 15-inch nonstick jelly-roll pan, and bake for 15 to 18 minutes, or until the layer is set, but not dry. The batter will rise about 1/2 inch while baking.

Let the cake cool, then cut it into 1- by 1 1/2-inch bars. Store them in the refrigerator or freezer.

Yields 100

CAROB PECAN COOKIES

These date-sweetened, pecan-topped cookies freeze well.

1 1/2 cups pitted dates, firmly packed down
1 cup water
1/2 cup carob powder
1 teaspoon dark molasses
1 tablespoon safflower or canola oil
2 teaspoons vanilla extract
1 teaspoon instant coffee substitute
1 cup whole wheat pastry flour
1 1/2 teaspoons baking soda
24 raw pecan halves

Preheat the oven to 400°.

In a medium saucepan, bring the dates and water to a boil. Simmer the dates, uncovered, for 5 minutes. Remove the pan from the heat, and stir in the next five ingredients. Purée the mixture in a food processor or blender, and put it into a large bowl.

In another bowl, mix together the flour and baking soda. Add them to the date-carob mixture, stirring only until the batter is blended. Drop the batter by rounded teaspoonfuls onto a nonstick baking sheet. Press one pecan half securely into the center of each cookie. Bake the cookies for about 10 minutes.

Yields 24 cookies

Wholesome Cookies, Pastries and Sweets 177

FRUIT-SWEETENED CAROB-WALNUT COOKIES

These cookies taste best right out of the freezer.

1/2 cup firmly packed pitted dates
1/2 cup black raisins
1/2 cup boiling water
1/2 cup carob powder
1/2 cup boiling water
1/2 teaspoon cider vinegar
1 teaspoon vanilla extract
1 tablespoon safflower or canola oil
1 1/2 teaspoons dark molasses
3/4 cup whole wheat flour
1 teaspoon baking soda
1/2 cup chopped walnuts

Preheat the oven to 400°.

In a medium saucepan, cook the dates and raisins in 1/2 cup boiling water, uncovered, over medium heat for 8 minutes. Stir in the carob powder. Purée the date-carob mixture in a food processor or blender, and put it into a large bowl. Stir in the next five ingredients until blended.

In another bowl, mix together the flour, baking soda, and walnuts. Add this mixture to the date-carob mixture, stirring only until the batter is blended.

Drop the batter by heaping teaspoonfuls onto two nonstick baking sheets. Bake the cookies for 15 minutes.

Yields 36 cookies

Note: You can omit the chopped walnuts, and instead lightly press a pecan half into the center of each cookie.

CAROB-PEPPERMINT-PECAN-RICE COOKIES

These mint-flavored cookies are wheat-free and very easy to prepare.

1/3 cup carob powder
1/3 cup boiling water
1 teaspoon dark molasses
1 teaspoon vanilla extract
1 tablespoon safflower or canola oil
1/2 teaspoon peppermint extract
2/3 cup frozen and thawed apple juice concentrate
2 tablespoons frozen and thawed pineapple juice concentrate
1/3 cup water
1 1/2 cups brown rice flour
1 teaspoon baking powder
1/2 cup chopped pecans

Preheat the oven to 400°.

In a large bowl, blend the carob powder with the boiling water. Stir in the next seven ingredients. In another bowl, mix together the rice flour, baking powder, and pecans. Add this mixture to the carob-juice mixture, and stir only until the batter is smooth.

Drop the batter by heaping tablespoonfuls, three across and three down, on two nonstick baking sheets. (These cookies spread out quite a bit.) Bake the cookies for 10 minutes.

Yields 18 cookies

WHEAT-FREE ORANGE-OAT BRAN COOKIES

These orange-flavored cookies are full of chewy oat bran, raisins, and walnuts.

1/2 cup frozen and thawed orange juice
   concentrate
2 tablespoons safflower or canola oil
2 tablespoons water
1 cup brown rice flour
2 teaspoons baking powder
1 cup oat bran
1/2 cup black raisins
1/4 cup chopped walnuts

Preheat the oven to 400°.

   In a medium bowl, mix together the orange juice, oil, and water. In another bowl, mix together the rice flour and baking powder, and add these to the orange juice mixture. Stir only until the batter is blended. Fold in the oat bran, raisins, and walnuts.

   Shape the dough into 1 1/2-inch round cookies and place the cookies on nonstick baking sheets. If the dough is too sticky, moisten your hands with a little water.

   Bake the cookies for 15 minutes, or until they are light brown.

Yields 36 cookies

WHEAT-FREE UNSWEETENED OAT BRAN-SPICE CRACKERS

These cookies are spicy but completely free of any sweeteners.

1 cup water
2 tablespoons safflower or canola oil
Grated zest of 1 lemon
Grated zest of 1 orange
1 cup brown rice flour
2 teaspoons baking powder
1 teaspoon ground cinnamon
1/4 teaspoon ground nutmeg
1/4 teaspoon ground ginger
1/8 teaspoon ground cloves
1/4 teaspoon ground coriander
1/4 teaspoon sea salt
1 cup oat bran
2 tablespoons sunflower seeds
2 tablespoons sesame seeds

Preheat the oven to 400°.

   In a medium bowl, mix the water, the oil, and the lemon and orange zests. In a small bowl, mix together the next eight dry ingredients. Add the dry ingredients to the liquid, stirring only until the batter is blended. Fold in the oat bran and seeds.

   Drop the batter by rounded teaspoonfuls onto two nonstick baking sheets. Bake the cookies for 25 minutes, or until they are brown.

Yields 24 cookies

WHEAT-FREE UNSWEETENED CARROT-SPICE COOKIES

These cookies have only carrots for sweetening.

3 large carrots (about 1/2 pound), peeled and cut into thick slices
1 cup water
2 tablespoons safflower or canola oil
Grated zest of 1 lemon
1 cup brown rice flour
2 teaspoons baking powder
1 teaspoon ground cinnamon
1/4 teaspoon ground nutmeg
1/4 teaspoon ground ginger
1/4 teaspoon ground cloves
1/4 teaspoon ground coriander
1 cup oat bran
1/2 cup rolled oats
1/2 cup chopped walnuts

In a medium covered saucepan, bring the carrots and water to a boil. Lower the heat, and simmer the carrots, covered, for about 15 minutes, or until the carrots are tender.

Preheat the oven to 400°.

Drain the carrots and reserve the liquid. You will need 3/4 cup liquid altogether. If less liquid remains, add water to make up the difference. Purée the carrots with 1/4 cup reserved carrot liquid in a food processor or blender. Put the puréed carrots into a large bowl. Stir in the oil, 1/2 cup carrot liquid, and the grated lemon zest.

In a small bowl, mix together the next seven ingredients, and add the dry ingredients to the carrot mixture. Stir until the ingredients are blended. Fold in the oat bran, rolled oats and walnuts.

Drop the batter by rounded tablespoonfuls onto nonstick baking sheets, shaping the batter into twenty-four large cookies. Bake the cookies for 20 minutes, or until they are brown.

Yields 24 cookies

CRUNCHY GRANOLA COOKIES

This recipe is for those who like really crunchy cookies. They freeze well.

1/2 cup pitted dates
3/4 cup black raisins
1/2 cup water
1 teaspoon vanilla extract
1/2 cup whole wheat flour
1 teaspoon baking powder
4 cups granola (preferably fruit juice-sweetened)

Preheat the oven to 350°.

In a food processor, coarsely chop the dates and raisins with the water and vanilla. Put the mixture into a large bowl. Mix together the flour and baking powder, and add these to the date-raisin mixture. Stir just until the ingredients are blended. Fold in the granola.

Drop the cookie batter by rounded teaspoonfuls onto nonstick baking sheets. Bake the cookies for 18 to 20 minutes, or until they are dark brown on top and around the edges.

Yields 36 cookies

BANANA-ORANGE PASSOVER COOKIES

These cookies are a pleasure to eat even when it's not Passover. They freeze well and are good right out of the freezer.

1 1/4 cups puréed bananas (about 2 large bananas)
1 tablespoon safflower or canola oil
1 teaspoon vanilla extract
1/4 cup orange marmalade, fruit-sweetened, if available
1/2 cup Passover cake meal (finely ground matzo, available in supermarkets at Passover season)
2 teaspoons ground cinnamon
3 1/2 cups crumbled whole wheat matzos
2/3 cup chopped pecans
Sprinkle of ground cinnamon

Preheat the oven to 400°.

In a large bowl, mix together the first four ingredients. Add the cake meal and cinnamon, and stir until the ingredients are blended. Fold in the crumbled matzos and chopped pecans. Shape the dough into twenty-four mounds the size of golf balls, and place the mounds on a lightly oiled nonstick baking sheet. (You can place the cookies close together, since they will not rise.) Sprinkle cinnamon on top of the cookies.

Bake the cookies for about twenty-five minutes, or until they are dark brown and crisp.

Yields 24 cookies

YAM-GINGERBREAD COOKIES

Gingerbread lovers will really enjoy these unusual cookies.

3/4 cup cooked mashed yams
2 tablespoons dark molasses
2 tablespoons maple syrup
1 1/2 tablespoons safflower or canola oil
1/4 cup water
2 cups plus 2 tablespoons whole wheat flour
1 1/2 teaspoons baking powder
2 teaspoons ground cinnamon
1 teaspoon ground ginger
1/8 teaspoon ground cloves

Preheat the oven to 375°.

In a large bowl, beat together the first five ingredients until the mixture is smooth. In another bowl, mix together the flour, baking powder, and spices. Add the dry ingredients to the yam mixture, and stir with a fork until the dough is blended. Shape the dough into a ball. Roll the dough out on a lightly floured board, and cut it into the shapes of your choice.

Place the cookies on nonstick baking sheets. Bake the cookies for about 15 minutes, or just until they are light golden brown.

Yield depends on size of cookies

GINGERBREAD RAISIN BARS

These molasses and date-sweetened bars are easy to prepare and so good to eat.

3/4 cup pitted dates
1 cup water
1/3 cup dark molasses
2/3 cup water
2 tablespoons safflower or canola oil
3 cups whole wheat flour
2 teaspoons baking soda
1 tablespoon ground cinnamon
2 teaspoons ground ginger
1/4 teaspoon ground cloves
1/2 cup black raisins

In a medium saucepan, cook the dates in the water, uncovered, over medium heat for 8 minutes. Purée the dates, and any liquid remaining in the saucepan, in a food processor or blender. Put the purée into a large bowl. Stir in the molasses, water, and oil, and blend the ingredients.

In another bowl, mix together the flour, baking soda, spices, and raisins. Stir the dry ingredients into the date purée, mixing only until the batter is smooth. Spread the batter in a lightly oiled 9- by 13-inch nonstick baking pan. Bake the cake for 12 minutes.

Let the cake cool before cutting it into bars.

Yields 24 bars

CHILDREN'S WHOLESOME GINGERBREAD COOKIES

Children really enjoy playing with this dough, creating their own shapes, and eating what they make.

1 1/2 cups cooked banana squash, or other sweet orange winter squash, or 1 12-ounce package frozen cooked orange squash, thawed
2 tablespoons safflower or canola oil
1/2 cup water
1/4 cup maple syrup
1/4 cup dark molasses
3 1/4 cups whole wheat flour
1 1/2 teaspoons baking soda
1 tablespoon ground cinnamon
2 teaspoons ground ginger
1/2 teaspoon ground cloves
1/2 cup black raisins, for decoration

Preheat the oven to 375°.

In a large bowl, beat together the first five ingredients until the mixture is smooth. In another bowl, mix together the flour, baking soda, and spices, and, with a fork, stir them into the squash mixture. Bring the dough together into a ball. Divide the dough into four or more parts, depending on the number of children present. Give each child a piece of dough and a chance to roll it out on a lightly floured board. The dough can be cut into gingerbread girls and boys, or into any shape. The cookies can be decorated with black raisins.

Bake the cookies on nonstick baking sheets for 7 to 10 minutes.

Yield depends on size of cookies

SWEET POTATO-GINGERBREAD COOKIES

Follow the preceding recipe, but substitute mashed sweet potatoes for squash, and reduce the amount of flour to 2 3/4 to 3 cups.

EASY BANANA GINGERBREAD COOKIES

These wholesome cookies are fun to make and fun to eat. Children love to eat pieces of the dough before it's baked.

1 1/4 cups puréed bananas (about 3 medium bananas)
1/3 cup dark molasses
2 tablespoons safflower or canola oil
3 cups whole wheat flour
1 teaspoon baking powder
1/2 teaspoon baking soda
2 teaspoons ground ginger
1 tablespoon ground cinnamon
1/2 teaspoon ground cloves

Preheat the oven to 375°.

In a large bowl, beat together the bananas, molasses, and oil. In another bowl, mix together the next six ingredients, and add them to the banana mixture. Stir until the dough is blended. Roll out the dough on a well-floured board. Cut out cookies with a cookie cutter or a drinking glass. Lay the cookies on nonstick baking sheets, and bake them for 8 minutes.

Yield depends on size of cookies

WHEAT-FREE GINGER SNAPS

Children love these spicy rye-flour cookies.

3/4 cup black raisins
1/2 cup water
1 teaspoon cider vinegar
1/2 cup dark molasses
1 tablespoon safflower or canola oil
2 1/2 cups rye flour
1 1/2 teaspoons baking powder
1 tablespoon ground cinnamon
1/2 teaspoon ground cloves
2 teaspoons ground ginger

Preheat the oven to 375°.

In a small saucepan, cook the raisins in the water, uncovered, over low heat for 8 minutes. Purée the raisins in a food processor or blender, and put the purée into a medium mixing bowl. Mix in the vinegar, molasses, and oil. In a smaller bowl, mix together the remaining ingredients. Add them to the raisin mixture while stirring with a fork. Stir until the dough is blended.

Drop the dough by teaspoonfuls onto non-stick baking sheets. Flatten the cookies with a fork, wetting the fork if the dough sticks. Bake the cookies for about 15 minutes.

Yields 48 cookies

WHEAT-FREE SQUASH-OAT BRAN-SPICE COOKIES

These spicy squash cookies are studded with raisins.

1 1/2 cups mashed cooked banana squash or other sweet orange winter squash, or 1 12-ounce package frozen orange squash, thawed
2/3 cup frozen and thawed apple juice concentrate
1 teaspoon vanilla extract
1 tablespoon safflower or canola oil
2/3 cup brown rice flour
1 1/2 cups oat bran
2 teaspoons baking powder
1 tablespoon ground cinnamon
1/2 teaspoon ground nutmeg
1 1/2 teaspoons ground ginger
1/4 teaspoon ground cloves
2/3 cup black raisins

Preheat the oven to 375°.

In a large bowl, beat together the squash, apple juice, vanilla, and oil until the mixture is smooth. Mix together the next seven ingredients, and stir the dry ingredients into the squash mixture. Stir until the batter is blended. Fold in the raisins.

Drop the batter by heaping teaspoonfuls onto two nonstick baking sheets. Press each cookie down lightly with a fork. Bake the cookies for 30 to 35 minutes, or until they are light brown.

Yields 60 cookies

EASY LEMON-WALNUT-OAT BRAN COOKIES

These healthful cookies, sweetened with pineapple juice, take only minutes to prepare.

3 tablespoons lemon juice
1/2 cup frozen and thawed pineapple concentrate
1/4 cup water
1 tablespoon safflower or canola oil
1/4 teaspoon almond extract
1/2 cup whole wheat flour
1 cup oat bran
2 teaspoons baking soda
1 cup rolled oats
1/2 cup chopped walnuts

Preheat the oven to 425°.

In a large bowl, beat together the lemon juice, pineapple juice, water, oil, and almond extract. In another bowl, mix together the flour, oat bran, and baking soda. Add the dry ingredients to the juice mixture, and stir until the batter is smooth. Fold in the oats and walnuts.

Drop the batter by rounded tablespoonfuls into twelve mounds on a nonstick baking sheet. Bake the cookies for about 12 minutes, or until they are light golden brown.

Yields 12 cookies

EASY ORANGE-CINNAMON-OATMEAL COOKIES

These cookies, made of whole wheat and oats, are sweetened with raisins and orange juice.

2/3 cup frozen and thawed orange juice concentrate
1/3 cup water
1 tablespoon safflower or canola oil
1 teaspoon vanilla extract
1/2 cup whole wheat flour
1 cup oat bran
1 cup rolled oats
2 teaspoons baking soda
1 tablespoon ground cinnamon
3/4 cup black raisins

Preheat the oven to 425°.

In a large bowl, beat together the orange juice, water, oil, and vanilla. In another bowl, mix together the next five ingredients, and add them to the juice mixture. Stir only until the batter is blended. Fold in the raisins.

Drop the batter by heaping tablespoonfuls onto a nonstick baking sheet. With a fork, shape the batter into twelve large cookies. Bake the cookies for about 15 minutes, or until medium brown.

Yields 12 cookies

Easy Banana-Walnut-Oat Bran Cookies

Bananas and walnuts give these easy-to-prepare, wholesome cookies a delightful flavor.

2 cups puréed bananas (about 4 medium
   bananas)
1 tablespoon safflower or canola oil
1 tablespoon maple syrup
1 teaspoon vanilla extract
1/2 cup whole wheat flour
2 cups rolled oats
1 tablespoon ground cinnamon
1 teaspoon baking soda
1/2 cup chopped walnuts

Preheat the oven to 425°.

   In a large bowl, beat together the bananas, oil, maple syrup, and vanilla. In another bowl, mix together the flour, oats, cinnamon, and baking soda. Add the dry ingredients to the banana mixture, stirring only until the batter is blended. Fold in the walnuts.

   Drop the batter by heaping tablespoonfuls onto a nonstick baking sheet. With a fork, shape the batter into twelve large cookies. Bake the cookies for 10 to 12 minutes, or until medium brown.

Yields 12 cookies

Easy Molasses-Raisin-Oat Bran Cookies

These raisin-, walnut-, and oat-filled cookies are chewy and sweet.

1/4 cup dark molasses
1/2 cup frozen and thawed apple juice
   concentrate
1/4 cup water
1 tablespoon safflower or canola oil
1/2 cup whole wheat flour
1 cup oat bran
1 cup rolled oats
2 teaspoons baking soda
1/2 cup black raisins
1/3 cup chopped walnuts

Preheat the oven to 425°.

   In a large bowl, beat together the molasses, apple juice, water, and oil. In another bowl, mix together the flour, oat bran, oats, and baking soda. Add the dry ingredients to the liquid, and stir only until the batter is blended. Fold in the raisins and walnuts.

   Drop the batter into twelve mounds on a nonstick baking sheet, and shape the cookies with a fork. Bake the cookies for about 15 minutes, or until dark brown.

Yields 12 cookies

Easy Carob-Pecan-Oat Bran Cookies

These pineapple juice-sweetened cookies take only minutes to prepare.

1/3 cup water
2/3 cup frozen and thawed pineapple juice concentrate
1 tablespoon safflower or canola oil
1 teaspoon dark molasses
1/4 teaspoon almond extract
1 teaspoon vanilla extract
1/2 cup whole wheat flour
3 tablespoons carob powder
2 teaspoons baking soda
1 cup oat bran
1 cup rolled oats
1/3 cup minced pecans

Preheat the oven to 425°.

In a large bowl, beat together the first six ingredients. In another bowl, mix together the flour, carob powder, and baking soda. Add the dry ingredients to the liquid, and stir just until the ingredients are blended. Fold in the oat bran, oats, and pecans.

Drop the batter into twelve large mounds on a nonstick baking sheet. Bake the cookies for about 18 minutes, or until dark brown.

Yields 12 cookies

Easy Banana Squash-Spice-Oatmeal Cookies

These cookies have a lovely flavor of maple syrup and squash, and they freeze well.

3/4 cup mashed cooked banana squash, or other sweet orange winter squash, or 1 12-ounce package frozen cooked orange squash, thawed
1/4 cup maple syrup
2 tablespoons safflower or canola oil
Grated zest of 1 lemon
1/2 cup whole wheat flour
2 teaspoons baking soda
2 teaspoons ground cinnamon
1 teaspoon ground ginger
1/4 teaspoon ground cloves
2 cups rolled oats
1/2 cup black raisins

Preheat the oven to 425°.

In a large bowl, beat together the squash, maple syrup, oil, and grated lemon zest until the mixture is smooth. In another bowl, mix together the flour, baking soda, and spices. Add the dry ingredients to the squash mixture, stirring only until the ingredients are blended. Fold in the oats and raisins. Drop the batter by rounded teaspoonfuls onto nonstick baking sheets, and press each cookie gently with a fork. Bake the cookies for about 12 minutes, or until medium brown in color.

Yields 36 cookies

EASY YAM-OATMEAL COOKIES

These spicy whole wheat cookies are a good use for leftover yams.

2/3 cup mashed cooked yams
1 tablespoon maple syrup
2 tablespoons dark molasses
2 tablespoons safflower or canola oil
1/4 cup water
1/2 cup whole wheat flour
2 teaspoons baking soda
2 teaspoons ground cinnamon
1 teaspoon ground ginger
1/8 teaspoon ground cloves
2 cups rolled oats
1/2 cup black raisins
1/3 cup chopped walnuts

Preheat the oven to 425°.

In a large bowl, beat together the yams, maple syrup, molasses, oil, and water until the mixture is smooth. In another bowl, mix together the flour, baking soda, and spices. Add the dry ingredients to the yam mixture, and stir only until the ingredients are blended. Fold in the oats, raisins, and walnuts.

Drop the batter by teaspoonfuls onto non-stick baking sheets, and press each cookie gently with a fork. Bake the cookies for about 15 minutes, or until medium brown in color.

Yields 36 cookies

EASY WHEAT-FREE YAM-SWEETENED OAT BRAN CHEWS

If you bake the yams ahead of time, these cookies will take only minutes to make.

1 1/2 cups mashed cooked yams
1/2 cup frozen and thawed apple juice
   concentrate
2 tablespoons frozen and thawed orange juice
   concentrate
1 teaspoon vanilla extract
2 tablespoons water
1 1/2 cups rolled oats
2 cups oat bran
1 teaspoon baking powder
1 tablespoon ground cinnamon
1 teaspoon ground nutmeg
1 teaspoon ground ginger
1 teaspoon ground coriander
1/4 teaspoon ground cloves
1/2 cup black raisins
1/2 cup chopped walnuts

Preheat the oven to 350°.

In a food processor or blender, purée the yams with the apple juice, orange juice, vanilla, and water. Put the mixture into a large bowl. In another bowl, mix together the remaining ingredients. Add them to the yam mixture, and stir until the batter is blended.

Drop the dough by rounded teaspoonfuls onto two nonstick baking sheets. Press each cookie gently with a fork. Bake the cookies for 25 to 30 minutes, or until they are crunchy.

Yields 48 cookies

EASY GRANOLA
BANANA SQUARES

1 1/2 cups mashed bananas (about 3 medium
    bananas)
1/2 cup frozen and thawed apple juice
    concentrate
1/4 cup frozen and thawed orange juice
    concentrate
2 tablespoons safflower or canola oil
3/4 cup whole wheat flour
1 1/2 teaspoons baking soda
1 1/2 teaspoons ground cinnamon
1/2 teaspoon ground nutmeg
4 cups granola (fruit-sweetened preferred)
Sprinkle of ground cinnamon

Preheat the oven to 400°.

In a large bowl, beat together the bananas,
apple juice, orange juice, and oil. Add the dry
ingredients to the banana mixture, and stir until the ingredients are blended. Fold in the
granola.

Spread the batter evenly in a 10- by 15-inch
nonstick jelly-roll pan. Sprinkle the cinnamon
generously over the batter. Bake the cake for 25
to 30 minutes, or until top is light golden brown.

When the cake is cool, cut it into squares.

Yields 24 squares

DATE-WALNUT
CRESCENT COOKIES

These crunchy cookies are among our favorites.

1 cup firmly packed pitted dates
1/2 cup water
2 tablespoons safflower or canola oil
1 teaspoon vanilla extract
Grated zest of 1 lemon
1 cup whole wheat pastry flour
1 1/2 teaspoons baking powder
1 cup finely chopped walnuts
1 teaspoon ground cinnamon
1/2 teaspoon ground ginger
1/2 teaspoon ground nutmeg

Preheat the oven to 375°.

In a small saucepan, cook the dates in the
water over medium heat, covered, for 8 minutes. Purée this mixture in a food processor or
blender, and put the purée into a medium bowl.
Stir in the oil, vanilla, and lemon zest.

In another bowl, mix together the flour, baking powder, walnuts, and spices. Add these all
at once, while stirring, to the date mixture. Stir
until the dough is blended.

Roll 1 tablespoon dough between the palms
of your hands to form a thin coil about 3 1/2
inches long. Bend the coil into a crescent shape,
and place the dough on a nonstick baking sheet.
Repeat this process with the remaining dough.

Bake the cookies for about 15 minutes.

Yields 36 cookies

BROWN RICE FLOUR-DATE-RAISIN-WALNUT COOKIES

These sweet, spicy cookies are wheat-free. They can be frozen, but heat the frozen cookies in an oven or toaster oven before serving.

1/2 cup black raisins
1/2 cup pitted dates
3/4 cup water
1/4 cup water
1 tablespoon safflower or canola oil
1 cup brown rice flour
2 tablespoons cornstarch
1 teaspoon ground ginger
1/4 teaspoon ground cloves
1 teaspoon ground cinnamon
1/3 cup chopped walnuts

Preheat the oven to 425°.

In a small saucepan, over low heat, cook the raisins and dates in 3/4 cup water, uncovered, for 10 minutes. Purée the mixture in a food processor or blender, and put it into a medium bowl. Stir in the water and oil.

In another bowl, mix together the next five ingredients, and add them to the raisin-date mixture. Fold in the chopped walnuts.

Drop the dough by teaspoonfuls onto nonstick baking sheets. Bake the cookies for 8 minutes.

Yields 36 cookies

DATE-RAISIN-SPICE COOKIES

These whole wheat cookies freeze well, but heat the frozen cookies in the oven or toaster oven before serving.

1 cup black raisins
1 cup pitted dates
1 1/2 cups water
1/2 cup water
2 tablespoons safflower or canola oil
2 cups whole wheat pastry flour
1 teaspoon baking soda
2 teaspoons ground ginger
1/2 teaspoon ground cloves
2 teaspoons ground cinnamon

Preheat the oven to 425°.

In a medium saucepan, over medium heat, cook the raisins and dates in 1 1/2 cups water, uncovered, for 15 minutes. Purée the mixture in a food processor or blender, and put it into a large bowl. Stir in the water and oil.

In another bowl, mix together the remaining ingredients. Add them to the raisin-date mixture, stirring only until the batter is smooth.

Drop the batter by heaping tablespoonfuls onto nonstick baking sheets. Shape the batter into rounded mounds. Bake the cookies for 15 minutes, or until light brown in color.

Yields 24 cookies

Brown Rice Flour-Nut-Marmalade Cookies

These crunchy, wheat-free cookies are very easy to prepare.

Double batch Brown Rice Flour-Nut Crust dough (page 157)
1/2 cup orange marmalade (preferably fruit juice-sweetened)

Preheat the oven to 400°.

Press 1 heaping tablespoonful dough between your hands, and shape the dough into a flat oval, about 1/2 inch thick. Lay the cookie on a nonstick baking sheet, and repeat the process with the rest of the dough. Dot the top of each cookie with 1 teaspoonful marmalade. Bake the cookies for 12 minutes.

Yields 24 cookies

Passover Haroset

Haroset is a wholesome and delicious Passover treat. For traditional Jews, it is served at the Passover table as a symbol of the mortar used in building the pyramids when Jews were enslaved in Egypt thousands of years ago.

3 cups grated apples
1 cup chopped walnuts
1/2 cup grape juice

In a medium bowl, mix the apples, walnuts, and grape juice together and chill.

Yields 4 cups

Passover Haroset Cookies

These cookies are easy to prepare, especially with leftover haroset, a special Passover treat.

4 cups Passover Haroset
1 1/2 cups Passover cake meal (finely ground matzo, available in supermarkets at Passover season)
2 tablespoons ground cinnamon
Grated zest of 1 lemon
Grated zest of 1 orange

Preheat the oven to 400°.

In a medium bowl, mix all the ingredients together. Drop the batter by rounded teaspoonfuls onto a lightly oiled nonstick baking sheet. Bake the cookies for about 30 minutes, or until they are dark brown.

Yields 48 cookies

Easy Brown Rice-Banana-Walnut Cookies

These simple wheat-free cookies are great for munching.

1/2 cup brown rice flour
1 teaspoon ground cinnamon
1/2 teaspoon ground coriander
2 tablespoons cornstarch
2 cups cooked brown rice
1/3 cup chopped walnuts
2/3 cup mashed bananas (about 2 medium
  bananas)
Sprinkle of ground cinnamon for top

Preheat the oven to 400°.

In a medium bowl, mix together the first six ingredients. Stir in the mashed bananas with a fork. Drop the dough by heaping teaspoonfuls onto nonstick baking sheets, and shape the dough into flat cookies about 2 inches in diameter. Sprinkle cinnamon over the cookies.

Bake the cookies for about 25 minutes, or until they are golden brown.

Yields 24 cookies

Brown Rice-Yam-Pecan Cookies

These wheat-free cookies, each adorned with a pecan, are a good use for leftover yams.

1 cup mashed cooked yams
1 tablespoon safflower or canola oil
1 cup brown rice flour
1 1/2 teaspoons ground cinnamon
1/4 teaspoon baking powder
30 pecan halves

Preheat the oven to 425°.

In a medium bowl, beat the mashed yams and oil with a fork. In another bowl, mix together the rice flour, cinnamon, and baking powder. With a fork, stir these into the yams. Stir until the mixture is smooth.

Shape the dough with your hands into walnut-size balls, and arrange the balls on nonstick baking sheets. Press the balls down with a fork into 1 3/4-inch round cookies. Press a pecan half in the center of each cookie.

Bake the cookies for 10 minutes.

Yields 30 cookies

Brown Rice Flour-Banana-Walnut Cookies

These are wheat-free.

1 cup puréed bananas (about 3 small bananas)
1 cup minced walnuts
1 cup brown rice flour
1 tablespoon ground cinnamon
1/2 teaspoon ground coriander
1/2 teaspoon baking soda
Sprinkles of ground cinnamon

Preheat the oven to 425°.

In a medium bowl, mix the puréed bananas and the walnuts. In another bowl, mix together the rice flour, cinnamon, coriander, and baking soda. Add the dry ingredients to the banana-walnut purée, and stir with a fork until the ingredients are blended. Let the dough rest for 15 minutes.

Shape the dough into balls the size of walnuts. Arrange the balls on nonstick baking sheets, flatten them each with a fork, and sprinkle cinnamon over them. Bake the cookies for 10 minutes.

Yields 36 cookies

Easy Glazed Oat Bran-Rice Cookies

Topped with marmalade, these wheat-free cookies make wholesome treats.

1/3 cup oat bran
2/3 cup water
3 tablespoons maple syrup
1 teaspoon vanilla extract
1 teaspoon safflower or canola oil
1 cup brown rice flour
1 teaspoon baking soda
1 tablespoon ground cinnamon
1/4 cup orange marmalade (preferably fruit juice-sweetened)
2 tablespoons frozen and thawed orange juice concentrate

Preheat the oven to 400°.

In a small saucepan, cook the oat bran and water over medium heat until the mixture is thick, stirring occasionally (this will take only a few minutes). Put the cooked oat bran into a medium bowl. Stir in the maple syrup, vanilla and oil.

Mix together the rice flour, baking soda, and cinnamon, and add the dry ingredients to the cooked oat bran, stirring with a fork until the dough is blended.

In a small bowl, mix together the marmalade and orange juice.

Drop the dough by teaspoonfuls onto nonstick baking sheets, and press the dough with a fork. Onto the center of each cookie, spoon a little of the orange-marmalade mixture. Bake the cookies for about 30 minutes, or until they are brown around the edges.

Yields about 24 cookies

CRUNCHY WHEAT-FREE PEANUT BUTTER COOKIES

These are for peanut butter lovers. Although the cookies are much higher in fat than most in this chapter, for an occasional splurge they are a delight.

1/2 cup unsalted peanut butter
1/2 cup frozen and thawed apple juice
  concentrate
1/4 cup maple syrup
2 tablespoons safflower or canola oil
1 1/2 cup rolled oats
1/2 cup oat bran

In a medium bowl, beat the first four ingredients with a fork until they are well blended. Stir in the rolled oats and the oat bran. Drop the cookie dough by tablespoonfuls onto two nonstick baking sheets, and flatten the cookies with a fork. Bake them for 10 to 12 minutes.

Yields 24 cookies

PASSOVER BANANA-PECAN-MATZO COOKIES

Chopped matzos take the place of flour in these Passover cookies, which you may enjoy throughout the year.

1 1/4 cups puréed bananas (about 2 large
  bananas)
1 teaspoon ground cinnamon
Grated zest of 1/2 lemon
2/3 cup finely crumbled whole wheat matzos
1/3 cup minced pecans
Sprinkles of ground cinnamon for top

Preheat the oven to 375°.

In a medium bowl, mix the bananas, cinnamon, and lemon zest. Stir in the chopped matzos and pecans.

Drop the batter by rounded teaspoonfuls onto a lightly oiled nonstick baking sheet. Flatten each cookie with a fork, and sprinkle cinnamon on the top. Bake the cookies for about 30 minutes, or until they are dark golden brown.

Yields 36 cookies

CRUNCHY BROWN RICE-OAT BRAN CRACKERS

These crackers are wheat-free.

1/2 cup oat bran
1 cup water
2 tablespoons sesame seeds
2 teaspoons onion powder
1 tablespoon safflower or canola oil
1/4 teaspoon sea salt
1 cup brown rice flour

Preheat the oven to 400°.

In a small saucepan, cook the oat bran in the water over medium heat, uncovered, for 2 minutes. Put the mixture into a medium bowl. With a fork, stir in the next four ingredients, then the rice flour.

Roll the dough between your hands into balls the size of walnuts. Arrange the balls on nonstick baking sheets, and press them flat into 1/3-inch crackers.

Bake the crackers for about 12 minutes.

Yields 30 crackers

WHEAT-FREE PUMPKIN-OAT CHEWS

Store these raisin-filled pumpkin cookies in the refrigerator or freezer.

1 cup pumpkin purée
2/3 cup frozen and thawed apple juice concentrate
1 teaspoon vanilla extract
1 tablespoon safflower or canola oil
1 cup oat flour
1 1/2 teaspoons baking soda
1 tablespoon ground cinnamon
1 teaspoon ground nutmeg
1 teaspoon ground ginger
1/4 teaspoon ground cloves
2 cups rolled oats
1/2 cup oat bran
1 cup black raisins
Sprinkles of ground cinnamon

Preheat the oven to 375°.

In a large bowl, beat together the pumpkin, apple juice, vanilla, and oil until they are well blended. In another bowl, mix together the next six ingredients. Add them to the pumpkin mixture, stirring only until the batter is smooth. Fold in the oats, oat bran, and raisins.

Drop the cookie dough by rounded teaspoonfuls onto two nonstick baking sheets. Flatten the cookies slightly with a fork, and sprinkle them lightly with the cinnamon. Bake them for about 30 minutes, or until they are brown.

Yields 48 cookies

FRUITY *MANDELBROT* (ALMOND COOKIES)

These crunchy almond cookies are sweetened with bananas. Store the *mandelbrot* in the refrigerator or freezer. Before serving, heat them until they are crisp.

1/3 cup mashed banana (about 1 medium banana)
1 cup frozen and thawed apple juice concentrate
1 teaspoon vanilla extract
2 tablespoons safflower or canola oil
Grated zest of 1 lemon
2 cups whole wheat flour
1 cup brown rice flour
2 teaspoons baking powder
2 tablespoons ground cinnamon
1 1/2 cups sliced almonds
Sprinkles of cinnamon

Preheat the oven to 350°.

In a large bowl, beat together the bananas, apple juice, vanilla, oil, and lemon zest until the mixture is blended. In another bowl, mix together the next four ingredients, and stir only until the batter is smooth. Fold in the almonds. Chill the dough for several hours or overnight.

Shape the dough into eight small loaves, each about 4 inches by 2 inches by 1 inch. Bake the loaves on a nonstick baking sheet for about 30 minutes, or until they are light brown. Reduce the oven temperature to 225°.

With a sharp serrated knife, cut each loaf into seven or eight slices. Arrange the slices on baking sheets, and sprinkle them lightly with cinnamon. Bake them for 2 hours.

Yields 60 cookies

CRUNCHY *MANDELBROT* (ALMOND COOKIES)

These almond-flavored cookies are very crunchy because they are baked twice.

2/3 cup water
1 tablespoon safflower or canola oil
2 tablespoons almond butter
1/4 cup maple syrup
1/4 teaspoon reduced-salt soy sauce or Bragg Liquid Aminos
1/2 teaspoon pure almond extract
Grated zest of 1 lemon
1 3/4 cups whole wheat flour
1 1/2 teaspoons baking powder
1/4 cup chopped or sliced raw almonds
1 1/2 tablespoons ground cinnamon

In a large bowl, whisk together the first seven ingredients. In a medium bowl, mix together the flour, baking powder, almonds, and cinnamon, and add them all at once to the liquid, while stirring with a fork. Bring the dough together, and chill it for several hours or overnight.

Preheat the oven to 375°.

Roll the chilled dough into two rolls about 8 inches long. Lay the rolls in a 10- by 15-inch non-stick baking pan. Press them to 8 inches long by 2 1/2 inches wide and 5/8 inch high. Bake the loaves for 25 minutes.

Let the loaves cool, then set the oven temperature at 350°. Cut the loaves into slices about 1/4 inch thick. Place the slices close together in the pan, and bake them for about 35 minutes, or until they are a light golden brown.

Let the cookies cool completely, then freeze or refrigerate them.

Yields about 60 cookies

CRUNCHY SESAME-SEED COOKIES

These crunchy cookies are a sesame version of *mandelbrot*.

2/3 cup water
1 tablespoon safflower or canola oil
2 tablespoons tahini
1/4 cup maple syrup
1/4 teaspoon reduced-salt soy sauce or Bragg
   Liquid Aminos
1 3/4 cups whole wheat flour
1 1/2 teaspoons baking powder
1/4 cup sesame seeds (hulled)

In a large bowl, whisk together the first five ingredients. In a small bowl, mix together the flour, baking powder, and sesame seeds. Add them all at once to the liquid, while stirring with a fork. Bring the dough together, and chill it for several hours or overnight.

Preheat the oven to 375°.

Roll and shape the chilled dough into two long rolls about 8 inches long. Lay the rolls in a 10- by 15-inch nonstick baking pan. Press them to 8 inches long by 2 1/2 inches wide and 5/8 inch high. Bake the loaves for 25 minutes.

Let the loaves cool, then set the oven temperature at 350°. Cut the loaves into slices about 1/4 inch thick. Place the slices close together the pan, and bake them for about 25 minutes, or until they are light golden brown around the edges.

Let the cookies cool completely, then freeze or refrigerate them.

Yields about 60 cookies.

SWEET YAM-CINNAMON-RAISIN BUNS

The syrup in and on these cinnamon buns is made of apple juice instead of refined sugar.

3/4 cup frozen and thawed apple juice
   concentrate
1/4 cup maple syrup
1 cup raisins
1 tablespoon ground cinnamon
Sweet Yam Pastry Dough (page 198)

In a medium saucepan, bring the juice, syrup, raisins, and cinnamon to a boil, then simmer the mixture, uncovered, for 5 minutes. Remove the pan from the heat, and let the mixture cool.

Measure out 1/2 cup of the syrupy liquid, and reserve this for the top of the buns.

Roll the dough out on a lightly floured board into a 14- by 8-inch rectangle. Spread the raisins and syrup over the dough, then roll the dough, starting from a long side, into a long roll. Cut the roll into eight slices, and lay the buns in a lightly oiled 9-inch round nonstick baking pan. Pour the reserved syrup evenly over the buns. Allow the buns to rise in a warm place until they are double in bulk.

Place the pan of buns in a cold oven, and place a large piece of foil at the bottom of the oven to catch any drips. Set the oven temperature to 375°, and bake the buns for about 30 minutes, or until light golden brown.

Yields 8 buns

Sweet Yam Pastry Dough

Yams make this dough moist and sweet; maple syrup makes it sweeter.

2 envelopes active dry yeast
1/2 cup lukewarm water
3 tablespoons maple syrup
2 tablespoons safflower or canola oil
1 teaspoon lemon juice
Grated zest of 1/2 lemon
1 cup whole wheat flour
2 teaspoons ground cinnamon
1/4 teaspoon sea salt
1 1/2 cups mashed cooked yams
2 1/2 cups whole wheat pastry flour

In a large bowl, dissolve the yeast in the warm water. Stir in the maple syrup, oil, lemon juice, and lemon zest. In another bowl, mix together 1 cup whole wheat flour, the cinnamon, and the salt. Add these to the liquid, stirring until the mixture is blended. Mix in the yams well, then, with a fork, stir in the pastry flour. Knead the dough in the bowl for 6 minutes, turning the bowl often. Cover the dough with plastic wrap, and chill it in the refrigerator for at least 2 hours or longer. The dough is now ready to use in any of the recipes that call for it. Follow the baking instructions for each recipe.

Yields dough for 24 buns

Sweet Yam Sticky Buns

These buns are sticky with maple-apple syrup.

1 1/2 cups black raisins
1 cup frozen and thawed apple juice
  concentrate
1 cup chopped pecans
1 tablespoon ground cinnamon
Sweet Yam Pastry Dough
1/4 cup maple syrup
1/3 cup chopped pecans for top

In a medium saucepan, bring the raisins and apple juice to a boil, then simmer the mixture, uncovered, for 15 minutes over low heat. Drain the raisins, reserving the syrup.

Put the raisins into a medium bowl, and stir in 1 cup pecans and the cinnamon.

Cut the dough into two equal parts, and, on a floured board, roll each piece into a 6- by 8-inch rectangle. Spread half the raisin-pecan filling on each rectangle. Roll each rectangle, starting from a long end, into a long roll, and cut each roll into twelve slices. Press the slices, cut side down, into twenty-four lightly oiled non-stick muffin cups.

In a small bowl, mix together the reserved liquid from the raisins with the maple syrup. Spoon 1 1/2 tablespoons syrup over each bun, and sprinkle the remaining pecans over each. Let the dough rise in a warm place until it has doubled in bulk.

Put the buns into a cold oven, then set the oven temperature at 375°. Bake the buns for exactly 20 minutes.

Yields 24 buns

CRESCENT-SHAPED COFFEE CAKE

Serve this lovely blueberry-and-almond-filled pastry warm from the oven.

Sweet Yam Pastry Dough (page 198)
1/3 cup blueberry jam (preferably fruit juice-
    sweetened)
1/4 cup sliced almonds
2 teaspoons maple syrup

Divide the dough in half. Reserve one half for another use. Roll the remaining dough into a 6-by 12-inch rectangle. Spread the blueberry jam over the dough, leaving 1/2 inch borders on all sides. Sprinkle the almonds over the jam. Roll up the dough, starting from a long side. Cut thirty slits along one side of the roll, as you would for a bear claw. In a 9-inch round nonstick baking pan, shape the dough into a crescent, with the ends almost touching each other. Brush the top of the crescent with the maple syrup.

Preheat the oven to 375°.

Let the dough rise in a warm place until it has doubled in bulk. Bake the crescent for exactly 25 minutes.

Serves 8

SWEET CINNAMON BUNS WITH RAISINS AND ALMONDS

These unglazed buns are sweetened with apple syrup.

1 1/2 cups black raisins
1 cup frozen and thawed apple juice
    concentrate
1 cup sliced almonds
1 tablespoon ground cinnamon
Sweet Yam Pastry Dough (page 198)

In a medium saucepan, bring the raisins and apple juice to a boil, then simmer them, covered, for 15 minutes over low heat. Drain the raisins, reserving the syrup. Put the raisins into a medium bowl, and stir in the almonds and cinnamon.

Cut the dough into two parts, and roll each piece on a floured board into a 6- by 8-inch rectangle. Spread half the raisin-almond filling over each rectangle. Roll up each rectangle, starting from a long side. Cut each roll into twelve slices. Put the slices cut side down into two lightly oiled 9-inch round nonstick baking pans. Let the dough rise in a warm place until it has doubled in bulk.

Put the pans of buns into a cold oven, then set the oven temperature at 375°. Bake the buns for exactly 20 minutes.

Yields 24 buns

APRICOT-NUT MINI SWEET ROLLS

Serve these apricot jam-filled pastries warm.

Sweet Yam Pastry Dough (page 198)
1 cup apricot jam (preferably fruit juice-sweetened)
1 cup chopped mixed nuts
1 cup black raisins
1 tablespoon ground cinnamon

On a lightly floured board, roll the dough into a 16- by 6-inch rectangle. Spread the jam over the dough, leaving a 1/2 inch border. In a bowl, mix together the chopped nuts, raisins, and cinnamon, and sprinkle the mixture over the jam. Roll up the rectangle, starting from a long side. Pinch the seam to keep the roll together. Stretch the roll out 2 inches longer. With a sharp serrated knife, cut roll into 1/2-inch slices.

Preheat the oven to 375°.

Place the slices on a lightly oiled nonstick baking sheet. Let the dough rise in a warm place until it has doubled in bulk. Bake the pastries for about 20 minutes, or just until they are light golden brown.

Yields 36 rolls

SWIRLED ORANGE-PECAN PASTRIES

These rolls have a simple filling of marmalade and pecans.

Sweet Yam Pastry Dough (page 198)
1 10-ounce jar orange marmalade (preferably fruit juice-sweetened)
1 1/2 cups minced pecans

Divide the dough in half, and roll each piece into a 6- by 10-inch rectangle. Spread half the marmalade and half the chopped pecans evenly on each rectangle. Roll up each rectangle, and cut each roll into twelve slices. Lay the slices on two lightly oiled nonstick baking sheets. Let the dough rise in a warm place until it has doubled in bulk.

Preheat the oven to 375°.

Bake the pastries for about 25 minutes, or just until they are light golden brown.

Yields 24 pastries

PRUNE-FILLED THREE-CORNERED PASTRIES

For each of these pastries, you can substitute 1 teaspoon jam and 1 teaspoon sliced almonds for the prune filling.

1 pound pitted prunes
1 cup water
2 teaspoons lemon juice
Grated zest of 1 lemon
2 tablespoons poppy seeds
Sweet Yam Pastry Dough (page 198)

In a saucepan, simmer the prunes in the water, uncovered, for 15 minutes, or until they are soft and the liquid is absorbed. Purée or mince the prunes. In a bowl, combine the prunes with the lemon juice, lemon zest, and poppy seeds.

Roll the dough 1/4 inch thick on a lightly floured board. With a biscuit cutter or drinking glass, cut the dough into 3-inch rounds. Stretch each round to 3 1/3 inches in diameter. Combine the scraps, roll out the dough again, and cut out more 3-inch rounds.

Drop 1 level tablespoon of the prune filling into the center of each round. Bring the dough together to form two sides of a triangle, and pinch the sides together. Then bring up the third side, and pinch it together with the other two, forming a three-cornered pastry. Let the pastries rise in a warm place until they have doubled in bulk. Bake the pastries for about 20 minutes, or until they are light golden brown.

Serve the pastries warm.

Yields 30 pastries

APPLE CINNAMON SWEET ROLLS

The dough for these delicious sweet rolls does not require kneading, and rises only once.

1 envelope active dry yeast
3/4 cup lukewarm water
2 tablespoons maple syrup
1/4 teaspoon sea salt
2 tablespoons safflower or canola oil
1 cup whole wheat flour
1 cup whole wheat pastry flour
1 large Red Delicious or Golden Delicious
   apple, chopped
1 tablespoon ground cinnamon
1/2 teaspoon ground coriander
1/4 cup frozen and thawed apple juice
   concentrate
1 teaspoon ground cinnamon

In a large bowl, stir the yeast into the warm water until the yeast is dissolved. Blend in the maple syrup, sea salt, and oil. In another bowl, mix together the next five ingredients. Add them to the liquid, and stir vigorously for 3 minutes. Divide the batter evenly among twelve lightly oiled nonstick muffin cups.

In a small bowl, mix together the apple juice and cinnamon. Spoon 1 teaspoon of the mixture on top of each roll.

Let the rolls rise in a warm place until they have doubled in bulk. Put the rolls into a cold oven, and set the oven temperature to 375°. Bake the rolls for about 20 minutes, or just until they are light golden brown.

Yields 12 rolls

QUICK BANANA-WALNUT COFFEE CAKE

This delicious banana-flavored coffee cake can be prepared in minutes.

1/2 cup frozen and thawed apple juice
   concentrate
1 tablespoon safflower or canola oil
2/3 cup mashed bananas
1 teaspoon vanilla extract
1 cup whole wheat pastry flour
1 teaspoon baking soda
1/2 teaspoon baking powder
2 teaspoons ground cinnamon
1/4 teaspoon ground coriander
1/2 cup chopped walnuts
1 tablespoon ground cinnamon
2 tablespoons chopped walnuts
Sprinkle of ground cinnamon

Preheat the oven to 350°.

In a large bowl, beat together the apple juice, oil, bananas, and vanilla. In another bowl, mix together the flour, baking soda, baking powder, and spices. Add the dry ingredients to the banana mixture, stirring only until the batter is blended.

Spread half the batter into a lightly oiled 9-inch round nonstick baking pan. Sprinkle the walnuts and cinnamon evenly over the batter, then spread the remaining batter evenly on top. Sprinkle chopped walnuts and cinnamon over the top. Bake the cake for about 25 minutes, or until it is golden brown on top.

Serves 6

QUICK JAM-WALNUT PASTRIES

These pastries taste delicious even when eaten frozen.

3 1/2 cups whole wheat pastry flour
1/2 cup oat bran
3 1/2 teaspoons baking powder
1 teaspoon ground cinnamon
1 1/4 cups water
1/4 cup frozen and thawed apple juice
   concentrate
2 tablespoons maple syrup
2 tablespoons safflower or canola oil
1 tablespoon maple syrup
1/2 cup berry or cherry jam (preferably fruit
   juice-sweetened)
1/2 cup orange marmalade (preferably fruit
   juice-sweetened)
1 cup chopped walnuts

In a large bowl, mix together the pastry flour, oat bran, baking powder, and cinnamon. In a small bowl, blend the water, apple juice, maple syrup, and oil. Stir the liquid into the dry ingredients with a fork. Bring the dough together, and, on a lightly floured board, roll it into a 10- by 18-inch rectangle.

Brush the entire surface of the dough with 1 tablespoon maple syrup, then spread berry or cherry jam on one 10- by 9-inch half of the dough, and marmalade on the other half. Sprinkle chopped walnuts evenly over the jam and marmalade. Roll up the dough, starting from a long side, and cut the roll into 1-inch slices. Arrange the slices on a lightly oiled nonstick baking sheet. Bake the pastries for 18 to 20 minutes, or until they are golden brown on top.

Yields 18 pastries

BANANA-APRICOT-ALMOND BUNS

3 envelopes active dry yeast
1/3 cup lukewarm water
2 cups puréed bananas (about 5 large
    bananas)
3 tablespoons safflower or canola oil
3 tablespoons lemon juice
Grated zest of 2 lemons
1 teaspoon ground coriander
3 cups whole wheat pastry flour
1/2 cup frozen concentrated pineapple juice
1 cup apricot jam (preferably fruit juice-
    sweetened)
1 cup sliced almonds

In the large bowl of an electric mixer, dissolve the yeast in the warm water. Beat in the next five ingredients. Continue beating until the mixture is smooth. Stop the mixer, and add the flour. Beat on medium speed for 5 minutes. Cover the dough, and let it rise in a warm place until it has doubled in bulk.

Punch the dough down, cut it into twenty-four equal pieces, and place each piece of dough in a lightly oiled nonstick muffin cup.

In a bowl, mix together the pineapple juice and apricot jam. Hollow each bun in the center with a finger, and fill each hollow with 1 tablespoon of the pineapple-apricot mixture. Sprinkle the sliced almonds on top of each bun. Let the buns rise in a warm place until they have doubled in bulk.

Preheat the oven to 350°.

Bake the buns for about 20 minutes, or until they are light golden brown.

Yields 24 buns

PINEAPPLE-OAT BRAN COFFEE CAKE SQUARES

2 cups oat-bran cereal flakes
1/4 cup frozen and thawed pineapple juice
    concentrate
2 teaspoons ground cinnamon
1/4 cup raw cashew pieces
2/3 cup water
1/2 cup frozen concentrated pineapple juice
1/4 cup frozen and thawed orange juice
    concentrate
1 teaspoon cider vinegar
1 cup whole wheat pastry flour
2 tablespoons cornstarch
2 teaspoons baking soda
1/2 cup black raisins
2 teaspoons ground cinnamon

Preheat the oven to 350°.

In a food processor, coarsely chop the cereal flakes, 1/4 cup pineapple juice, and 2 teaspoons cinnamon. Spread half this mixture in the bottom of a lightly oiled 9- by 9-inch nonstick baking pan, reserving the other half for the top.

In a food processor or blender, blend the cashews and water, and put this mixture into a large bowl. Stir in 1/2 cup pineapple juice, the orange juice, and the vinegar.

Mix together the flour, the cornstarch, the soda, the raisins, and 2 teaspoons cinnamon, and add to the cashew-juice mixture, mixing until the batter is smooth. Spread the batter on top of the cereal in the baking pan, and sprinkle the reserved cereal mixture on top. Bake the cake for about 35 minutes, or until cake tests done.

Let the cake cool, then cut it into squares.

Yields 9 squares

Date Carob Fudge Balls

These uncooked candies are a treat at any time. They should be stored in the refrigerator or freezer, and served chilled.

2 cups pitted dates
1/4 cup water
4 tablespoons carob powder
1 teaspoon dark molasses
1 teaspoon vanilla extract
1/4 cup boiling water
1 tablespoon almond butter or peanut butter
1/2 teaspoon cider vinegar
1/2 cup chopped pecans

In a medium saucepan, simmer the dates in 1/4 cup water, covered, for 8 minutes. Purée the dates in a food processor or blender, then blend in the carob powder, molasses, vanilla, boiling water, nut butter, and vinegar. Put the mixture into a medium bowl, and stir in the chopped pecans. Chill the dough for about 1 hour, or until it is firm.

With moistened hands, shape the dough into balls the size of small walnuts. Arrange the balls in a wax paper-lined baking pan. Cover the pan, and chill or freeze balls until serving time.

Yields about 30 candies

Note: For an added treat roll half the balls in 1/2 cup minced pecans. Walnuts can also be substituted for the pecans in the dough.

Frozen Bananas with Easy Carob Fudge Sauce

1/2 cup maple syrup
3 tablespoons carob powder
1 1/2 tablespoons cornstarch
1/2 tablespoon dark molasses
1/2 tablespoon safflower or canola oil
1/2 teaspoon cider vinegar
1/3 cup boiling water
4 medium bananas, peeled, wrapped in plastic, and frozen
Easy Carob Fudge Sauce (page 205)
1/4 cup chopped walnuts, pecans, or almonds

In a small nonstick saucepan, mix together the first six ingredients with a wooden or plastic spoon. Add the boiling water, and stir until the mixture is smooth. Heat the mixture over medium heat until it is thick. Chill.

Twenty minutes before serving, place each frozen banana on a dessert plate. Top each banana with a portion of the carob sauce, and sprinkle over it some of the nuts.

Serves 4

Easy Carob Fudge Sauce

This sauce is marvelous over poached pears and fresh fruit.

1/3 cup maple syrup
3 tablespoons carob powder
1 tablespoon cornstarch
1/2 tablespoon dark molasses
1 teaspoon safflower or canola oil
1/2 teaspoon cider vinegar
1/2 cup boiling water

In a small nonstick saucepan, blend together all the ingredients. Heat the sauce over medium heat, stirring constantly, until it thickens.

Serves 4

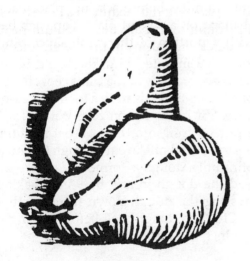

Carob-Nut Clusters

For an occasional splurge, these candies are superb. Keep them in the freezer. They are best eaten frozen, since they become sticky when thawed.

Prepare Easy Carob Fudge Sauce (see preceding recipe) according to the instructions, but omit the boiling water. Stir constantly over medium heat as the mixture comes to a full boil, and continue heating and stirring until the sauce becomes very dark and glossy. (This will take about 2 minutes. The mixture will not thicken while hot.) Pour the sauce into a small bowl, and stir in 1 1/2 cups walnuts, almonds, or pecan chunks. Drop the mixture by teaspoonfuls onto a foil- or plastic wrap-lined 10- by 15-inch baking pan with 1/2 inch sides. Cover the pan with a layer of foil or plastic wrap, and put the pan in the freezer. When the candies are frozen, transfer them to a smaller container, but keep them separated, because they can stick together even when frozen.

Yields 16 candies

Carob-Raisin Clusters

Follow the recipe for Carob Nut Clusters, but substitute black raisins for the nuts.

Poached Winter Pears with Easy Carob Fudge Sauce

This elegant dessert can be prepared well in advance.

2 large firm green winter pears, peeled, halved, and cored (or 4 small pears, peeled but left whole, with stems intact)
1/4 cup frozen concentrated pineapple juice
2 tablespoons water
1/4 teaspoon ground coriander
Easy Carob Fudge Sauce (page 205)
1/4 cup chopped nuts

In a 4- to 5-quart covered saucepan, simmer the pears in the juice, water, and coriander for 10 minutes. Turn the pears over, and simmer them for an additional 10 to 15 minutes, or until they are tender but not too soft. Chill the pears in juice until you are ready to serve them.

At serving time, drain the pears and arrange a half pear, cut side down, (or 1 whole pear if you're using smaller pears) on each dessert plate. Spoon the carob sauce over each serving, and sprinkle the top with the chopped nuts.

Serves 4

Date-Sunflower-Sesame Candy Squares

Healthful candy is hard to find. It's nice to be able to make your own.

1 cup raw shelled sunflower seeds
1/2 cup raw sesame seeds
1 cup rolled oats
1 cup pitted dates, packed down
1/2 cup black raisins
1/4 cup water
Grated zest of 1/2 lemon

Preheat the oven to 400°.

In a 10- by 15-inch nonstick jelly-roll pan with 1/2-inch sides, bake the seeds and oats together for 12 to 15 minutes, or until they are lightly browned, stirring once. Let the toasted seeds and oats cool for a few minutes, then mince them in a food processor. Put the mixture in a large bowl.

In a medium saucepan, over medium heat, cook the dates and raisins in the water, uncovered, for 5 to 7 minutes, until the liquid is absorbed. Stir occasionally as the fruits cook. Blend the cooked dates and raisins in a food processor or blender. Stir in the lemon zest. With a fork, stir the puréed fruit into the seed-oat mixture. (If necessary, use a knife to cut through this mixture.) Stir until a dough is formed.

Spread the dough in a 9- by 9-inch baking pan, pressing the dough down firmly with a spatula. Chill the dough well before cutting it into 1 1/2-inch squares.

Yields 36 squares

RAISIN-NUT-SEED-OAT BRAN CRUNCHIES

This wheat-free snack is good for you and fun to eat.

3/4 cup black raisins
3/4 cup water
1/2 cup mixed nuts (walnuts, cashews, almonds)
1/2 cup mixed seeds (sunflower, pumpkin, sesame)
1/4 cup pure maple syrup
2 cups rolled oats
1 cup oat bran

Preheat the oven to 450°.

In a medium saucepan, bring the raisins and water to a boil, then simmer the mixture, uncovered, for 5 minutes. In a food processor or blender purée the raisins with the liquid left in the pan. Put the purée into a large bowl.

In a food processor, finely chop the nuts and seeds, and stir this mixture into the puréed raisins. Stir in the maple syrup.

In another bowl, mix together the oats and oat bran. Stir these into the raisin-nut-seed mixture until the ingredients are well blended.

Spread the mixture in a 10- by 15-inch nonstick jelly-roll pan. Bake the mixture for about 15 minutes, or until brown on the top.

When the mixture is cool, break it into pieces. Store the Crunchies in a closed container in the refrigerator or freezer.

Serves 8

DATE-WALNUT PARTY TREATS

These simple, healthful treats are as sweet as candy. They can be prepared up to one week before serving.

1 pound walnut halves, or large pieces
1 pound large medjool dates

Preheat the oven to 350°.

Spread the walnut halves in a 9- by 13-inch baking pan. Bake them for 10 minutes. Remove the pan from the oven, and let the walnuts cool for 10 minutes.

Cut the dates in half lengthwise, and remove their pits. Gently press one walnut half into the center of each date. Arrange the stuffed dates in a covered storage container, separating the layers with wax paper or plastic wrap. Cover the container tightly, and store it in the refrigerator until you're ready to serve.

Yields about 36 stuffed dates

Note: You can modify this recipe to use small dates. Cut the dates only partly through—not completely in half—and stuff their centers with walnut pieces instead of walnut halves.

DELUXE TRAIL MIX

This snack mix is as welcome at parties as on the trail.

1 1/2 cups almonds
1 1/2 cups walnuts
1 cup pecans
1 cup sunflower seeds
1 cup pitted dates, quartered
2 1/2 cups black raisins

Preheat the oven to 350°.

In a 10- by 15-inch nonstick jelly-roll pan, bake the almonds, walnuts, and pecans for 5 minutes. Add the sunflower seeds, and bake 5 minutes longer. Let the nuts cool.

In a large bowl, mix together the dates and raisins, then stir in the nuts and seeds.

Store the trail mix in airtight jars in the refrigerator.

Yields 8 cups

EASY STEWED PLUMS

Stewed plums make a simple, refreshing, tart dessert.

6 large or 10 small whole red or yellow plums
1/2 cup frozen and thawed apple juice
  concentrate
1/4 teaspoon ground coriander

In a 4- to 5-quart covered saucepan, bring the plums, apple juice and coriander to a boil. Simmer the mixture until the plums begin to fall apart. Remove the pan from the heat, and let the plums cool. Chill them well before serving.

Serves 6

SIMPLY DELICIOUS BAKED APPLES

Serve these baked apples warm or chilled with Easy Cashew Cream or Vanilla Cashew Cream (page 173).

5 large Rome Beauty apples
2 1/4 teaspoons ground cinnamon
2 cups water

Preheat the oven to 375°.

Partly core the apples, leaving the bottom 1/2 inch intact. Place the apples in a 10-inch oven-proof glass deep-dish pie plate. Put 1/4 teaspoon cinnamon in each apple, and 1 teaspoon cinnamon in the pie plate. Fill the center of each apple with water, and pour the remaining water into the pie plate.

Bake the apples, uncovered, for about 1 1/2 hours, or until they are soft.

Serves 5

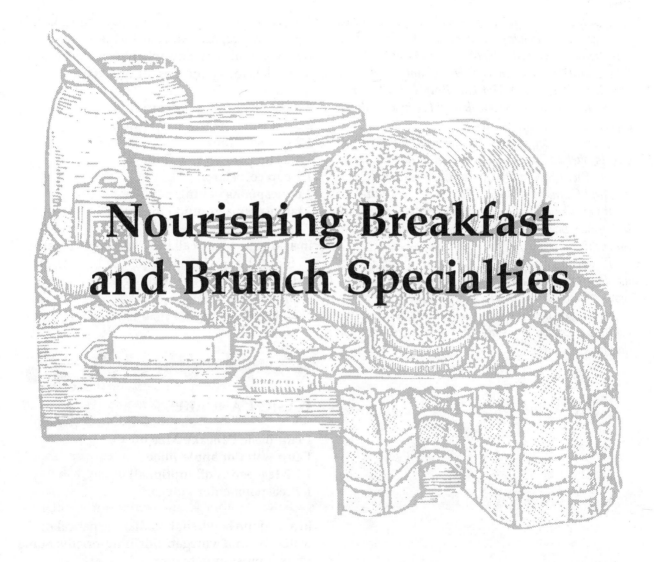

Nourishing Breakfast and Brunch Specialties

Imagine waking up to make marvelous multigrain pancakes in minutes. You can do this using one of the pancake mixes in this chapter, and you can serve your pancakes with our Fresh Strawberry Sauce or Easy Berry Sauce.

If you and your loved ones wake up in the mood for a heartier breakfast, you might try Spicy Tofu Ranchero, or Scrambled Tofu and Onions and Fat-Free Country Fries. Then again, a steamy bowl of hot cereal, such as Quick Hot Oat Bran Cereal, or Hot Oatmeal and Oat Bran Cereal, might be just the thing, especially in fall and winter.

There are recipes here, too, for healthful breakfast sweets, such as Passover Banana-Pecan Fritters; Sweet Brown Rice Cereal with Coconut, Dates, and Coriander; and Cinnamon-Raisin-Brown Rice Pudding.

If you like to drink your breakfast, you may wish to try our Banana Shake for Two, or our Hawaiian Smoothie.

If you are in the mood for healthy home-baked whole-grain bread, muffins, or pastries, you will find recipes for those in the preceding chapters.

Whatever you do, don't skip breakfast. Enjoy a healthful, hearty breakfast, and you'll feel better all day long.

BASIC PANCAKE MIX

This versatile, nondairy, multigrain pancake mix is easy to prepare. Store it in the refrigerator, where it will be ready whenever you wish to make delicious pancakes for breakfast.

2 cups *masa harina* or corn flour
2 cups whole wheat pastry flour
1/2 cup soy flour
1 1/2 cups brown rice flour
1/2 cup cornstarch
3 tablespoons baking powder
2 tablespoons ground cinnamon

In a large bowl, mix all the ingredients together.

Store the mixture in a plastic bag, or other airtight container, in the refrigerator.

Yields 8 cups

BASIC PANCAKES

1 cup Basic Pancake Mix
1 cup water or apple juice
1 1/2 teaspoons oil (optional)
1/2 teaspoon cider vinegar

In a medium bowl, stir together the pancake mix, water, oil and vinegar. Stir only briefly; some small lumps can remain.

Fry the pancakes over medium heat in a hot, lightly oiled nonstick griddle, or frying pan, until they are brown on both sides.

Yields 8

Banana Pancakes

Bananas add a sweet, delicious flavor to pancakes. Serve these with pure maple syrup, or, for a special treat, with Fresh Strawberry Sauce or Easy Berry Sauce.

1 ripe medium banana, mashed
1 cup Basic Pancake Mix (page 210)
1 1/4 cups water or apple juice
1 teaspoon safflower or canola oil (optional)
1/2 teaspoon cider vinegar

In a medium bowl, mix all the ingredients together, stirring as little as necessary (some lumps can remain). Fry the pancakes over medium heat on a hot, lightly oiled nonstick griddle or large frying pan over medium heat until the pancakes are brown on both sides. (Some nonstick frying pans or griddles will not require the use of any oil.)

Yields 8 pancakes

Banana-Blueberry Pancakes

Follow the recipe for Banana Pancakes, adding 1/2 cup of fresh or frozen blueberries to the batter.

Fresh Strawberry Sauce

1 cup hulled fresh strawberries
2 tablespoons frozen and thawed apple juice concentrate

In a food processor, purée the strawberries and the apple juice. Chill the sauce, and serve it over pancakes.

Serves 2 to 3

Easy Berry Sauce

1 cup fresh or frozen strawberries
1 cup fresh or frozen blueberries
1/3 cup frozen and thawed apple juice concentrate
1/4 teaspoon ground coriander

Purée all the ingredients in a food processor or blender. Chill the sauce, and serve it over pancakes.

Serves 4 to 6

Easy Peach Topping

1 medium peach, cut into pieces (1 cup)
2 tablespoons frozen concentrated pineapple juice

Purée the peach and the pineapple juice in a food processor or blender. Chill the sauce, and serve it over pancakes.

Serves 2 to 3

BASIC WHEAT-FREE PANCAKE MIX

This wheat-free and dairy-free mix makes great pancakes. Store the mix in the refrigerator.

2 cups brown rice flour
2 cups *masa harina* or corn flour
1/4 cup cornstarch
2 1/2 tablespoons baking powder
1 1/2 tablespoons ground cinnamon
1 teaspoon ground coriander

In a medium bowl, mix all the ingredients together. Store the mixture in an airtight container until you are ready to use it.

Yields 5 cups

BASIC WHEAT-FREE PANCAKES

1 cup Basic Wheat-Free Pancake Mix
1 cup apple juice (or 1/4 cup frozen and thawed apple juice concentrate and 3/4 cup water)
1/2 teaspoon cider vinegar
1 teaspoon safflower or canola oil

In a medium bowl, beat the pancake mix with the next three ingredients. Stir only until the mixture is blended.

Fry the pancakes on a hot nonstick griddle or frying pan until they are brown on both sides.

Yields 8 to 12

WHEAT-FREE BANANA PANCAKES

Serve these with Fresh Strawberry Sauce or blueberry jam.

1/2 mashed medium banana
1 cup Basic Wheat-Free Pancake Mix
1 cup apple juice (or 1/4 cup frozen and thawed apple juice concentrate and 3/4 cup water)
1/2 teaspoon cider vinegar
1 teaspoon safflower or canola oil

In a medium bowl, mix all the ingredients except 1/2 teaspoon oil together, as little as necessary (some lumps can remain). Over medium heat, heat a nonstick griddle or a large nonstick frying pan. Brush the heated surface with 1/2 teaspoon oil, and fry the pancakes, turning once, until they are brown on both sides.

Yields 8 to 12 pancakes

APPLE CINNAMON PECAN PANCAKES

Serve these pancakes with pure maple syrup, or with heated apple juice concentrate with a dash of cinnamon added.

1/2 cup frozen and thawed apple juice concentrate
3/4 cup water
1 tablespoon plus 1/2 teaspoon safflower or canola oil
3/4 cup whole wheat flour
1 1/2 teaspoons baking powder
1/4 cup chopped pecans
1 tablespoon ground cinnamon
1 tablespoon cornstarch

Whisk together the apple juice, water, and 1 tablespoon oil in a medium bowl. In another bowl, mix together the next five ingredients. Add the dry ingredients to the liquid all at once, stirring with a whisk just until the ingredients are blended.

Over medium heat, heat a nonstick griddle or a large nonstick frying pan. Brush the heated surface with 1/2 teaspoon oil, and fry the pancakes, turning once, until they are brown on both sides.

Serves 2

ORANGE-SESAME PANCAKES

Serve easy-to-prepare pancakes with marmalade or maple syrup.

1 cup fresh orange juice (or 1/4 cup frozen and thawed orange juice concentrate, plus 3/4 cup water)
1 tablespoon safflower or canola oil
Grated zest of 1/2 lemon
3/4 cup whole wheat flour
1 1/2 teaspoons baking powder
2 tablespoons hulled sesame seeds
1 tablespoon cornstarch
1/2 teaspoon oil for pan

In a medium size bowl, whisk together the orange juice, 1 tablespoon oil, and the lemon zest. In another bowl, mix together the remaining ingredients, and add them all at once to the juice mixture, stirring with a whisk just until the batter is blended. Over medium heat, heat a nonstick griddle or large nonstick frying pan. Brush the heated surface with 1/2 teaspoon oil, and fry the pancakes, turning once, until they are brown on both sides.

Serves 2

SCRAMBLED TOFU AND ONIONS

This recipe makes a high-protein breakfast or brunch dish. Serve it with whole-grain toast and sliced tomatoes. The turmeric will turn the tofu from white to yellow as it heats.

1 14-ounce package firm tofu, rinsed and well drained
1 tablespoon reduced-salt soy sauce or Bragg Liquid Aminos
1 teaspoon cider vinegar
2 teaspoons onion powder
Pinch ground black pepper
1 teaspoon Vegit
1 teaspoon cornstarch
1/4 teaspoon turmeric
1 teaspoon water
1 medium onion, coarsely chopped
2 tablespoons water

Crumble the tofu into a medium bowl. Stir in the next five ingredients. In a small bowl, mix together the cornstarch, turmeric, and 1 teaspoon water, and stir this mixture into the tofu mixture.

In a preheated medium nonstick frying pan, sauté the chopped onion over medium heat, without oil, until the onion begins to brown and stick to the pan. Stir in 2 tablespoons water, and cook the onion 1 minute longer. Stir in the tofu mixture, and cook until the tofu is well heated. Serve the tofu hot.

Serves 2 to 3

SCRAMBLED TOFU RANCHERO

For brunch, serve this Mexican-flavored scrambled tofu with warm tortillas, guacamole, and salsa.

1 14-ounce package regular tofu, rinsed and well drained
1 tablespoon reduced-salt soy sauce or Bragg Liquid Aminos
2 teaspoons chili powder
1/4 teaspoon dried oregano
2/3 cup chopped fresh tomatoes
1/2 medium onion, coarsely chopped
2 large cloves garlic, coarsely chopped
1/2 jalapeño pepper, seeded, coarsely chopped
1/2 medium red or green bell pepper, coarsely chopped
1/2 cup firmly packed cilantro leaves
2 tablespoons water

Crumble the tofu into a medium bowl. Stir in the soy sauce or Bragg, chili powder, oregano, and chopped tomatoes, and set the bowl aside. In a preheated nonstick frying pan without oil, sauté the onion, garlic, peppers, and cilantro. When the onion begins to stick, stir in 2 tablespoons water, and continue sautéing until the onions and garlic are soft. Stir in the tofu mixture. Heat the mixture over medium heat for about 10 minutes, or just until it is heated through. Serve the tofu hot.

Serves 2 to 4

EASY SCRAMBLED TOFU

Here is an extra quick version of scrambled tofu. Rinse the tofu the night before, and let it drain overnight, so it will be ready to cook in the morning. Serve with Easy Hash Browns and sliced tomatoes.

1 14-ounce package firm tofu, rinsed and well
    drained
1 tablespoon reduced-salt soy sauce or Bragg
    Liquid Aminos
1 teaspoon cider vinegar
2 teaspoons onion powder
Pinch black pepper
1/4 teaspoon turmeric
1 teaspoon cornstarch

Crumble the tofu into a medium bowl. Stir in the remaining ingredients.

Preheat a medium nonstick frying pan. Cook the tofu, without oil, over medium heat, until it is well heated, stirring occasionally. Serve the tofu hot.

Serves 2 to 3

SCRAMBLED TOFU AND VEGETABLES

You'll enjoy this scrambled tofu for breakfast or for any meal. The turmeric will turn the tofu from white to yellow as it heats.

1/4 large onion, coarsely chopped
1 large celery stalk, coarsely chopped
1/4 large red bell pepper, coarsely chopped
1/4 large green bell pepper, coarsely chopped
2 tablespoons water
1 14-ounce package firm tofu, rinsed and well
    drained
1 tablespoon reduced-salt soy sauce or Bragg
    Liquid Aminos
2 teaspoons onion powder
1 teaspoon cider vinegar
1 teaspoon cornstarch
1/4 teaspoon turmeric

In a preheated nonstick frying pan, sauté the vegetables in 2 tablespoons water until the pan becomes dry.

Into a medium bowl, crumble the tofu. Stir the soy sauce or Bragg, onion powder, cider vinegar, cornstarch, and turmeric. Add the tofu mixture to the sautéed vegetables in the frying pan. Cook the mixture over medium heat, stirring occasionally, until the tofu is heated through and turns yellow.

Serves 2 to 3

Easy Hash Browns

Eating these hash browns won't make you feel guilty; they're cooked without oil. Enjoy them for breakfast or brunch with Easy Scrambled Tofu (page 215).

5 small boiling potatoes, peeled and coarsely chopped
1 tablespoon reduced-salt soy sauce or Bragg Liquid Aminos
1 teaspoon cider vinegar
1/8 teaspoon ground black pepper
1/2 teaspoon safflower or canola oil

Put the chopped potatoes into a medium bowl, and stir in the next four ingredients.

Preheat a large nonstick frying pan or griddle, and spread the potatoes evenly in the pan or on the griddle. Cook the potatoes over medium heat until they are brown on both sides.

Serves 2 to 3

Sweet Crunchy Millet Cereal

For those who enjoy a sweet cold cereal, this millet mixture is just the thing. It takes only minutes to prepare, and you can store it in the refrigerator or freezer.

8 cups puffed millet (available in health-food stores)
1/4 cup dark molasses
1/4 cup maple syrup
1/4 teaspoon ground ginger
1/2 teaspoon ground cinnamon

Preheat the oven to 350°.

Put the puffed millet into a large bowl. In a small nonstick saucepan, bring the remaining ingredients to a boil. Cook the mixture over medium heat for 3 to 5 minutes, until it rises and bubbles. Slowly pour the hot syrup into the puffed millet, while stirring constantly with a fork. Stir until all the millet is evenly coated.

Spread the millet evenly in a 10- by 15-inch jelly-roll pan. Bake the cereal for 15 minutes.

Let the cereal cool, then store it in the refrigerator or freezer.

Yields 8 cups

Sweet Crunchy Corn Cereal

Follow the recipe for Sweet Crunchy Millet Cereal, but substitute puffed corn for the puffed millet.

Yields 8 cups

High-Fiber Dry Cereal

This recipe makes eight servings of wholesome high-fiber cereal. Enjoy this cereal with water, fruit juice, or any milk substitute.

2 cups rolled oats
1 1/3 cups oat bran
1/4 cup sunflower seeds
2/3 cup black raisins
1/4 cup sliced or whole almonds

Mix all the ingredients together. Store the cereal mix in the refrigerator.

Yields 4 cups

High-Energy Granola

This hearty granola can keep you going all morning. Enjoy it with soy milk or any milk substitute.

4 cups oatmeal (rolled oats or oat flakes)
1 1/3 cups oat bran
2 tablespoons ground cinnamon
1/4 cup soy flour
1/4 cup grated coconut (optional)
1/4 cup sunflower seeds
1 cup frozen and thawed apple juice
    concentrate
2 tablespoons frozen and thawed orange juice
    concentrate
1/4 cup maple syrup

In a large bowl, mix together the first six ingredients. Add the apple juice, orange juice, and maple syrup, and stir until the mixture is blended. Bake the granola, half at a time, in a 10- by 15-inch nonstick jelly-roll pan for 25 to 35 minutes, or until the granola is golden brown. As it bakes, turn the granola every 8 to 10 minutes, so it browns evenly. Toward the end of the baking time, check often to see that the granola isn't burning or getting too brown.

Let the granola cool, then store it in the refrigerator or freezer.

Yields about 6 cups

Quick Hot Oat Bran Cereal

This pleasant hot cereal has a texture like Cream of Wheat. Pour 1 teaspoon maple syrup on top of each serving.

3/4 cup oat bran
2 cups cold water

Mix together the oat bran and water in a small nonstick saucepan. Heat the mixture over medium heat, while stirring with a wooden or plastic spoon, for 2 minutes. Lower the heat, and simmer the cereal for 1 minute longer. Serve the cereal hot.

Serves 2

Note: This recipe makes a thick hot cereal. For a thinner cereal, add 1/4 cup more water, and cook to the desired consistency.

Oat Bran and Wheat Bran Cereal

Serve this with maple syrup, or with bananas and raisins.

1 cup oat bran
1/2 cup wheat bran
3 cups cold water

Mix the oat bran, wheat bran, and water together in a medium nonstick saucepan. Heat the mixture over medium heat, while stirring with a wooden or plastic spoon, until the cereal thickens. Serve the cereal hot.

Serves 3 to 4

Note: This recipe makes a thick hot cereal. For a thinner cereal, add 1/4 cup more water, and cook to the desired consistency.

Hot Oatmeal-Oat Bran Cereal for Two

This hot cereal can be ready to enjoy in under 10 minutes. Serve it with maple syrup, sunflower seeds, and raisins.

1 cup rolled oats
3 cups water
1/2 cup oat bran

Mix the rolled oats and water together in a small nonstick saucepan. Bring the cereal to a boil, then reduce the heat to low. Cook the oatmeal over low heat for 5 minutes, uncovered, then stir in the oat bran. Continue to cook, stirring constantly, until the cereal thickens.
    Serve the cereal immediately.

Serves 3 to 4

Note: This recipe makes a thick hot cereal. For a thinner cereal, add 1/4 cup more water, and cook to the desired consistency.

Easy Hot Oat Bran-Oatmeal Cereal for One

Enjoy this cereal with a teaspoon of pure maple syrup, or sunflower seeds and raisins.

1/4 cup oat bran
1/4 cup rolled oats
1 cup water

In a small saucepan, mix together the oat bran, rolled oats, and water. Bring the mixture to a boil, uncovered, over medium heat. Then reduce the heat to low, and cook the cereal for 2 to 3 minutes, just until it thickens. Remove the pan from the heat, cover the pan, and let the cereal steam for a few minutes. Serve the cereal hot.

Serves 1

Easy Hot Oat Bran Cereal for One

1/2 cup oat bran
1 cup water

In a small saucepan, mix together the oat bran and water. Bring the mixture to a boil over medium heat. Then lower the heat, and simmer the cereal, uncovered, for 2 to 3 minutes, stirring occasionally.

Serve the cereal at once, or cover it and let it stand for a few minutes.

Serves 1

Note: For a thinner cereal, add a little more water.

Passover Banana-Pecan-Matzo "Fritters"

These make a delicious breakfast alternative. Serve them with fresh fruit or jam.

**Batter for Passover Banana-Pecan-Matzo
  Cookies (page 194)**

Drop the batter by rounded teaspoonfuls into a hot, lightly oiled nonstick frying pan. Fry the "fritters," turning them once, until they are brown on both sides. Serve them hot.

Yields 12 "fritters"

Sweet Brown Rice with Coconut, Dates, and Coriander

This sweet rice pudding is a special treat for breakfast. It keeps well in the refrigerator for about five days.

1 cup fresh coconut pieces
1 cup water
1/4 cup pitted dates
1 cup water
1 cup uncooked brown rice
1 teaspoon ground cinnamon
1/2 teaspoon ground coriander
1/4 cup black raisins

In a food processor, blend the coconut, 1 cup water, and the pitted dates until the coconut is finely ground. Pour the mixture into a 3-quart covered saucepan. Stir in an additional 1 cup water, the brown rice, spices and raisins. Bring the rice to a boil over medium heat, stirring occasionally. Lower the heat, cover the pan, and simmer the mixture over low heat for 20 minutes. Remove the pan from the heat, but keep the lid on. Set the rice aside for about 1 hour, or until the liquid is absorbed.

Fluff the rice with a fork. Serve it warm or cold.

Serves 6

Brown Rice-Soy Pudding with Black Currants

This rice pudding is great warm or cold for breakfast.

2 cups cooked brown rice
2 tablespoons cornstarch
1 cup soy milk
1/4 cup pure maple syrup
1 1/2 teaspoons vanilla extract
1/4 teaspoon ground coriander
1 1/2 teaspoons ground cinnamon
1/2 cup black currants (or black raisins)
1/2 cup chopped walnuts
Sprinkle of nutmeg

Preheat the oven to 375°.

In a large bowl, blend together all the ingredients except the nutmeg. Spread the mixture in a 1-quart ovenproof casserole dish, and sprinkle the nutmeg on top. Bake the pudding for about 35 minutes, or until it is light brown on top and bubbling around the edges. The pudding will be loosely set in the middle, but it will thicken as it cools.

Serves 4

Soft Brown Rice with Cinnamon and Nutmeg

This extra moist rice can be used as a base for a variety of dishes such as Vanilla Brown Rice Drink and Cinnamon-Raisin-Brown Rice Pudding. You can store it in the refrigerator for up to one week, or freeze it for later use.

1 pound uncooked brown rice
7 cups water
2 whole cinnamon sticks
1 teaspoon ground nutmeg

In a 4- to 5-quart saucepan, bring all the ingredients to a boil. Cover the pan, lower the heat, and simmer the rice for 1 hour, or until the liquid is absorbed.

Yields 8 cups

Vanilla Brown Rice Drink

You can enjoy this healthful beverage over cold cereal, or as a base for Carob Brown Rice Drink, Hot Carob Beverage for Two, or Banana Shake for Two.

1 1/2 cups uncooked brown rice
4 cups water
1/8 teaspoon almond extract
1 1/2 teaspoons vanilla extract
1/8 teaspoon sea salt (optional)
1 to 2 tablespoons maple syrup, to taste

In a large mixing bowl, soak the rice in water in the refrigerator for 48 hours. In a food processor or blender, blend the rice with 2 cups water, almond extract, vanilla, salt, and maple syrup. Strain the mixture into a 4-cup measure. Add enough additional water to equal 1 quart.

Store the rice drink in the refrigerator. Shake or stir it well before serving.

Yields 1 quart

Carob Brown Rice Drink

This healthy drink can be enjoyed all year-round.

Vanilla Brown Rice Drink
1 tablespoon carob powder

In a food processor or blender, blend 1 cup of Vanilla Brown Rice Drink and the carob powder. Add this mixture to the remaining 3 cups of Vanilla Brown Rice Drink.

Store the rice drink in the refrigerator. Shake or stir it well before serving.

Yields 1 quart

CINNAMON-RAISIN-BROWN RICE PUDDING

This maple-sweetened brown rice pudding is good hot or cold for breakfast, for dessert, or for snacks.

6 cups Soft Brown Rice with Cinnamon and Nutmeg (page 221)
1 3/4 cups water
1 tablespoon ground cinnamon
1/2 teaspoon ground coriander
2 tablespoons cornstarch
1 teaspoon baking powder
2 teaspoons safflower or canola oil
1/2 cup maple syrup
1 tablespoon vanilla extract
1 cup black raisins
1/2 cup chopped walnuts
Sprinkle of nutmeg

Preheat the oven to 400°.

Put 4 cups Soft Brown Rice with Cinnamon and Nutmeg into a large bowl. In a food processor or blender, blend 2 cups Soft Brown Rice with Cinnamon and Nutmeg along with the water, cinnamon, coriander, cornstarch, and baking powder. Stir this mixture into the rice in the bowl until the ingredients are well blended, then stir in the next five ingredients.

Put the mixture into a 3-quart ovenproof soufflé dish, and sprinkle the top with nutmeg. Bake the rice pudding uncovered for 50 to 60 minutes, or until it is brown on top and set around edges.

Serve the pudding hot or cold.

Serves 8 to 10

BANANA SHAKE FOR TWO

2 large ripe bananas
1 cup Vanilla Brown Rice Drink (page 221), or other milk substitute
4 to 6 ice cubes

In a food processor or blender, blend the bananas, the Vanilla Brown Rice Drink or other milk substitute, and the ice cubes.

Serves 2

HOT CAROB DRINK FOR TWO

1 cup water
1 cup Vanilla Brown Rice Drink (page 221), or other milk substitute
1 tablespoon carob powder
1 teaspoon dark molasses

Heat the ingredients in a small saucepan. Strain the mixture into 2 mugs. Serve at once.

Serves 2

Easy Hot Carob Breakfast Drink

2 tablespoons carob powder
2 cups hot water
2 teaspoons maple syrup
2 teaspoons molasses
1 cup soy milk or other milk substitute

Heat all the ingredients in a medium size saucepan until the mixture is piping hot. Serve immediately.

Serves 2 to 3

Hawaiian Smoothie

1/2 ripe Hawaiian papaya, seeded
1 large banana
1/3 cup frozen and thawed pineapple juice
  concentrate
1/2 cup water
4 ice cubes (optional)

Scoop out the papaya flesh, and put it into a food processor or blender. Add the remaining ingredients, and purée until the mixture is smooth. Serve at once.

Serves 2

Easy Soy Milk

This pleasant-tasting, wholesome soy milk takes only minutes to prepare.

3 cups water
1/2 cup soy flour
1 tablespoon maple syrup
1/2 teaspoon cider vinegar
1 teaspoon vanilla extract

In a medium bowl, blend all the ingredients with a whisk. If any lumps remain, pour the mixture through a strainer. Store the soy milk in the refrigerator in a covered jar. Shake the jar well before serving.

Yields 3 1/2 cups

Index

A

Almond Cookies, 196
Almond Mocha Torte, 152
Appetizers, 2-10
    artichokes with lemon-tahini dressing, 10
    babaganoosh, 5
    eggplant dip, Middle Eastern 5
    eggplant-bell pepper dip, Bulgarian, 8
    garbanzo bean dips, 5, 6
    hummus, 5
    lentil-nut-oat bran balls, 6
    marinated and steamed vegetables, 9
    Middle Eastern, on a platter, 8
    oven-barbecued tofu, 7
    pita bread, toasted, 8
    quiche, 4
    tofu "egg salad," 2
    tofu wieners in dough, 7
    vegetables, raw, on a platter, 10
Apple Delight Torte, 149
Apple-Cinnamon Sweet Rolls, 201
Apple-Cinnamon-Pecan Pancakes, 213
Apple-Pecan Torte, 148
Apples, baked, 208
Apricot Pie, 155
Apricot-Nut Mini Sweet Rolls, 200
Artichokes with Lemon-Tahini Dressing, 10
Asian-style dishes, 89-101
Asian-style Sweet and Sour Tofu with Pineapple and Bell Peppers, 91
Avocado-Mustard Dressing, 12

B

Babaganoosh (Middle Eastern eggplant dip), 5
Baked Tofu Slices with Garlic-Ginger Sauce, 88
Baking powder, xii
Baking tips, xi-xii
Banana Pancakes, 211
Banana Shake for Two, 222
Banana Squash Passover Rolls, 130
Banana Squash-Raisin-Nut Bread, 124
Banana(s)
    -apricot-almond buns, 203
    blueberry pancakes, 211
    -brown-rice flour-walnut cookies, 192
    frozen, with carob fudge topping, 204
    gingerbread cookies, 183
    pancakes, 211, 212
    -pecan-matzo cookies, 194
    -pecan-matzo Passover cookies, 194
    shake, 222
    -walnut coffee cake, 202
    -walnut-oat bran cookies, 186
Banana-Apricot-Almond Buns, 203
Banana-Orange Passover Cookies, 181
Banana-Raisin-Pear-Oat Bran Muffins, 131
Banana-Squash Pudding, 78
Banana-Walnut Cake with Blueberry-Banana Filling and Easy Blueberry Topping, 142
Banana-Wheat Bran-Raisin Muffins, 129
Barley
    in burgers, 109
    and rice, Indian-style, 53
    in soups, 35, 39
    in stew, with beans, 60, 61
Basic Black Beans, 75

Basic Brown Rice, 76
Basic Pancake Mix, 210
Basic Pancakes, 210
Basic Wheat-Free Pancake Mix, 212
Basic Wheat-Free Pancakes, 212
Bean-Barley-Oat Bran Burgers, 109
Bean(s)
    black, 71, 75
    in burgers, 109, 110, 111
    dips, 5,6
    dry, how to cook, xi
    garbanzo, 5, 6, 31, 58, 109, 110, 111
    green, salad, 22
    kidney, 31, 33
    lima, 61
    pinto, 60, 66, 67, 68, 73
    red, 39, 67, 68
    refried, 66
    in soups, 31-33, 39
    sprouting, 111
    in stews, 58, 60, 61, 67-68
    in tamale pie, 73
    in tostadas, 71
    white, 32, 62
Beet salad
    pickled, 25
    zucchini-carrot-, 20
Bell pepper(s)
    -broccoli sauté, 92
    -eggplant stew, 63
    salad, 21
    stuffed, 102-4
    and tofu, sautéed, 93, 97
Bell Peppers Stuffed with Lentils, Rice, Vegetables, and Pine Nuts, 103
Bell Peppers Stuffed with Tofu and Walnuts, 102
Best Tofu Enchilada Casserole, 64
Biscuits
    baking-powder, 133, 134

carrot-spice, 133
wheat-free, 133
Black beans, 75
in tostadas, 71
Bragg Liquid Aminos, ix, x
Braided Whole Wheat-Yam-Raisin
Bread, 123
Braided Whole-Wheat Cashew-
Onion Loaf, 120
Braided Whole-Wheat Sabbath
Loaves, 119
Breaded Veggie "Wiener Schnitzel,"
108
Bread(s). *See also* Buns; Muffins;
Scones
baking, tips for, xi-xii
banana, 124
banana squash cornbread, 126
banana squash Passover rolls,
130
banana squash-raisin-nut, 124
brown-rice flour-banana, 125
cashew-onion, braided, 120
cornbread, 125, 126
corn-rye-oat bran, 118
Italian, 128
oat, 117
oat bran-pumpkin, 123
paratha, 127
quick, 117, 123, 124, 125, 126
reheating, vi
Sabbath, braided, 119
Scotch oat-rye, 117
sour onion-corn-rye, 121
storing, xii
sweet-potato cornbread, 126
wheat-free, 117, 118, 123,
125, 126
yam, coiled, 122
yam-raisin, 123
yeast, 116, 117, 118-22, 123,
124, 128
seed, 116
Breakfast dishes, 211-23
Broccoli

and bell-pepper sauté, 92
-mushroom-tofu sauté, 101
and vegetable salad, 12
Broccoli-Bell Pepper Sauté, 92
Broccoli-Vegetable Salad, 12
Broiled High-Energy Slices with
Barbecued Flavor, 86
Broiled High-Energy Slices with
Garlic and Ginger, 84
Broth
quick, 40
vegetable, 36
Brown Rice-Soy Pudding with Black
Currants, 220
Brown Rice-Yam-Pecan Cookies, 192
Brown-Rice Flour Crust, 156
Brown-Rice Flour-Banana Bread, 125
Brown-Rice Flour-Banana-Walnut
Cookies, 193
Brown-Rice Flour-Date-Raisin-
Walnut Cookies, 190
Brown-Rice Flour-Nut Crust, 157
Brown-Rice Flour-Nut-Marmalade
Cookies, 191
Brown-Rice Flour-Sweet Potato
Scones with Raisins or Currants,
135
Brownies, carob-pecan, 176
Buckwheat
groats with noodles, 77
noodles, 22, 40
steamed, with brown rice, 88
Buckwheat-Noodle Salad with
Ginger-Orange-Pecan Dressing,
22
Bulgar Wheat Salad, 11
Bulgarian Eggplant-Bell Pepper Dip,
8
Buns. *See also* Rolls
banana-apricot-almond, 203
cinnamon with raisins and
almonds, 199
yam sticky, 198
yam-cinnamon-raisin, 197
Burgers, 108-13

C
Cabbage rolls, sweet and sour, 80
Cabbage soups, 37, 39
Cake(s). *See also* Tortes
baking, tips for, xii-xiii
banana squash fruitcake, 140
banana-walnut with blue-
berry-banana filling, 142
carob-cherry-date, 143
carrot-raisin-walnut, 146
date-carrot, 147
fig-carob fudge, 144
lemon-walnut, 145
Passover date-walnut pudding,
148
pear-raisin-nut, 141
storing, xii
yam-raisin-spice, 141
Candies
carob-nut clusters, 205
carob-raisin clusters, 205
date-carob fudge balls, 204
date-sunflower-sesame squares,
206
Carbohydrates, simple versus
complex, ix
Carob breakfast drinks, 222, 223
Carob Brown Rice Drink, 221
Carob-Cherry-Date Cake, 143
Carob-Mocha Mousse with Sliced
Almonds, 174
Carob-Nut Clusters, 205
Carob-Oat Bran Muffins, 130
Carob-Pecan Cookies, 177
Carob-Pecan-Brown-Rice Flour
Crust, 167
Carob-Peppermint-Pecan-Rice
Cookies, 178
Carob-Raisin Clusters, 205
Carrot Spice Biscuits, 133
Carrot-celery-raisin salad, 19
Carrot-Raisin-Walnut Cake, 146
Carrot-spice cookies, 180
Carrot-sweet potato-prune stew
(*tzimmes*), 77

Cashew-mushroom sauce, 107
Casseroles
    apple, 165
    brown rice-vegetable, 76
    Mexican-style tofu, 69
    tofu enchilada, 64
    tofu-tamale pie, 72
Cauliflower, potato, and pea curry, 50
Celery-root salad, 24
Cereal
    corn, 216
    dry, 216-217
    granola, 217
    high-fiber, 217
    hot, 218-219
    millet, 216
    oat-bran, 218-219
    oatmeal-oat bran, 218, 219
Children's Wholesome Gingerbread,
    183
Chili beans, 67-68
Chinese-style Salad with Marinated
    Tofu, 24
Cholesterol, iii
Chopped Salad for Two, 13
Chopped Vegetable Salad for Two
    with Lemon-Tahini Dressing, 16
Chopped Vegetable-Pasta Salad, 16
Chutney
    coconut, 53
    mango, 53
Cinnamon-Raisin-Brown Rice
    Pudding, 222
Classic Pesto, 52
Classic Tofu Lasagna, 47
Cobbler
    pear, 160
    summer fruit, 154
Coconut Chutney, 53
Coffee cake. See also Bread(s), quick
    banana-walnut, 202
    crescent-shaped, 199
    pineapple-oat bran, 203
Coiled Sweet Whole-Wheat Yam
    Bread, 122

Coleslaw
    with carrots, 19
    with red cabbage, 18
Coleslaw with Carrots, Ginger, and
    Sunflower Seeds, 19
Colorful Grated Vegetable Salad, 26
Cookies
    almond, 196
    banana gingerbread, 183
    banana-orange Passover, 181
    banana-pecan-matzo, 194
    banana squash-spice-oatmeal,
        187
    banana-walnut-oat bran, 186
    brown-rice flour-banana-
        walnut, 192
    brown-rice flour-banana-
        walnut, 193
    brown-rice flour-date-raisin-
        walnut, 190
    brown-rice flour-nut-marma-
        lade, 191
    brown-rice flour-yam-pecan,
        192
    carob-pecan, 177
    carob-pecan brownies, 176
    carob-pecan-oat bran, 187
    carob-peppermint-pecan-rice,
        178
    carob-walnut, 178
    carrot-spice, 180
    date-carob-pecan bars, 177
    date-raisin-spice, 190
    date-walnut crescent, 189
    ginger snaps, 184
    gingerbread-raisin bars, 182
    glazed oat bran-rice, 193
    granola, 180
    haroset, 191
    lemon-walnut-oat bran, 185
    mandelbrot, 196
    molasses-raisin-oat bran, 186
    orange-cinnamon-oatmeal,
        185
    orange-oat bran, 179

    peanut butter, 194
    pumpkin-oat, 196
    sesame-seed, 197
    squash-oat bran-spice, 184
    sweet-potato gingerbread, 183
    wheat-free, 178-180, 184, 188,
        190, 191, 192-194, 195
    yam gingerbread, 182
Corn cereal, 216
Cornbread, 125-127
Country-style White Beans, 62
Crackers
    brown rice-oat bran, 195
    oat bran-spice, 179
Creamy Carob Mousse Pie, 167
Creamy Carob Mousse Pudding, 174
Creamy Pineapple-Tofu Frosting, 147
Creamy Tofu-Curry Dressing (or
    Dip), 11
Crêpes, Indian-style potato, 56-57
Crescent-shaped Coffee Cake, 199
Crispy Pita Bread, 8
Crockpot dishes, 60, 67, 68
Crowd-Size Wheat-Free Apple
    Casserole, 165
Crunchy Brown Rice-Oat Bran
    Crackers, 195
Crunchy Brown-Rice Flour Topping,
    156
Crunchy Brown-Rice Flour-Nut
    Topping, 158
Crunchy Granola Cookies, 180
Crunchy Mandelbrot, 196
Crunchy Marinated Cucumber Salad,
    21
Crunchy Sesame-Seed Cookies, 197
Crunchy Sprouted Garbanzo Beans,
    111
Crunchy Wheat-Free Peanut Butter
    Cookies, 194
Crustless Gelled Banana-Blueberry
    Pie, 163
Crustless Gelled Kiwi-Banana Pie,
    163
Crustless Gelled Mixed-Fruit Pie, 163

Crustless Gelled Strawberry-Banana
    Pie, 162
Cucumber, Cherry Tomato, and
    Romaine Salad, 15
Cucumber salad
        with dill, 13
        crunchy marinated, 21
        sweet, 25
Cucumber Salad with Fresh Dill, 13
Curried Cauliflower, Potatoes, and
    Peas, 54
Curried Rice and Eggplant Casserole,
    55
Curries, 54, 55, 59
Curry-Ginger-Tofu-Vegetable
    Quiche, 4

D

Dal (Indian lentil soup), 28, 29
Date Brownie Torte with Bananas
    and Boysenberry Topping, 151
Date-Almond-Brown Rice Pudding,
    172
Date-Carob Fudge Balls, 204
Date-Carrot Cake, 147
Date-Raisin-Spice Cookies, 190
Date-Sunflower-Sesame Candy
    Squares, 206
Date-Sweetened Tofu "Cheese" Pie,
    171
Date-Walnut Crescent Cookies, 189
Date-Walnut Party Treats, 207
Deluxe Chinese-style Vegetables
    with Tofu, 94
Deluxe Dutch Apple Pie, 157
Deluxe Poached Pear Pie, 159
Deluxe Trail Mix, 208
Diet for a New America (John Robbins),
    88
Dips
        babaganoosh, 5
        eggplant, Middle Eastern, 5
        eggplant-bell pepper,
            Bulgarian, 8

garbanzo bean, 5, 6
hummus, 5
Indian, 6
lemon-tahini-garlic, 10
Middle Eastern, 5
tofu-curry, 11
Dressing
        avocado-lemon-herb, 17
        avocado-mustard, 12
        ginger-orange-pecan, 22
        lemon-Dijon, 15
        lemon-tahini, 16
        red bell pepper, 14
        sesame-ginger, 24
        tofu-curry, 11
        vinaigrette, 15
Drinks, 221, 222-23

E

Easy Baking-Powder Biscuits, 134
Easy Banana Bread, 124
Easy Banana Gingerbread Cookies,
    183
Easy Banana Squash-Spice-Oatmeal
    Cookies, 187
Easy Banana-Walnut-Oat Bran
    Cookies, 186
Easy Barley and Brown Rice, 89
Easy Berry Sauce, 211
Easy Black-Bean Tostadas, 71
Easy Brown-Lentil *Dal*, 29
Easy Brown-Rice Flour Gravy, 105
Easy Brown-Rice Flour-Banana-
    Walnut Cookies, 192
Easy Carob Fudge Sauce, 205
Easy Carob-Pecan-Oat Bran Cookies,
    187
Easy Cashew Cream, 173
Easy Chopped Vegetable Salad, 20
Easy Coleslaw with Carrots, 19
Easy Colorful Pasta Salad, 14
Easy Enchilada Sauce, 66
Easy Glazed Oat Bran-Rice Cookies,
    193

Easy Granola Banana Squares, 189
Easy Grated Carrot-Celery-Raisin
    Salad, 19
Easy Grated Raw Vegetable Salad, 20
Easy Guacamole, 65
Easy Hashbrowns, 216
Easy Hearts of Romaine Salad, 15
Easy High-Protein Lentil-Soy
    Burgers, 112
Easy Hot Carob Breakfast Drink, 223
Easy Hot Oat Bran-Oatmeal Cereal
    for One, 219
Easy Hot Oat-Bran Cereal for One,
    219
Easy Italian-style Lentil Soup, 30
Easy Lemon-Walnut-Oat Bran
    Cookies, 185
Easy Lentil Soup, 29
Easy Lentil-Cabbage Stew, 60
Easy Lentil-Vegetable Soup, 30
Easy Marinara Sauce, 102
Easy Marinated Tomato and Cucum-
    ber Salad, 12
Easy Mexican Sauce, 65
Easy Molasses-Raisin-Oat Bran
    Cookies, 186
Easy Onion-Poppy Seed Scones, 134
Easy Orange-Cinnamon-Oatmeal
    Cookies, 185
Easy Peach Topping, 211
Easy Potato Pancakes, 114
Easy Sautéed Tofu and Vegetables,
    90
Easy Scrambled Tofu, 215
Easy Soy Milk, 223
Easy Spanish Rice, 74
Easy Steamed Brown Rice with
    Celery, Onion, and Carrots, 89
Easy Steamed Vegetables, 92
Easy Stewed Plums, 208
Easy Strawberry-Blueberry Pie, 161
Easy Sweet and Sour Sauce, 85
Easy Tofu and Veggies for Two, 98
Easy Tofu-Tamale Pie Casserole, 72
Easy Veggie Tofu Cutlets, 105

Easy Wheat-Free Apple-Pecan Pie, 165
Easy Wheat-Free Oat Loaf, 117
Easy Wheat-Free Oat-Bran Muffins, 138
Easy Wheat-Free Peach Pie, 164
Easy Wheat-Free Yam-Sweetened Oat-Bran Chews, 188
Easy Yam-Oatmeal Cookies, 188
Eggplant
    curry, 55
    dips, 5, 8
    salad, exotic, 17
    stew, with bell peppers, 63
    stuffed, 104
    -zucchini salad, 17
Eggplant-Bell Pepper Stew, 63
Eggplant Curry, 55
"Egg salad," tofu, 2
Enchilada sauce, 73
Enchiladas, tofu, 64
Exotic Eggplant Salad, 17

F
Fat, dietary, ix
Fat-Free Hashbrowns with Onions, 114
Flavorful Celery-Root Salad, 24
Flavorful Vegetable Broth or Soup Stock, 36
Flavorful Vegetable Broth with Noodles, 36
Flour, whole-grain, xi-xii
    pastry, xi
    sifting, xii
    storing, xi
Fresh Cilantro Salsa, 65
Fresh Herb Marinade, 9
Fresh Spicy Salsa, 65
Fresh Strawberry Sauce, 211
Fresh Vegetable Platter, 10
"Fritters," banana-pecan-matzo, 219
Frozen Bananas with Easy Carob Fudge Sauce, 204

Fruit and Vegetable Salad, 25
Fruitcake, banana squash, 140
Fruit-Sweetened Almond Torte, 152
Fruit-Sweetened Carob-Walnut Cookies, 178
Fruit-Sweetened Wheat-Free Oat-Bran Muffins, 138
Fruity *Mandelbrot*, 196

G
Garbanzo Bean Veggie Burgers, 110
Garbanzo Bean-Garlic Burgers, 111
Garbanzo beans
    in burgers, 109, 110, 111
    in dips, 5, 6
    in soup, 31, 33
    sprouts, 111
    in stew, Indian-style, 58
Garlic-Ginger-Tofu Dinner Slices, 93
Gelled Fresh Peach Pie, 164
Gingerroot, freezing, xi
Ginger snaps, 184
Ginger-Red Bell Pepper-Tofu Sauté, 97
Gingerbread, 183
    cookies, 182, 182, 183, 183
Gingerbread-Raisin Bars, 182
Glazed Fresh Strawberry Pie, 162
Glazed Poached Apple Pie, 158
Gnocchi, potato-oat bran, 51
Granola, 217
    banana squares, 189
    cookies, 180
Grated Fresh Vegetable Salad, 20
Gravy
    brown-rice flour, 105
    mushroom-onion-garlic, 106
Greek Potato Salad with Fresh Mint, 23
Green Split-Pea Soup, 34

H
Haroset (apple-walnut Passover mix), 191
Haroset cookies, 191
Hashbrowns, 216
Hawaiian Smoothie, 223
Heart disease, ix
Hearty Bean and Pasta Soup, 31
Hearty Cabbage-Potato Soup, 37
Hearty Chili Beans, 68
Hearty Crockpot Bean-Barley Stew, 60
Hearty Split-Pea Soup, 33
Herb marinade, 9
Herbs, freezing, xi
High-Energy Granola, 217
High-Energy Protein Loaf, 82
High-Energy Stew, 63
High-energy loaves, 82-86, 107
High-Fiber Dry Cereal, 217
High-Protein Lentil-Vegetable Loaf, 107
Holiday Baked Squash with Curried Brown-Rice Stuffing, 79
Holiday Banana Squash Fruit Cake, 140
Holiday Brown Rice-Vegetable Casserole, 76
Holiday Buckwheat Groats with Noodles, 77
Holiday Carrot-Sweet Potato-Prune Stew, 77
Holiday Sweet and Sour Cabbage Rolls, 80
Hot Carob Drink for Two, 222
Hot Oatmeal-Oat Bran Cereal for Two, 218
Hummus, 5

I
Indian Garbanzo Bean Dip, 6
Indian-style Brown Rice and Barley, 53

Indian-style dishes, 6, 28-29, 50, 53-58
Indian-style Garbanzo Bean Stew, 58
Indian-style Potato Crêpes, 56-57
Italian-style dishes, 42-50, 51-52, 87
Italian-style Eggplant-Tofu Casserole, 50

J
Jalapeno peppers, freezing, xi

K
Kasha Varnishkas (Holiday Buckwheat Groats with Noodles), 77

L
Lasagna, 47-49
Lasagna Florentine, 49
Leek-Potato-Onion Soup, 38
Lemon Pudding Pie, 169
Lemon Tofu Custard Sauce, 170
Lemon Tofu Pie, 169
Lemon Tofu Pie with Lemon Glaze, 170
Lemon-Tahini Dressing, 16
Lemon-Tahini-Garlic Dip, 10
Lemon-Walnut Cake with Creamy Lemon-Walnut-Tofu Frosting, 145
Lentil
    balls, with spaghetti, 43
    curry, 59
    -nut burgers, 108
    -nut loaf, 106
    -nut-oat bran balls, 6
    -rice burgers, 113
    soups, 28-31, 35, 36
    stews, 59, 60, 61
    stuffing, for bell peppers, 103
    -vegetable loaf, 107
Lentil-Nut Loaf, 106
Lentil-Spinach Soup, 31

Lettuce, Broccoli, and Tomato Salad, 14
Light Sweet and Sour Cabbage Borscht, 39
Lima bean stew, with barley and rice, 61
Live Longer Now (Nathan Pritikin), 88

M
Marinade, herb, 9
Marinated and Steamed Vegetables, 9
Marinated Green Bean Salad, 22
Masala Dosa (Indian-style Potato Crepes), 56
Mexican-style dishes, 64-75
Mexican-style Tofu Casserole for Four, 69
Middle Eastern Appetizer Platter, 8
Middle Eastern Dip (hummus), 5
Mild Crockpot Chili Beans, 68
Millet cereal, 216
Mocha Tofu Pie, 166
Moist Carob-Pecan Brownies, 176
Moist Fig-Carob Fudge Cake, 144
Moroccan Bell Pepper Salad, 21
Mousse
    carob-mocha, 174
    creamy carob, 174
    strawberry tofu, 173
Muffins
    banana-apple-oat bran, 137
    banana-blueberry-oat bran, 129
    banana-raisin-pear-oat bran, 131
    banana-wheat bran-raisin, 129
    carob-oat bran, 130
    corn, 128
    fruit-sweetened, 138
    oat-bran, 138

onion-poppy seed-oat bran, 135
    wheat-free, 137, 138
    whole wheat-banana-pineapple, 132
Mushroom
    gravy, 106
    soups, 35, 37
Mushroom-Barley Soup, 35
Mushroom-Barley-Lentil Soup, 35
Mushroom-Broccoli-Tofu Saute, 101
Mushroom-Cashew Sauce, 107
Mushroom-Onion-Garlic Gravy, 106
Mushroom-Potato Curry, 54
Mushroom-Potato-Vegetable Soup, 37

N
Nutty Steamed Brown Rice, 97

O
Oat bran
    in breads, 118, 123
    cereals, 218-219
    in cookies, 179, 194, 195, 186, 187, 193
    in gnocchi, 51
    -lentil-nut balls, 6
    in muffins, 129, 130, 131, 135, 137
    in scones, 136, 137
Oat Bran-Banana Muffins, 131
Oat Bran-Pumpkin Bread, 123
Oat-Bran and Wheat-Bran Cereal, 218
Oat-Pecan Crust, 168
Oils, cold-pressed, ix-x
Onion-Poppy Seed-Oat Bran Muffins, 135
Orange Halves Stuffed with Banana-Squash Pudding, 78
Orange-pecan pastries, 200
Orange-Sesame Pancakes, 213

Organic produce, xi
Oval Whole-Wheat Italian Loaves, 128
Oven-Baked Garbanzo Bean Burgers, 109
Oven-Baked Potato Chips, 114
Oven-Barbecued Tofu "Steaks," 100
Oven-Barbecued Tofu Appetizers, 7
Oven-Barbecued Tofu on Skewers, 99
Oven-Browned Red Potatoes and Onions, 113

P

Pancake mixes
    basic, 210
    wheat-free, 212
Pancake toppings, 211
Pancakes
    apple-cinnamon-pecan, 213
    banana, 211, 212
    banana blueberry, 211
    basic, 210
    frying without oil, xi
    orange-sesame, 213
    potato, 114
    wheat-free, 212
Paratha (Whole-Wheat Indian Bread), 127
Passover Banana-Pecan-Matzo "Fritters," 219
Passover Banana-Pecan-Matzo Cookies, 194
Passover Date-Walnut Pudding Cake, 148
Passover Haroset, 191
Passover Haroset Cookies, 191
Pasta dishes
    eggplant-tofu casserole, 50
    gnocchi, potato-oat bran, with spinach pesto, 51
    lasagna Florentine, 49
    pasta marinara with zucchini and asparagus, 45

pasta pomodora, 44
pasta primavera with pine nuts, 42
pasta with eggplant and tomato-bell pepper sauce, 43
pasta with tomatoes, garlic, and basil, 44
pasta with tomatoes, basil, and pine nuts, 46
pasta salad, 14
spaghetti with lentil balls, 43
tofu lasagna, classic, 47
tofu-broccoli lasagna, 48
Pasta Marinara with Zucchini and Asparagus, 45
Pasta Pomodora, 44
Pasta Primavera with Pine Nuts, 42
Pasta salad, 14
Pasta with Eggplant and Tomato-Bell Pepper Sauce, 43
Pasta with Tomatoes, Garlic, and Basil, 44
Pasta with Tomatoes, Basil, and Pine Nuts, 46
Pastries. *See also* Buns; Pies
    apple-cinnamon sweet rolls, 201
    apricot-nut mini sweet rolls, 200
    jam-walnut, 202
    prune-filled three-cornered, 201
    swirled orange-pecan, 200
Pastry dough, sweet yam, 198. *See also* Pie crusts
Peach topping, for pancakes, 211
Peanut butter cookies, 194
Pear-Raisin-Nut Cake, 141
Pears, poached, with carob fudge sauce, 206
Peas
    in burgers, 112
    in soups, 33-34

    in stew, with lentils and barley, 61
Pesto
    spinach, 51, 52
    classic, 52
Petite Date-Carob-Pecan Bars, 177
Pickled Beet Salad, 25
Pie crusts
    brown-rice flour, 156
    brown-rice flour-nut, 157
    brown-rice flour-nut topping, 158
    carob-pecan-brown-rice flour, 167
    brown-rice flour topping, 156
    oat-pecan, 168
    pineapple-almond-brown-rice flour, 159
    wheat-free, 156, 157, 158, 159, 167, 168
    whole wheat-pecan, 172
Pie(s). *See also* Cobbler
    apple, 154, 155, 157, 158, 165
    apple-pecan, 165
    apricot, 155
    banana-blueberry, 163
    carob mousse, 167
    crustless, 162-64
    kiwi-banana, 163
    lemon pudding, 169
    lemon tofu, 169, 170, 171
    mixed-fruit, 163
    mocha tofu, 166
    peach, 164
    pear, 159, 160, 161
    pear-almond, 161
    strawberry, 161, 162
    strawberry-banana, 162
    strawberry-blueberry, 161
    tofu "cheese," with blueberry glaze, 168
    wheat-free, 154, 155, 157, 158, 159, 160-65, 166, 167, 168, 169, 170, 171
    yam-pecan, 166

Pilaf, 86
Pineapple-Almond-Brown Rice
 Crust, 159
Pineapple-Oat Bran Coffee Cake
 Squares, 203
Pinto beans, 60, 66, 67, 68, 73
Pita bread, toasted, 8
Plum Torte with Brown-Rice Flour-
 Almond Butter Crust, 150
Plums, stewed, 208
Poached Pear Pie, 160
Poached Winter Pears with Easy
 Carob Fudge Sauce, 206
Polenta, 87
Polenta Topped with Vegetables and
 Pine Nuts, 87
Potato(es)
 chips, oven-baked, 114
 crêpes, Indian-style, 56-57
 curries, 54
 hash-browned, 114, 216
 oven-browned, 113
 pancakes, 114
 salads, 23
 soups, 37, 38
Potato-Leek Soup, 38
Prakus (Holiday Sweet and Sour
 Cabbage Rolls), 80
Pritikin, Nathan, ix
Protein loaves, 82-86
Prune-filled Three-Cornered Pastries,
 201
Puddings
 banana squash, 78
 brown-rice, with coconut,
dates, and coriander, 220
 brown rice-soy, with black
currants, 220
 carob-mocha mousse, 174
 carob mousse, 174
 cinnamon-raisin-brown rice,
 222
 date-almond-brown rice, 172
 strawberry tofu mousse, 173
Pumpkin-oat chews, wheat-free, 195

Q
Quiche, Curry-Ginger-Tofu-
 Vegetable, 4
Quick and Easy Broth, 40
Quick and Easy Broth with Buck-
 wheat Noodles, 40
Quick and Easy Curried Lentils, 59
Quick and Easy Hot Enchilada
 Sauce, 73
Quick Banana-Walnut Coffee Cake,
 202
Quick Hot Oat-Bran Cereal, 218
Quick Jam-Walnut Pastries, 202
Quick Thick Lima Bean-Barley-Rice
 Stew, 61

R
Raisin-Nut-Seed-Oat Bran
 Crunchies, 207
Red bell pepper dressing, 14
Refried beans, 66
 in tamale pie, 73
Reheating solid foods, xi
Rice
 and barley, easy, 89
 and buckwheat, 88
 casseroles, 55, 76
 with celery, onion and carrots,
 89
 drink, 221
 Indian-style, with barley, 53
 pilaf, 86
 soft, with cinnamon and
nutmeg, 221
 Spanish, 74, 75
 steamed, 97
 stew, with lima beans and
 barley, 61
 stuffing, 79, 103
Robbins, John, ix
Rolls, bread
 apple-cinnamon, 201
 banana squash, 130

Romaine, Tomato, and Carrot Salad,
 11
Romaine and Tomato Salad with
 Avocado-Lemon-Herb Dressing,
 17
Romaine Salad with Lemon-Dijon
 Dressing, 15

S
Salaan Vegetables (Curried Cauliflower and Peas), 50
Salad(s)
 beet-zucchini-carrot, 20
 broccoli-vegetable, 12
 buckwheat-noodle, 22
 bulgar, 11
 carrot-celery-raisin, 19
 celery-root, 24
 Chinese-style, 24
 chopped vegetable, 13, 16, 20
 chopped vegetable and pasta,
 16
 coleslaw, 18, 19
 cucumber, cherry tomato, and
 romaine, 15
 cucumber with dill, 13
 eggplant, 17
 eggplant-zucchini, 18
 fruit and vegetable, 25
 grated vegetable, 20, 26
 green bean, 22
 heart of romaine, 15
 lettuce, broccoli, and tomato,
 14
 marinated cucumber, 21
 Moroccan bell pepper, 21
 pasta, 14
 pickled beet, 25
 potato, 23
 romaine, tomato, and carrot,
 11
 romaine and tomato, 17
 romaine with lemon-Dijon
 dressing, 15

sweet and sour high-energy, 26
sweet cucumber, 25
tabouli, 11
tomato and cucumber, 12
Salsas. *See also* Sauces
    cilantro, 65
    guacamole, 65
    spicy, 65
Sauces. *See also* Salsas
    barbecue, 100
    berry, 211
    cashew cream, 173
    carob fudge, 205
    dessert, 170, 173, 205
    enchilada, 66, 73
    lemon tofu custard, 170
    marinara, 102
    Mexican, 65
    mushroom-cashew, 107
    for pancakes, 211
    peach pancake topping, 211
    strawberry, 211
    sweet and sour, 81, 85
    tomato-basil, 46
    vanilla cashew cream, 173
Sautéed Tofu and Bell Peppers with
    Garlic and Ginger, 93
"Sautéing" without oil, xi
Scones
    banana-raisin-nut, 132
    brown-rice flour-sweet potato,
      135
    oat-bran, 137
    oat-bran-sweet potato, 136
    onion-poppy seed, 134
    wheat-free, 136, 137
    whole wheat-orange-sweet
      potato, 136
Scrambled Tofu and Onions, 214
Scrambled Tofu and Vegetables, 215
Scrambled Tofu Ranchero, 214
Sesame-Ginger Dressing, 24
Sesame-seed cookies, 197
Shake, banana, 222
Simply Delicious Baked Apples, 208

Sliced Tofu Wieners in Dough, 7
Smoothie, Hawaiian, 223
Snacks
    raisin-nut-seed-oat bran
      crunchies, 207
    date-walnut party treats, 207
    trail mix, 208
Soft Brown Rice with Cinnamon and
    Nutmeg, 221
Soups
    bean and pasta, 31
    broth with noodles, 36, 40
    cabbage borscht, 39
    cabbage-potato, 37
    dal, 28, 29
    easy broth, 40
    easy lentil, 29
    Indian-style lentil, 28, 29
    Italian-style lentil, 30, 36
    leek-potato-onion, 38
    lentil-spinach, 31
    lentil-vegetable, 30
    mushroom-barley, 35
    mushroom-barley-lentil, 35
    mushroom-potato-vegetable,
      37
    potato-leek, 38
    red bean-barley-vegetable, 39
    split-pea, 33, 34
    split-pea with fresh peas, 34
    stock for, 36
    three-bean vegetable, 33
    vegetable broth, 36
    white-bean, with leeks and
      vegetables, 32
Sour Onion-Corn-Rye Bread, 121
Soy milk, 223
Spaghetti with Lentil Balls, 43
Spanish rice, 74, 75
Spanish Rice with Fresh Cilantro, 74
Spicy Barbecue Sauce, 100
Spicy Chili Beans, 67
Spicy *Dal* (Indian Lentil Soup), 28
Spicy High-Energy Protein Loaf, 83
Spicy High-Energy Slices, 84

Spicy Lentil Stew, 59
Spicy Spanish Rice, 75
Spicy Tofu "Egg Salad," 2
Spicy Vegetarian Tamales, 70
Spinach Pesto, 52
Split-Pea Soup with Fresh Peas, 34
Split-Pea Veggie Nut Burgers, 112
Split-peas
    in burgers, 112
    in soups, 33-34
    in stew, with lentils and
      barley, 61
Squash, stuffed with rice, 79
Squash
    acorn, stuffed with rice, 79
    steamed, 92
Steamed Brown Rice, 97
Steamed Buckwheat and Brown Rice,
    88
Stew
    bean-barley, 60
    carrot-sweet potato-prune, 77
    eggplant-bell pepper, 63
    garbanzo bean, Indian-style,
      58
    high-energy, 63
    lentil, spicy, 59
    lentil-cabbage, 60
    lentil-split pea-barley, 61
    lima bean-barley-rice, 61
    tzimmes, 77
Stock, vegetable, 36
Strawberry Tofu Mousse, 173
Summer Pear Cobbler, 160
Sweet and Sour High-Energy Salad,
    26
Sweet and Sour High-Energy Slices,
    85
Sweet and Sour Sauce, 81
Sweet and Tangy White Beans, 62
Sweet Brown-Rice Pudding with
    Coconut, Dates, and Coriander,
    220
Sweet Cinnamon Buns with Raisins
    and Almonds, 199

Sweet Corn Muffins, 128
    Banana-Blueberry-Oat Bran
      Muffins, 129
Sweet Crunchy Corn Cereal, 216
Sweet Crunchy Millet Cereal, 216
Sweet Cucumber Salad, 25
Sweet Mango Chutney, 53
Sweet Yam Pastry Dough, 198
Sweet Yam Sticky Buns, 198
Sweet Yam-Cinnamon-Raisin Buns,
    197
Sweet-Potato Cornbread, 126
Sweet-Potato Gingerbread Cookies,
    183
Swirled Orange-Pecan Pastries, 200

T

Tabouli, 11
Tamale pies, 71, 72, 73
Tamales, 70
Tangy Eggplant-Zucchini Salad, 18
Tangy Red Bell Pepper Dressing, 14
Tart Summer Fruit Cobbler, 154
Tasty Lentil-Nut Burgers, 108
Tasty Potato Salad, 23
Tasty Red Coleslaw, 18
Tasty Refried Beans, 66
Thick Italian-style Lentil Soup, 36
Thick Lentil-Split Pea-Barley Stew,
    61
Thick Red Bean-Barley-Vegetable
    Soup, 39
Three-Bean Vegetable Soup, 33
Three-cornered pastries, prune-filled,
    201
Tofu
    appetizers, oven-barbecued, 7
    in Chinese-style salad, 24
    and curry dip, 11
    and curry dressing, 11
    "egg salad," 2
    in enchilada casserole, 64
    how to prepare, v
    in Mexican-style casserole, 69

oven-barbecued, 99, 100
sautéed, with vegetables, 89,
    90, 93, 94, 95, 97, 98,
    101
scrambled, 214-15
skewered, 99
slices, baked, 88, 93
stuffing, for bell peppers, 102
sweet and sour, Asian-style, 91
wieners in dough, 7
Tofu "Cheese" Pie with Blueberry
    Glaze, 168
Tofu Tamale Pie, 71
Tofu with Vegetables and Cashews,
    89
Tofu-Broccoli Lasagna, 48
Tofu-curry dip, 11
Tofu-curry dressing, 11
Tomato and cucumber salad, 12
Tomato-Basil Sauce, 46
Torte(s). *See also* Cake(s)
    apple delight, 149
    apple-pecan, 148
    date brownie, 151
    date-carob-walnut, 149
    plum, 150
    wheat-free, 148, 149, 150
Tostadas, 71
Trail mix, 208
Turkish Stuffed Eggplant and Bell
    Peppers, 104
Tzimmes, 77

U

Unsweetened Wheat-Free Oat-Bran
    Scones, 137

V

Vanilla Brown-Rice Drink, 221
Vanilla Cashew Cream, 173
Vegan Mexican-style Casserole, 69
Vegetable platter, 10

Vegetables. *See also* Salads; specific
    vegetables
      browning, xi
      marinated and steamed, 9
      raw, on a platter, 10
      sautéed, with tofu, 89-92, 93,
        94, 95, 97, 98, 101
Vegetarianism, health benefits, of, ix
Vegit, ix
Vinaigrette Dressing, 15

W

Wheat-Free Almond-Pear Torte, 153
Wheat-Free Baking-Powder Biscuits,
    133
Wheat-Free Banana Pancakes, 212
Wheat-Free Banana Squash
    Cornbread, 126
Wheat-Free Banana-Apple-Oat Bran
    Muffins, 137
Wheat-Free Banana-Raisin-Nut
    Scones, 132
Wheat-Free Carob-Almond Torte,
    153
Wheat-Free Corn-Rye-Oat Bran
    Bread with Caraway Seeds, 118
Wheat-Free Creamy Lemon Pie, 171
Wheat-Free Date-Carob-Walnut
    Torte, 149
Wheat-Free Dutch Apple Pie, 154
Wheat-Free Tart Dutch Apple Pie,
    155
Wheat-Free Fancy Yam-Pecan Pie,
    166
Wheat-Free Ginger Snaps, 184
Wheat-Free Lentil-Nut-Oat Bran
    Balls, 6
Wheat-Free Oat Bran-Sweet Potato
    Scones, 136
Wheat-Free Orange-Oat Bran
    Cookies, 179
Wheat-Free Poached Pear-Almond
    Pie, 161

Wheat-Free Potato-Oat Bran Gnocchi with Spinach Pesto, 51
Wheat-Free Pumpkin-Oat Chews, 195
Wheat-Free Scotch Oat-Rye Bread, 117
Wheat-Free Squash-Oat Bran-Spice Cookies, 184
Wheat-Free Unsweetened Carrot-Spice Cookies, 180
Wheat-Free Unsweetened Oat Bran-Spice Crackers, 179
White beans, 32, 62
White-Bean Soup with Leeks and Vegetables, 32
Whole Wheat-Almond-Pineapple Crust, 172

Whole Wheat-Banana-Pineapple Muffins, 132
Whole Wheat-Orange-Sweet Potato Scones, 136
Whole Wheat-Pecan Crust, 172
Whole-Wheat Indian Bread, 127
Whole-Wheat Seed Bread, 116
Wholesome Cornbread, 125
"Wiener schnitzel," 108

Y
Yam
   -brown-rice flour-pecan cookies, 192
    -cinnamon-raisin buns, 197

gingerbread cookies, 182
-oatmeal cookies, 188
pastry dough, 198
raisin-spice cake, 141
sticky buns, 198
-sweetened oat-bran chews, 188
Yam Gingerbread Cookies, 182
Yams, how to prepare for recipes, v
Yeast, xii
Yeast doughs, kneading and rising of, xii

Z
Zesty Bean Tamale Pie, 73

The Crossing Press
publishes a full selection
of cookbooks.
For a current catalog,
please call toll-free
800-777-1048